Indian Baskets of Central California

To Yvonne —
Hope this furthers
your knowledge of
Basketry.
Best wishes —
Ralph Shanks
&
Lisa Woo Shanks

With a large winnower under her arm and a seedbeater in her hand, the gathering season has arrived for California Indian women. The striking model is Joseppa Dick, a well-known Pomo weaver. A Grace Carpenter Hudson oil on canvas painting done in 1908. (Collection of the Grace Hudson Museum and the Sun House, Ukiah, California)

INDIAN BASKETS OF CENTRAL CALIFORNIA

Art, Culture, and History

Native American Basketry from San Francisco Bay and Monterey Bay
North to Mendocino and East to the Sierras

Ralph Shanks ✺ Lisa Woo Shanks, Editor

First Edition

Volume I of the Indian Baskets of California and Oregon Series

**Costaño Books in association with
Miwok Archeological Preserve of Marin (MAPOM)**
MAPOM Publication Number 8

Costaño Books, P.O. Box 2206, Novato, CA 94948-2206

**Distributed by:
University of Washington Press
P.O. Box 50096
Seattle, WA 98145-5096
www. washington.edu/uwpress**

ISBN: 978-0-930268-18-3   (13 digit)
ISBN: 0-930268-18-0   (10 digit)

Library of Congress Control Number: 2005907400

Publisher's Cataloging in Publication
Shanks, Ralph C.
Indian baskets of central California : art, culture, and history : native American basketry from San Francisco Bay and Monterey Bay north to Mendocino and east to the Sierras / Ralph Shanks ; Lisa Woo Shanks, editor. -- 1st ed. -- Novato, CA : Costaño Books in association with the Miwok Archeological Preserve of Marin (MAPOM), 2006.
p. ; cm.
(Indian baskets of California and Oregon ; v. 1)
ISBN-13: 978-0-930268-18-3
ISBN-10: 0-930268-18-0
Includes bibliographical references and index.
1. Indian baskets--California. 2. Basket making--California. 3. Indians of North America--California. I. Shanks, Lisa Woo. II. Title. III. Series.
E98.B3 S33 2006   2005907400
746.41'2'0899707943--dc22   CIP

Design by Jacci Summers, Healdsburg, California
Printed and bound in Hong Kong through Global Interprint, Inc., of Santa Rosa, California

Dedicated to the great California Indian basket weavers
of past generations, of today and of the future.

With deep appreciation to the late Larry Dawson
for decades of patiently teaching me to be a basketry scholar.

"The Wedding Guest" by Grace Carpenter Hudson. A beautiful young Pomo woman admires the California Indian baskets presented as wedding gifts. The lovely model is believed to be Rosa Peters of Yokayo Rancheria in Mendocino County. The portrait was done in bitumen on canvas in 1932. (Collection of the Grace Hudson Museum and the Sun House, Ukiah, California)

Front cover and title page: "The Dowry" by Grace Carpenter Hudson (Private collection)
Cover imprint: Maidu basket
Back cover: "The Wedding Guest" by Grace Carpenter Hudson (Collection of the Grace Hudson Museum and Sun House, Ukiah, California)

INDIAN BASKETS
OF CENTRAL CALIFORNIA

TABLE OF CONTENTS

A California Indian weaver pauses while gathering seeds on a summer day. She holds her seedbeater in one hand and has her burden basket at her feet. Seed processing was the central purpose of most California baskets. The beautiful model is Eva Scott, a Pomo. The painting is in oil on canvas by artist Grace Carpenter Hudson, 1905. (Collection of the Grace Hudson Museum and the Sun House, Ukiah, California)

BASKETRY IN NATIVE CALIFORNIA

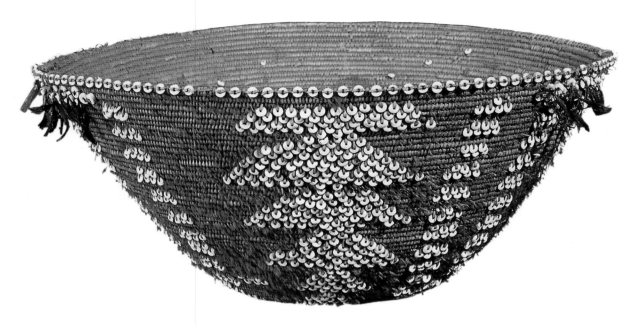

Great art thrived among the California Indian people. This is an Ohlone/Costanoan coiled basket from the San Francisco Bay Area. It is decorated with olivella shell disc beads and woodpecker feathers. California Native American baskets are a fine art that combines beauty, form and function. The San Francisco Bay and Monterey Bay areas are the home of the Ohlone people. (Musee de l'Homme, Paris, #09-19-53)

Basketry is of supreme importance in Native California. It is valuable for understanding daily life, cultural change, cultural values, art, history, belief, settlement patterns, migrations and the transmission of ideas. Basketry speaks of the life and history of a people.

A Wintu elder said it well. "I live in a basket," she observed. It was true. Baskets were vital and were used every day in all aspects of people's lives.

Nearly every meal of a person's life involved baskets in numerous ways. Baskets were used for cooking, gathering, carrying, storing, winnowing, sifting, trapping and fishing. There were huge feast baskets so large that when filled with acorn mush it took several men to lift one. There were baskets so tiny they could sit on the head of a pin.

Each Indian homemaker had her set of beautiful baskets that were the pride of her family. Baskets marked the entire lifespan of every California Indian person. From a newborn's first basketry cradle on through life to the baskets burned in honor at death, many types of baskets were required.

A father might say of his daughter when she was born, "I wish she would be a good basket-maker and a good girl"

(Goldschmidt 1951, 372). Such wishes were usually fulfilled. Young girls spent countless hours watching their mothers, aunts and grandmothers weave. Young women became accomplished basket weavers by the time they married. Husbands then watched with admiration and love as their wives created baskets of beauty and honor.

The men were often more than bystanders; in some cultures they were weavers. The men typically made rugged utilitarian baskets and sometimes baby cradles. Men might help their wives, mothers and daughters gather basketry materials. A few men became expert weavers themselves. Some are weavers to this day.

Baskets were important in the routine of daily life. But they were also vital in times of joy and in times of crisis. Baskets were the most treasured of wedding gifts. A person's most beloved possessions were often baskets. There were memories of joy, love, heritage and pride in those baskets. As if to celebrate life, most baskets had stunning geometric designs arranged with the best artistic taste.

Baskets could also help the people through even the most difficult of times. Among the Nomlaki, for example,

CALIFORNIA INDIAN NATIONS
Central California
Basketry Area

Central California Basketry Area

Possibly Central California
Basketry Area

Other California Basketry Areas

Karuk
Chimariko
Tolowa
Yurok
Chilula
Hupa
Wiyot
Whilkut
Nongatl
Bear River
Mattole
Lassik
Sinkyone
Wailaki
Cahto
Coast Yuki
Huchnom
Lake Miwok
Wappo
Coast Miwok
Bay Miwok
Ohlone
(Costanoan)
Esselen

Shasta
Modoc
Achumawi
Northern
Paiute
Wintu
Atsugewi
Yana
Mountain
Maidu
Nomlaki
Konkow
Maidu
Yuki
Washoe
Patwin
Nisenan
Maidu
Pomo
Mono Lake
Paiute
Western
Mono
Plains
Miwok
Sierra
Miwok
Owens
Valley
Paiute
Foothill Yokuts
Tubatulabal
Panamint Shoshone
Northern
Valley
Yokuts
Southern
Valley
Yokuts
Salinan
Kawaiisu
Chemehuevi
Mohave
Chumash
Serrano
Halchidhoma
Kitanemuk
Gabrielino
(Tongva)
Cahuilla
Tataviam
Juaneño
Luiseño
Cupeño
Kumeyaay
(Dieguéño)
Quechan
(Yuma)

Native California homes blended with the environment. The Wappo, Pomo and some other North Central Californians made large multi-family tule houses such as this one. If you look carefully, you can see a mortar hopper and a winnower hanging on the side of this home. Baskets were essential in every California Indian home. (University of Pennsylvania Museum of Archaeology and Anthropology, #54-148224)

a woman made a basket if she was planning to divorce her husband. She gave the basket to him as a departing gift for his mother to encourage a friendly separation (Margolin 1981, 35). At funerals to express grief for their deceased loved one, especially fine baskets might be burned. If a person was known to be dying, a weaver might work ceaselessly. The weaver was risking ruining her eyesight in order to have a basket ready to honor her loved one. Lives began and ended with baskets.

Baskets are from this Land

Baskets were in part the art of the individual weaver. They could be fragile works of art or simple utilitarian objects. But in every case, they were unique products of the land.

Today a painter's brushes, oils and canvas use materials that could come from anywhere in the world. In contrast, California Indian baskets blossom entirely from the soil of this state. Weavers always had special places where they nurtured and gathered shoots, rushes, roots or grasses. Each region of California produced its own preferred basketry materials.

Native Californians carefully managed the land. Selective burning was practiced both to encourage growth of certain plants and to reduce pests. Desired and much needed plants were protected, nurtured and carefully utilized using sophisticated horticultural knowledge.

Ultimately, the plants selected for basketry had the color tones, shapes, smell and look of each special part of

California. Each basket reflected the beauty of the land interpreted through the eye of the Native artist. Weavers approached plants respectfully and offered prayers of thanks as they gathered materials. Thus, baskets reflected the beauty that results when the environment is treated with respect, kindness and gratitude.

The Diversity of the People and of the Art

Great art usually comes from areas that are special in some way. California is one of these unique places. The land itself is diverse. There are great valleys, mountains, deserts, rivers and coastline. There are regions that receive two inches of rain a year and those that receive over one hundred inches. There are valleys that drop below sea level and mountains that are the highest in the forty-eight contiguous states. The plants are equally unusual and include the world's tallest trees and the world's oldest trees and shrubs. California has the rarest oak, fir, pine, manzanita and barberry in the world. California has a greater diversity of plant life than any other state.

It was in this land that Native Californians flourished. More Indians lived (and still live) in California than in any other state in America. There was perhaps no other comparably sized area in the world with so many cultures speaking so many different languages (Merriam 1966, 44). Even in physical terms, California Native people were diverse: the Yuki were the shortest and the Mohave the tallest Native Americans (Spencer 1977, 201). The richness and diversity of the land, the plants and the people combined to produce diverse cultures and great art.

An Ancient Art with an Uninterrupted History

Some Native American art forms are quite old; others are relatively new. For example, silverwork, beadwork and Navajo rugs are all post-European arts. Even Hopi pottery is a revival. All these and others are beautiful and admirable arts, but few have the long, uninterrupted history of California basketry.

Baskets are among the most ancient of all arts. Basketry has existed in California for thousands of years. Its history is uninterrupted and the bonds from one generation to the next span centuries and even millennia. These ties exist to this day.

Where archeological findings provide a record, we often find basketry dating back thousands of years that is nearly identical to that being made today. Basketry from the Modoc and Klamath is a good example. From cave deposits in southeastern Oregon and western Nevada we have a basketry record extending back over 3,000 years. Archeological pieces dating back to 1,000 B.C. are almost identical to modern Klamath and Modoc basketry (Dawson, Bancroft notes).

In Chimariko tradition, the spider's web was the inspiration for openwork basketry (Silver 1978, 207). California basketry is old, although as the Chimariko noted not as old as the spider web. The two main basketry traditions in California, twining and coiling, are both very old. Twining arrived in California first. No one is sure when twining began in California, but it may have been

With baskets in hand, the joy and beauty of the Sierra Miwok basket dance can be seen in the faces of the dancers. This is Bill Franklin's dance group at the California State Indian Museum, Sacramento. (Photo use courtesy of Bill Franklin—photo by Ralph Shanks)

ten thousand years or more ago. Coiling began arriving in California much later, about 4,000 years ago (Heizer 1949-1953, 27; Dawson, "Fields of Clover," n.d.).

Among Central and Southern California cultures, coiled baskets displaced some of the older twined basket types. This was a long, slow replacement period, taking 800 to 1,000 years (Dawson p.c.). All major California basketry traditions represent very long time periods.

But California basketry was always a dynamic art. A people's basketry has a history. It is the result of influences and innovations that take place over the centuries. By carefully studying basketry it is possible to better understand and appreciate a culture's history. Basketry studies can be as valuable as studies in linguistics and archeology. Linguistic studies help show the history of a language and the people who speak it. Archeological studies find changes in layers of strata and other data that illuminate the lives of a people. Basketry studies are similar to both linguistics and archeology in that the history of cultural changes over time can be seen.

As with determining the origins of words or the finding of datable artifacts, baskets teach us their history. California basketry was not static. It developed in a series of cultural contacts, migrations and exchanges of ideas. Each class of basketry type was modified, added to, and either increased or diminished in importance over time. Because of basketry's unparalleled importance in Native California life,

Honored elder Laura Fish Somersal, a famed Wappo master weaver. She generously shared her basketry skills and worked with linguists to preserve her Wappo language. Mrs. Somersal was Alexander Valley Wappo and Southern Pomo. (Ralph Shanks photo)

it is unexcelled as a subject of study. It is also fascinating to see how the studies of linguists, archeologists and basketry scholars so often have similar, mutually supporting findings. Often the voices of the tribal elders speak through the centuries in the findings of these studies.

Basketry and Pottery in California

Basketry predates pottery. Basketry is more structured than pottery in terms of the steps of the process and, as a result, is more resistant to change (Greevy 2001, 10). The exceptionally high development of basketry in California must in part account for the failure of pottery to replace basketry (Bennyhoff 1977, 13). Pottery had some advantages: it could be made faster and was fireproof and insect-proof. But California basket weavers had long ago discovered how to overcome these issues. Pottery was not essential and all food processing could easily be done without it. Pottery also had the liability of being easily broken and heavier to carry than baskets. Pottery is inferior to baskets for gathering, carrying, winnowing, fishing, trapping and other uses. In California,

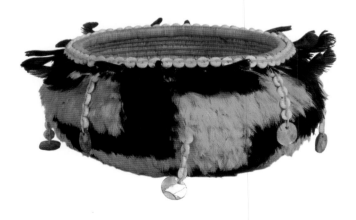

This Pomo feather basket makes it easy to understand why Native California basketry is renowned worldwide. Pendants of clamshell disc beads tipped with large abalone shell discs accent meadowlark, mallard and quail feathers. D: 4.5", H: 2.75" (Milwaukee Public Museum, #15121/4250, Lisa Woo Shanks photo file)

pottery largely replaced basketry only among the people who lived along the Colorado River such as the Mohave and Quechan (Yuma). Along the California-Oregon state line among the Shasta and Takelma, pottery was invented and then apparently discontinued as non-essential. Basketry was the supreme art of Native California.

World Class Art

Native American basketry reaches its highest development in California (Merrill 1923, 215). It could as accurately be said that the world's basketry reaches its highest development in California.

California Indian basketry is much more than just exceptional local art. California Indian basketry ranks as one of the great art forms in the world. It greets the eye, mind

California Indian basketry is a living art due to those who weave, teach and demonstrate. Beloved elder and teacher Julia Parker is representative of the many gracious and talented weavers of the twenty-first century. She is shown here weaving a coiled basket. Coiling is a sewing technique that is a markedly different technique from the twining shown in the adjacent photo (Lisa Woo Shanks)

and heart with the same unforgettable beauty as European, Chinese and Japanese paintings or Mayan, Aztec, Greek and Egyptian sculptures or African woodcarvings or the feather-work of Polynesia.

Native people have long appreciated Native California basketry. But from the very first contact, California Indian basketry also stunned the first European visitors with its beauty. They had never seen baskets of such quality in Europe or anywhere else in the world. Beginning with the first overland expedition in California, the Spanish de Anza expedition of 1775-1776, visitors were overwhelmed by their beauty. The de Anza expedition bought so many beautiful baskets that entire villages were sold out (Dawson and Deetz 1965, 200). British, French, Russian and American voyagers eagerly sought these remarkable artworks.

Famed anthropologist Alfred L. Kroeber wrote "basketry is unquestionably the most developed art in California" (Kroeber 1925, 819). At the beginning of the last class he taught at the University of California at Berkeley, Professor Kroeber brought a large Pomo basket into class and filled it with water. He then covered it with glass and there it sat in front of the class week after week. On the final day of his last class, Dr. Kroeber lifted up the glass and the water was still there. It was a graphic illustration of the magnificent weaving abilities of California Indian women. It was the final point the "Dean of American Anthropologists" wanted to make to his students. It is understandable that a basket would epitomize what Kroeber would want his students to remember. Nothing better represents the cultural achievements and complexity of Native California life.

Besides their cultural importance, baskets are great art. Today, many California Indian baskets are prized jewels in the collections of museums in more than twenty countries (Blackburn and Hudson, 1990). California Indian baskets are found in great museums in England, Russia, France, Germany, Japan, The Czech Republic, Switzerland, New Zealand, Australia, and across the United States. While many of the earliest baskets are found in European museums, the most extensive and best-documented collections are here in America.

The research for this three volume series began in the late 1960s at Hearst (then Lowie) Museum of Anthropology at the University of California at Berkeley. I began as a graduate student working with museum anthropologist Lawrence Dawson. Larry and I worked together during the 1960s, 1970s and again in the 1990s through to 2003. Along with my

The warps of twined baskets generally radiate out from a central starting knot. During the weaving process, twined basket warps spread out much more spectacularly than do the tightly clustered foundation warps of coiled baskets. Coast Miwok/Kashaya Pomo weaver Julia Parker demonstrates this fact using a partially completed tule basket at a Miwok Archeological Preserve of Marin (MAPOM) class at Point Reyes National Seashore. (Lisa Woo Shanks)

wife Lisa Woo Shanks, we have spent decades of researching and photographing these great baskets in the United States and in Europe. This research has resulted in our present three volume series on California Indian basketry. Most of the finest and rarest baskets found are illustrated here. We have also spent years visiting with California Indian people. These cultural leaders and weavers graciously offered much guidance and assistance. Most importantly, many became our friends.

It should be noted, too, that the Indian elders were really co-authors for most of the early anthropology books cited. These long-ago elders, whose births often predated the Gold Rush, had unequaled cultural knowledge. Their generous sharing of their heritage was a great gift to the world. When reading information from an early anthropologist it is good to remember that it was the generous sharing by the elders that made this information available to all. Both the elders and the authors are to be honored.

Courageous Artists and the Time of Horror

To be a weaver required artistic skill, courage and specialized knowledge. Women were the ethno-botanists of their communities (Barrows 1967, 51). They knew where, when and how to gather all the plants the tribe needed. But gathering food and basketry materials also meant entering the territory of grizzly bears, mountain lions and rattlesnakes. After the 1849 Gold Rush, it also meant risking being kidnapped, raped or murdered by marauding miners. As late as the start of the Civil War in 1861, indenturing Indians was legal in California, which meant virtual enslavement (Waterman 1918, 43). From the days of the Spanish missions through the period of American settlement, California Indians faced European diseases, relentless attack, enslavement, loss of land and endless indignities. When self-appointed "volunteers" or army troops attacked villages, one military tactic was to burn all the baskets. For without baskets, California Indian life was not possible (Beckham 1971, 27).

Yet, through all the horror, courageous Native California weavers kept basketry traditions alive. Suffering artists have never endured more difficult or heartbreaking times than what Native people experienced. The weavers were heroic women and men. Some weavers managed to survive this time of horror. By around 1900, basketry was becoming an important source of income for Indian people. As Indian people continued to adopt metal culinary utensils, most California Indian baskets began to be made primarily for sale. Even rugged utility baskets such as seed beaters, mortar hoppers and openwork burden baskets were made for sale (see for example: "Catalogue of F. M. Gilham," an early dealer in Indian baskets, n.d.). During the late 19th century and early 20th century there was even "a basket craze" in which private collectors and museums competed in purchasing thousands of baskets from weavers.

Aspects of some cultures' basketry did change after sales to non-Indians became important (see for example: Bates, Cohodas, Slater and Smith-Ferri). European inspired designs and forms began appearing among some groups. But almost all older baskets and many newer baskets were made to please Native artistic tastes. To this day many California cultures make many baskets remarkably similar to those of the elders. Yet basketry has always been dynamic and changing. In this book we trace changes that occurred prior to European arrival.

Please be assured that if known, the names of weavers of the baskets illustrated in this volume are given. Sadly, this is all too uncommon.

California Indian Basketry Today: A Living Art

After a long period of declining production, California Indian artists are again actively carrying on and reviving basket making. Native California basketry is an ancient art, yet one kept alive today by hundreds of contemporary basket weavers throughout the state. Even some cultures where basketry had totally ceased have now revived the art. Weavers, both young and old, female and male, from cultures in most parts of the state now actively weave. Weavers carry on this art despite heavy responsibilities of work, education and child rearing. The enthusiasm and love of basketry by present-day weavers is soon apparent. Each weaver honors the great weavers of the past that brought the art to us today.

Many basket weavers have joined the **California Indian Basketweavers Association (CIBA)**. Members share the joy and challenges of basketry in today's world. CIBA works to encourage Native basketry traditions. Problems of access to material, herbicide use and many other vital issues are addressed. Each year CIBA holds an annual gathering that

An exquisite winnowing tray made by Nora Maxmillion, a Southern Pomo weaver born in 1878 in Sebastopol, Sonoma County. Note the bands of varying shades of redbud and the background of sedge root. D: 21", H: 6.5" (Private Collection)

includes demonstrations, exhibits and other events open to the public. This is a wonderful opportunity to meet the artists, see beautiful baskets being made and help support CIBA. If you are a California Indian weaver you can join as a regular member. Non-Indians and non-weavers are welcome as non-voting associate members. Everyone receives an informative newsletter. Your CIBA membership helps support and encourage the work of today's dedicated weavers and ensure that future generations will continue this vibrant, living art.

In addition, some weavers teach classes in California Indian basketry. The Miwok Archeological Preserve of Marin (MAPOM), for example, regularly offers classes open to all that teach how to weave California Indian baskets, shell bead making and other skills. MAPOM's board of directors is made up of both California Indian and non-Indian members. Both MAPOM and CIBA have Internet web sites.

Museum collections are also an extremely important part of keeping basketry alive. After expressing the importance of studying early baskets in museums, a friend who is one of the finest contemporary California Indian weavers said, "the museums are our teachers now! I think the Indian people are

Mortar hoppers were strong, purposely made bottomless baskets. Mortar hoppers were placed atop stone slabs or mortars when pounding dried acorns into flour using a pestle. This Pomo mortar hopper has redbud designs on a background of sedge root, D: 22", H: 6" (Maryhill Museum of Art, Goldendale, Washington, #53-33)

Acorn mush is shown being prepared using heated cooking stones. At right, a sizzling hot cooking stone is briefly dipped in water to remove any ash it has acquired while being heated in the fire. At left, a cooking stone is being removed from the coiled cooking pot since the rock has transferred its heat. This is a Miwok Archeological Preserve of Marin (MAPOM) cooking demonstration at Point Reyes National Seashore. (Lisa Shanks)

finally realizing what they have. Now days everyone wants to be a weaver." By calling the museums our teachers, she is emphasizing that early baskets made by the elders need to be carefully studied if the art is to flourish. One of the goals of this book is to help contemporary weavers and all others to understand the baskets of the great weavers of the past.

The Organization of this Book and the Three Volume Series

Each chapter covers the basketry of a people. Chapters are grouped based on how the cultures are related in terms of basketry. In most cases this is also geographic. We plan to cover California in a three volume series. The present volume covers Central California, except for the Yokuts, Salinan and Western Mono. The basketry of these three South Central California peoples has strong ties to Southern California and properly belongs in the volume on the southern half of the state. Northwestern and Northeastern California basketry is most closely related to the basketry of Western Oregon and will be studied in the third volume, covering Northern California and Oregon.

The California Indian chapters that are the heart of this book interrelate as the lives of the people were related. For most cultures, this book offers the most detailed account of their basketry ever presented. It is hoped that the information will be of value to Native People and to people the world over. It is also hoped that California Indians, weavers, art lovers,

anthropologists, museum staff and visitors, historians, linguists, teachers and students, basketry collectors and everyone who admires Native California will enjoy the rich illustrations and text.

MAJOR TYPES OF CALIFORNIA INDIAN BASKETS

We focus on traditional baskets rather than later types made in response to European taste. Traditional basketry includes those baskets and techniques that most clearly approximate the pre-European contact or early post-contact period (Fowler and Dawson 1986, 705). Such baskets originally served vital functions in each culture, especially for seed processing. They are of special importance in understanding and appreciating each culture. We begin by discussing widely used types of California baskets.

Burden Baskets are large, conical or flat-bottomed baskets used to carry heavy loads. The burden basket was carried on a person's back. Smaller **gathering baskets** were held in the hand. Often the contents of gathering baskets were used to fill the big burden baskets. **Seedbeaters** were also used in conjunction with burden baskets. Seed beaters were spoon-shaped or round baskets with sturdy woven handles. They were used to knock smaller seeds off plants into the burden basket.

Basketry Traps were made to catch fish, birds and other animals. Most traps were long and narrow, but forms varied.

Storage Baskets were used to hold foods until needed. Storage baskets were carefully designed to match the preservation requirements of whatever type of food was being stored. For example, some food required openwork baskets that allow for air circulation to prevent decay. Other kinds of food needed tight containers to protect them from loss or from animals. Storage baskets were often quite large since the family had to get through winter using primarily the food they had gathered earlier.

Mortar Hoppers were specially made bottomless baskets placed atop a stone slab or stone mortar. When acorns were being pounded into flour, mortar hoppers kept the flour from blowing out and debris from blowing in. After the acorn flour was finely pounded, it had to be sifted.

Winnowing, Sifting and Parching Trays served several key uses in food processing. Sometimes the same tray served for all three purposes. **Winnowing trays** were used to toss seeds in the air as part of the process of removing husks and eliminating unwanted material such as small leaves that were accidentally included during gathering. Winnowers were also used as **parching trays** to cook various foods. Hot

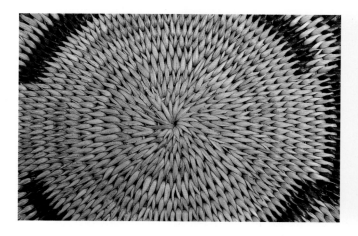

The start of a coiled basket. By looking at the bottom of a coiled basket the foundation warps can be seen to spiral out from the basket's center like a coiled rope. This coiled basket has a single rod foundation that causes the weft designs to blend like the teeth of a comb with the background color. Three-rod and grass bundle foundations in contrast are very evenly separated from the background weft color. The light colored wefts on this photo are of sedge root; the dark color design is dyed bulrush root. (Private collection)

The start of a twined basket. Notice how countless warp sticks radiate from the central starting knot. This starting knot is the crossed warp type; note the sets of bare warps crossing at the center where no wefts were wrapped around them. This is a Southern Pomo basket done in plain twining, except for a ring of lattice twining used in the circular design of alternating red and white that surrounds the starting knot. (Private collection)

coals from a fire were placed on the tray. By keeping the coals moving on the tray, all the seeds on it were exposed to the heat and cooked. The constant movement prevented the basket from being burned. Nearly flat **sifting trays** were gently tapped so that the acorn flour on them moved into separate piles of fine and coarse particles. The larger particles were put back in the mortar hopper for further pounding. Acorn flour as fine as commercial flour was soon completely separated from coarse particles. This fine acorn flour was then ready for leaching.

Acorn flour has a bitter tannic acid in it that must be removed before eating. The tannic acid was removed by leaching; that is, pouring water gently through it. Some cultures used **leaching baskets** to hold the flour while water was poured through to wash away the tannic acid. The acorn flour is then ready to cook.

Cooking Pots were used to boil acorn mush as well as many other foods. Using stirring sticks, hot stones were placed in the cooking pot. The cooking stones, constantly stirred along with the food to prevent burning the basket, brought the food to a boil quickly and efficiently. **Feast Baskets** were huge cooking pots reserved for special occasions when large numbers of people gathered for a "Big Time" or other important event.

Water Bottles were especially useful when traveling in the desert and among the Channel Islands. Indian people needed fresh water to survive when traveling in hot, waterless areas or on ocean voyages to offshore islands. A lightweight, tightly woven basketry container was ideal for bringing water along. These short-necked baskets could be round, oval or have pointed bottoms. They were coated with pine pitch or asphaltum to ensure that no water loss occurred. Water bottles were probably the single most important invention in allowing desert areas such as the Great Basin to be settled by Native peoples (Dawson p.c.).

Women's Hats were baskets of great beauty. They were often worn in ceremonies, especially in Northwestern California. But hats were also important during food gathering. Hats were worn by women to protect their heads from the pack strap or tumpline that ran around the forehead when carrying a burden basket on the back. Hats also protected hair from pitch while gathering pine nuts, especially in desert areas. Some cultures also used hats for serving food, a convenient use on gathering trips.

All of the above basket types were used in some aspect of food processing. But baskets were also made for other purposes.

Treasure Baskets (Bottleneck Baskets) were finely made baskets with shoulders and short necks. They were used to hold valued possessions, were sometimes used ceremonially and later became immensely popular items made for sale. These baskets often had quail plumes or red yarn as decorative additions around the shoulder.

Basketry Baby Cradles were used from the first days of life to provide safe, comfortable and convenient carriers for babies. All cradles were carefully designed for the health of the child and for ease of handling by the mother. Commonly, one type of cradle was made for newborns and subsequent larger cradles for older infants. Some cradles had beads, tiny baskets or other interesting items hanging from a sunshade or rod to entertain the baby.

There were three basic types of California Indian cradles: sitting cradles, lying cradles and ladder-back cradles. In woven sitting cradles, the basketry cradle provided a seat for the snugly wrapped child. In both the woven lying cradles and the more structural-type ladder-back cradles, the child lays on its back comfortably wrapped on a padded flat surface (Bibby 2004, 5-6).

Other Types of Baskets were made. These specialized types of baskets are discussed as they are encountered in each culture. The specific characteristics of each culture's wonderful baskets are detailed in the tribal chapters.

Understanding California Indian Basketry: The Technical Features

California Indian Basketry is a sophisticated, highly developed art. When we spoke with two friends about the technical features of basketry, they said that in the past they had a difficult time understanding them. One friend is one of the best contemporary California Indian basket weavers in the state and the other friend has a doctorate in anthropology. Gulp! This inspired us to attempt to present a more understandable description of these features than has generally been done in the past.

Some choices were matters of individual taste, such as which designs to use. But both technical and artistic decisions were clearly guided by honored traditions of the people (see for example: O'Neale, 1995 and Dawson and Deetz, 1965). Respected elders knew how baskets should be made in the proper way of their culture. These rules were carefully taught to each generation. The wisdom of the elders was appreciated and honored.

Every basket has certain construction features that result from the steps a weaver goes through to produce a basket. By using baskets documented as to which culture made them,

Coiled baskets are sewn in a spiral with a bottom that resembles a coiled rope. Note how this coiled Yuki basket begins at the center with the starting knot and progresses in ever-widening circles. The red designs on this basket are unpeeled redbud and the yellowish background is peeled redbud. (Michael Smith Gallery, Santa Fe)

we can identify the construction features of each culture's baskets. In this way we can attribute (identify) additional baskets from each culture and add to our knowledge. This helps us to more fully understand the cultural history and art. Increasing knowledge can excite and enrich everyone, especially California Indian people.

The time-honored weaving steps chosen by each culture enable us to recognize the culture or region where a basket was made. Even baskets traded from one culture to another can usually be identified as to where they originated (see for example, Merriam 1962, 50).

Identifying baskets (attribution) increases our knowledge not only of basketry, but it also gives us an appreciation and greater understanding of people's daily lives. Since baskets were the most important objects made by California Native peoples, no other objects can provide comparable insight. Beyond this, understanding the heritage, art and the use of baskets makes our appreciation of the baskets themselves more accurate, deeper and enjoyable.

Documented and Attributed Baskets

Baskets can be classified as documented or attributed. Documented pieces have specific information on where or who made them. Indian elders who recognize a weaver's work can also sometimes identify baskets, which is also important documentation. Attributed pieces are baskets lacking documentation, but where, based on its culturally selected technical features and materials, the basket can be said to have likely been made by one or more cultures. Each

The work direction of a basket is an important indicator of a weaver's cultural heritage and a key feature in attributing baskets. Notice that on this basket's rim the top coil tapers down to the leftward to form the coil ending. Note, too, the rim ticks (stripes), a nice artistic touch the Maidu sometimes did near the coil ending.

Most coiled baskets could be sewn from either the exterior or interior side. Which side was used was a cultural choice specified by honored tradition. On this basket the exterior of the basket is the smoother, more carefully finished work face, indicating that it was sewn from the outside. A basket's work face is the side that faced the weaver. Since she could see this side best, it almost always is the smoother, more finely finished side of the basket.

Once we determine which side of the basket was the work face, we can look to see what its work direction is. Since we are viewing this basket from the weaver's perspective, the direction the coil ending is pointing indicates that the basket was woven in a leftward work direction.

With the notable exception of the Yuki who wove 85% of their baskets to the right, all North Central California cultures regularly coiled to the left. With the exception of the Western Mono, who worked in both left and right work directions, all South Central and Southern California cultures regularly coiled to the right.

The basket shown here is a Valley Maidu basket with redbud designs on a sedge root background. D: 19", H: 11" (Courtesy of Len Wood's Indian Territory, Laguna Beach, California)

attribution is a probability statement, not something carved in stone.

Unfortunately, mislabeled baskets often occur even in museum collections. An important benefit of learning the technical features of each culture's basketry is to be able to recognize any errors and correct them. By knowing basketry technical features, baskets that were traded can also be recognized and properly identified.

Creating Woven Art: Selecting, Gathering, Preparing and Storing Materials

The work of creating a basket begins long before the weaving starts. Basket materials must be located, selected, gathered, prepared and properly stored. These materials must have proper length, width, strength, flexibility and beauty. With the exception of decorative elements such as feathers, beads and yarn, all California baskets were made of plant material.

Plant materials naturally vary by season. They must be gathered in the right season to have the desired characteristics of color, flexibility, ease of peeling and the like. Often favored materials were gathered annually from cultivated beds or from carefully selected trees, shrubs or beds of plants. Gathering was often hard work, particularly when digging was involved. Long trips might be required. Obtaining materials could also be dangerous work as rattlesnakes, bears and human enemies might be encountered.

Once materials were gathered, they had to be prepared and cleaned, split, peeled, soaked or undergo some other time

  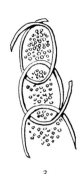  

1   *2*   *3*   *4*   *5*

Major Types of California Coiled Basketry Foundations

California Indian coiled baskets used several basic types of coil foundations. Wefts, which are roughly comparable to the role that thread plays in sewing a fabric, run through and/or around the foundation to hold the basket together. In North Central California, a three-rod foundation was most commonly used (1). Note that one rod is placed atop two rods in a triangular pattern. The wefts run between the rods of adjoining weft rows so that the basket is held tightly together. Single-rod foundations were also used. In this type only one rod forms the foundation of each weft row (2). Grass bundle foundations used a cluster of grass stems for a foundation. The weft would pass through some of the grass stems in each adjoining coiling row (3). The Yuki used splint foundations, which were thin strips shaped like tiny boards (4). Sometimes the Yuki would combine the splints with rods to form a rod and splint foundation (5). (After Mason, 1902, 247)

consuming process such as dyeing. These preparations had to be done before the actual weaving began. Some weavers felt gathering and preparing materials was an especially hard part of making baskets (Mabel McKay and Laura Fish Somersal, p.c.). When finally ready to start weaving, family or cultural obligations might intervene. Additionally, a weaver always had to be careful to protect her eyes from strain.

CALIFORNIA COILED BASKETS:
Key Features

Coiled baskets are made with a foundation that spirals from the bottom to the rim. Coiled baskets can be easily recognized by looking at their bottom. The spiral begins at a starting knot at the center of the basket's bottom. Beginning at the starting knot, the rope-like foundation will spiral around and around in ever larger circles. This foundation is made of small shoots (thin branches), a bundle of grass or other materials.

To hold the foundation together, sewing material called the weft is used. The weft consists of thin strands of plant material. The thin weft strand is a sewing element and each weft passes through or under the foundation in the preceding coil. The weft is the wrapping and binding material that holds the basket together.

A thin, sharp pointed awl is used to make small holes in the foundation through which the weft is inserted by hand. Coiling is a type of sewing, and as holes are made along the foundation the weft is inserted so as to bind the coils together. Coiled baskets have a corrugated feel to them. When carefully done, the result can be a basket sewn so tightly that it can hold water.

In California, coiled baskets were virtually always close-coiled with no openings between the coils. Openwork coiling, however, was done elsewhere (see Mason 1902, plate 31 for an example of openwork coiling done outside California).

Major Culturally Determined Features of Basketry

Nationally recognized basketry scholar Lawrence Dawson, the noted University of California museum anthropologist, developed the concept of "culturally determined categories" of coiled and twined basketry. There are certain technological steps required to create a coiled or twined basket. How these steps are implemented was a matter of cultural choice, but doing these steps was necessary to produce the basket. The culturally guided categories of basketry are discussed below. We begin with coiled basketry.

Specific Technical Features of California Coiled Basketry

It is impossible to understand California basketry without a grasp of their technical features. The following is an introduction to a complex subject.

Starting Knots

All coiled baskets begin with some type of starting knot. Coiled starting knots can be made using: (1) overhand knots (where a strand just loops back through itself), (2) tight pinhole spirals, (3) twined starts (some coiled baskets have twined or partially twined starts), (4) a start shaped like a clock spring (here, the materials used are placed closely back to back like the pages of a book), or (5) other types of starts. Some starting knots are stitched over so there is no hole in the bottom of the basket.

Work Position and Work Face

The weaver must choose how to hold the basket. The basket's **work position** can be either with the basket's outside toward her or with the interior toward her. This is in part cultural choice. Some tribes always weave bowl-shaped baskets from the exterior while others work from the interior side. However, globular-shaped baskets with small mouths will have to be worked from the exterior because there is not enough room to work from the inside. Which work position the weaver chooses determines the basket's work face.

The **work face** is the side of the basket held toward the weaver as she works. In coiling, for example, the work face is the side of the basket in which the weaver inserts the awl. Since this side faces the weaver, it is the side where she has the best control over how the awl enters the basket. She has less control in how the awl exits the basket on the **back face**, the side of the basket facing away from the weaver. Consequently, the **work face** almost always ends up as the smoother, most finished side of the basket.

Rim finishes on baskets are one of the key elements in identifying (attributing) baskets. This coiled basket has a plain wrapped rim (also called a self-rim). Note that at the coil ending, a short section of over-stitching can be seen atop the coil. (Michael Smith Gallery, Santa Fe)

Work Direction

Coiling is a form of sewing. **Work direction** is the direction the weaver progresses with when sewing the basket. The weaver will work either to her left or to her right. You must first determine the work face of the basket before you can determine a basket's work direction. Work direction was either to the weaver's left or to her right as she looked at the basket. The choice of work direction was a cultural one. It was not affected by whether the weaver was right or left-handed. Most cultures in California coiled in only one direction.

If the mouth (the open side toward her) of the basket was held toward the weaver and she works rightward, the coil would be clockwise as you looked into the basket. But if the weaver instead held the basket with the bottom end toward her (the open end away from her) and still worked rightward, the coil would be counter clockwise as you looked into the basket. Thus, it makes little sense to speak of "clockwise" or "counter clockwise" work direction. Simply determine the work face (normally the smoother side of the basket) and then look at that side to see if the basket was coiled leftward or rightward.

Foundations

When coiling, you sew horizontally along the foundation. You can visualize the foundation by extending your arm and wrapping it with a string. Your arm would be the foundation coil. In basketry, however, the string also would have to pass over at least two rows of foundation coils to hold the basket together. Think of holding both your arms out and wrapping the string around both of them to hold your arms in place.

There were different **foundation types** in coiled California Indian baskets. These consisted of: (1) one, two (rare) or three small rods, (2) grass bundles, (3) juncus stems, (4) splints (broad, flat materials like tiny boards), (5) rods and splints used together, or (6) a rod and grass mixed together in the same bundle. The most common foundations were three-rod and grass bundle. In California, three-rod foundations were with one rod atop the other two rods. The foundation diameter determined the thickness of the bottom and side of the basket. Usually grass bundle foundations provided the thinnest walls.

Warps

The coiling foundation serves the same general purpose as **warps** do in twining: they each provide structure to the basket. Just as wefts are wrapped around the foundation on coiled baskets, wefts are wrapped around **warp sticks** on twined baskets. Coil foundations and warps are both passive, non-moving elements. Similarly, in both coiling and twining wefts are the active, moving element in the weaving process.

Wefts

Wefts are the strands used to wrap around the foundation. They hold the coils together by linking each coil to the next. When the coiled basket is being sewn, the foundation is more or less horizontal and the wefts are wrapped vertically.

The most common types of wefts include: (1) split shoots (very thin, young branches or new sprouts from the base of the trunk split in half length wise by the weaver), (2) rushes (pliable, round stemmed plants), (3) roots (also split), (4) peeled bark, and (5) the basal leaves of rushes. Note that round shoots and roots when split will have a round side and a flat side. The weaver, depending on cultural preference, may choose either side to face outward and be visible.

Weft Fag Ends

A weft strand must first be anchored to the basket to keep it in place. The end that is anchored is called the **fag end**. Coiled weft fag ends are always on the work face of the basket; that is, the side of the basket facing the weaver. Common **weft fag end types** include: (1) those inserted in the foundation and then trimmed on the work face, (2) those bound in place under successive weft stitches in the foundation, (3) those hidden in the foundation, and other variations. Trimmed fag ends (often called clipped fag ends) are sometimes simply snapped off after they have dried rather than being cut off.

Weft Moving Ends

The **moving end** of a weft is the forward end of the weft strand. While fag end anchors the start of the weft strand, the moving end of the weft is repeatedly inserted through successive holes made by the awl as the sewing progresses horizontally. When the length of weft strand runs out, the moving end also must be anchored by splicing it in. **Common types of moving ends** include: (1) those simply trimmed or snapped off on the back face of the basket, (2) those bound under successive weft stitches, and (3) those trimmed with the stub of the moving end covered by a successive stitch on the back face.

Stitch Types

There are three main types of stitches that were used to wrap the foundation and to hold the basket together. **Non-interlocking stitches** are the most common. Here the weft stitches do not pass through each other but only loop around or through the foundation rods. You can picture this by

Twined basketry has a woven look to it somewhat similar to clothing fabric. A major identifying feature of a twined basket is whether the slant of weft twist is up-to-the-right or down-to-the-right. Note that on this plain twined Wappo basket, the wefts slant down-to-the-right. The design is in redbud and the background in sedge root. (Phoebe Apperson Hearst Museum of Anthropology and Regents of the University of California, #1-14512)

laying a pencil across the fingers of your right hand with the palm up. Place one end of the pencil near your thumb and the other end near your little finger. Now insert the fingers of your left hand between the other hand's fingers wrapping all the fingers of both hands around the pencil. Notice how firmly everything holds together. **Interlocking stitches** are done the same way, but instead of the wefts being side by side they pass through each other like links in a chain. You can get the idea by simply making a circle with your thumb and the finger next to it. Then take your other hand and place the thumb and finger through the first loop and close them. You have an interlocking stitch. All or part of the foundation also passes through the interlocked stitches. If you pass a pencil through both pairs of your interlocked fingers, you will understand this technique. Note that the fingers (wefts) lock in both each other and the pencil (warp). **Split stitches** are intermediate between interlocking and non-interlocking stitches. Instead of being side-by-side or looping through each other, split stitches actually pass through a hole made in the weft in the adjoining coil. The foundation, of course, again passes through the looped weft stitches to hold the basket together.

There are good ways to identify these stitch types. Carefully hold the basket and line the side up with your line of vision so you can look along the side at a right angle to the rim. **Non-interlocking stitches** will appear to have neat, even rows leading up to the rim. Most coiled California baskets will show this weft arrangement. **Interlocking stitches** will not. Instead, interlocking stitches can be seen to line up only by looking toward the rim at a diagonal angle. The stitches will line up across the basket's side both on your left and right in a V-pattern. Most Sierra Miwok and Washoe coiled baskets have this stitch type. **Split stitches** can best be seen by looking on the back face of the basket. This will normally be the rougher looking side of the basket. You can look at the wefts and see where the awl was used to split them. Determining stitch type is a valuable step in identifying tribal styles. For example, the Valley Maidu and Patwin split their weft stitches on the back face, but the Yokuts, Western Mono and Southwestern Californians (Mission) did not normally split their stitches (see: Elsasser 1978, 633).

Weft Spacing and Fineness of Stitching

Weft spacing refers to how close wefts are to each other. Most coiled baskets have wefts tightly sewn right next to each other. Weft spacing is important if a basket is meant to hold water or small seeds. However, some cultures spaced their wefts further apart than others. A few coiled baskets, usually made for sale, had very widely spaced wefts. **Fineness of stitching** refers to the width of each weft strand. Some cultures emphasized extremely fine stitch work with very narrow wefts placed close together. Others used wider wefts. Some cultures placed wefts far enough apart that the foundation can easily be seen between each weft. Remarkably, all three approaches resulted in beautiful baskets.

Rim Finish

Rims, the top coil of a basket, can have wefts wrapped in different ways. By far the most common type of rim is what is called a **plain rim** or a **self rim**. A plain or self rim is nothing more than a plainly wrapped rim. The wefts are just wrapped in the same way the entire basket is done—with wefts parallel to the wefts below (that is, at a right angle to the foundation and rim).

Sometimes on top of the plain wrapped rim **over-stitching** will be done. The plain wrapped weft can be seen beneath the over-stitching, thus the name "over-stitching." The over-stitching can either go all the way around the rim or occur just at the coil ending, often in the last inch or less. The types of over-stitching on top of a rim may be: (1) diagonal over-stitching, (2) herringbone (V-shaped) over-stitching, or (3) over-stitching parallel to the weft immediately below it.

Coil Endings are the last inch or so of the final coil. Coil endings can: (1) be plain wrapped, (2) have backstitches that are diagonal or parallel to the other wefts, or (3) have a herringbone finish. Coil endings may be tapered or blunt.

Shapes and Design Layouts

Each culture chooses its own basket shapes and overall design layouts. Baskets designed to perform the same purpose often vary in shape, technique and designs from one culture to the next. These variations are described in detail in each tribal chapter. Interestingly, coiling permits a more abrupt change of contour than twining does and this difference can be seen in coiled basketry forms.

Decoration Techniques

Designs were created as the basket was being made. The most common technique used to create designs on California Indian baskets is called weft substitution. **Weft substitution** involves changing the weft from one material to another of a different color. Each time a color change occurs a new weft strand must be substituted. Weft substitution itself does not weaken a basket, although some weft materials are stronger than others. Native Californian weavers generally worked using designs of red, black or both. These colors were used on a white or buff colored background. Besides the color provided by wefts, shell or glass beads, feathers and feather shafts were also used to decorate fancy baskets. Over-stitching on rims or at coil endings also provided artistic touches on some baskets in certain cultures. After European contact, commercial trade beads and red fabric were occasionally used by some tribes for decoration.

Names

Each type of basket had a name in the language of the weaver. To name something helps define what it is like. Associated with the name were concepts of artistic good taste, cultural rules of how to make the basket and feelings about what the finished basket should look like. **Religious observances** might occur during the gathering of materials and during weaving. For example, a prayer of appreciation might be said thanking the plant for providing material.

TWINED BASKETS:
The Technical Features

Twined baskets have a woven look to them. Twining involves weaving two or more pliable weft strands horizontally over and under vertical stable warp sticks. Twined baskets have many warp sticks rising upward from a starting knot. The warps provide the basket's structure and the wefts hold the basket together.

Additional warp sticks are added as the basket continues to increase in size. The warps typically extend out from the starting knot like the spokes of a wagon wheel. Two or three weft strands are woven horizontally around the vertical warps.

Work Face and Work Position

Work face is the side of the basket toward the weaver. **Work position** determines whether the open side of the bowl is facing toward or away from the weaver. Some twined baskets were turned over during weaving to obtain a desired weft slant or to facilitate weaving.

Starting Knots

Starting knots are necessary to align the warps and to hold them steady while the weft strands are woven among them. Starting knots can, for example, be layers of crossed warps, a bundle of fibers or even a material folded back on itself. Warps extended out from the starting knot in parallel, fan-like or radiating arrangements.

Warp Arrangements

Twining warps provide a framework upon which the weft can be woven. Warps can be bound in parallel, radial or hourglass arrangements. Therefore, warps can come straight out from the starting knot in: (1) a radiating pattern (used typically for bowls or round winnowers), (2) in a parallel pattern (used often for shallow trays and seed beaters), or (3) a fan-shaped arrangement (used typically for oval shapes). As the basket progressed, a weaver often worked with dozens of warps extending out from the basket's center like beautiful rays.

Warp Types

Twining warps were most commonly made of whole peeled shoots, such as young, thin willow or hazel branches. Rushes, such as tule or juncus, were used for warps, too. When juncus was used, the whole stem was used as the warp. When tule was used, it was twisted into cordage, which made a pliable warp.

Insertion of New Warps and the Removal of Excess Warps

Properly adding or subtracting warps is vital to creating the desired basket shape. As a twined basket grows in size, new warps are added. When adding warps, the warp ends were sometimes sharpened or chewed to flatten them to make inserting easier. Warps may also have to be subtracted. If the basket narrows toward the rim, warps must be removed as the diameter decreases.

Dozens of warp sticks rise from this unfinished Pomo lattice twined basket. (Southwest Museum of the American Indian, Autry National Center, #149-G-122)

Wefts

Wefts are the moving elements in twining. Wefts hold the warps together and provide a solid wall in close twining. Often, split shoots (very thin, young branches) were used for wefts. A shoot split lengthwise has a flat side and a round side. Either the round or flat weft side, or a mixture of both sides, can be used as the outward, visible side of the weft. Wefts can be made of roots, shoots, bark, rushes or even beargrass (the latter for overlay).

Weft Overlay

Some cultures chose to cover their wefts with an overlay material. Overlay is not a structural necessity, but it is beautifully decorative. Flat, thin materials such as beargrass fern stems, the inner strands from inside Woodwardia fern stems, or very thinly peeled redbud bark could be woven atop wefts to provide designs. The overlay strands were thinner and flatter than the basic structural weft underneath them. Overlay materials were selected or naturally pre-dyed to produce bright, high contrast designs on the blander colored wefts.

Types of Overlay

There were three types of overlay: the single side, the double side and the irregular overlay. On **single side overlay**, the design shows fully only on one side of the basket, usually the exterior. The Northwestern California tribes regularly used single face overlay. On **double side overlay**, the design shows on both the exterior and interior of the basket. Northeastern Californians and the Mountain Maidu regularly used double side overlay. **Irregular overlay** occurs when the design shows fully on one side of the basket, but shows only irregularly on the other side. This irregularity of overlay face usually occurs on Southern Humboldt Athapaskan baskets, but is also found on some Northwestern California baskets.

Slant of Weft Twist

By looking carefully at a twined basket you can observe that the wefts slant **up-to-the-left** or **up-to-the-right**. The slant of twist is culturally determined and generally is quite consistent within a culture. Slant of weft does not result from the weaver being left-handed or right-handed, but was purely a cultural choice and was done quite consistently within each tribe.

Each culture chose to slant their twining wefts either up-to-the-left, up-to-the-right or even both directions. The Ohlone (Costanoan) and Esselen creatively used both slants of twist as decorative patterns on the same basket. Slant of weft is an important and useful feature in attributing baskets.

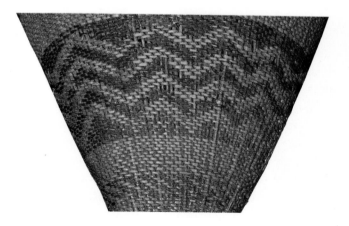

Diagonal twining is another major twining technique. Diagonal twining can be recognized by its visual similarity to brickwork since the ends of each weft are at the mid-point of the weft above and below it. This is a detail of a diagonally twined Valley Maidu burden basket's bottom. (California State Parks, Bidwell Mansion State Historic Park, #139-19-40)

Twined Fag Ends and Their Splices

Weft fag ends (the beginning end of the weft strand) can be anchored in several ways. For example, fag ends can be caught under the preceding weft turn on either the work face or the back of a basket. Fag ends can also be wrapped around one or two warps and any leftover remnant of strand was trimmed or snapped off on the work face for neatness. Fag ends were also sometimes caught between tight warp sticks and held in place.

Twined Moving Ends and Their Splices

The weft **moving end** is the end of the weft strand that moves along through the warps. Moving ends could be paired with a new weft strand and anchored to the basket along with the new fag end. Moving ends might also be caught between tight warps and held in place. Any excess strand was then trimmed on the back face of the basket. Moving ends could additionally be turned upward and secured by incorporating them with the warps. Sometimes a moving end and a new fag end were overlapped for strength.

Close Twining Versus Openwork Twining

Wefts were placed very close together on baskets meant to hold water, small seeds or valued objects. Baskets meant to be beautiful show pieces, such as women's hats, were also tightly woven. Such tightly woven baskets are called **close-twined baskets**.

In **openwork twining**, the wefts are widely spaced so that there were open areas between the warp sticks. These are called **openwork baskets**. Their warps can always be plainly seen. In fact, many Northwestern California weavers call openwork baskets "stick baskets" because the warp sticks are so conspicuous.

Openwork baskets had open spaces between wefts and warps. This open spacing was needed to: (1) allow air circulation, (2) let water to pass through (such as on fish traps) or (3) simply because they were used to carry large items that did not require close twining. Openwork weaving allowed a basket to be made more quickly than a comparable close-twined basket. Many kinds of openwork baskets were quite large, and this technique also helped minimize the basket's weight.

Fineness of Weave

Baskets varied in the size of the weft. Some had very fine wefts, while others had quite large wefts. A mortar hopper or burden basket destined for very hard use, for example, would have larger wefts than, say, a fine tobacco basket or a

Three major types of twining can be seen in this photo. (1) Plain twining with two weft strands is used at the top where the long, dark rectangles appear. Note the neat, stacked look up the weft rows. (2) Immediately below the plain twining are five rows of lattice twining. If you look carefully at the uppermost row of lattice twining, you can see the horizontal reinforcing rod that runs through all exterior lattice twined wefts. Lattice twining occurs in another band of six weft rows farther down the basket's side. Interestingly, on the opposite side (the basket's interior), lattice twining will look like ordinary plain twining. (3) At the very bottom of the basket two or three weft rows of plain twining can be seen. Just above this, five rows of three-strand twining can be seen. Three-strand twining is easily recognizable since the wefts look much more horizontally elongated than in either the lattice twining immediately above or the plain twining below. This photo is a detail of a Pomo mortar hopper and dramatically illustrates Pomo virtuosity in twining. (Private collection)

hat. How fine each type of basket was woven was a cultural choice influenced by function and individual skill and taste.

Warp Selvages

The rim of twined baskets must be finished in a secure way so that it will not unravel or loosen. The woven rim finish on a basket is called the selvage (also spelled selvedge). Twined

basket rims can be finished in several ways, including: (1) trimmed rims, where the warps were all cut off evenly and the wefts brought up to or near the trim line, (2) coiled rims, where the warps were turned horizontally and used as a coiling foundation one coil wide, or (3) braided, twined or plaited rims, where warps are woven together over one another to form an edge. Rims are also often reinforced with attached rods to strengthen baskets destined for hard use. Termination of the last weft row must be done in a way to keep the wefts from unraveling.

Shape

The shape selected was influenced by the basket's purpose, culturally preferred form and the weaver's own artistic tastes. Weavers in each culture had clear ideas, handed down through generations, as to what was a proper shape for a particular type of basket. There was room for individual variation, but the traditions were clear enough that community members would know if the basket conformed to the normal idea of a proper basket of its type.

Designs

Designs were made within the boundaries of cultural traditions and taste (see: O'Neale, 1994, 62-104). Designs were carefully selected, considered as a part of the entire work of art and placed in culturally appropriate locations. They were normally woven into the basket rather than added after it was finished. Red, black or both were the most common design colors. In North Central California, designs of only one color, either red or black, were almost always preferred. In South Central California designs of both red and black together were commonly used together. Everywhere the background color was almost always the lighter color, usually white, brown or yellow (in the case of older beargrass overlay material). Sometimes the opposite sides of the same peeled material were alternated to give different colors, as with peeled redbud which has a red side and a white side. **Design layouts** were usually very clearly specified by respected cultural tradition. For example, Pomo design layouts were quite different from those of the Maidu. These are discussed later for each culture. All or most designs had names, but few designs had symbolic meaning (Kroeber in Barrett 1996, 90; Barrett 1996, 251-256; Dawson and Deetz, 1965, 204; Smith-Ferri 1998, 38).

Names

As with coiled baskets, each twined basket type had a name. Names are often remembered by elders, recorded in early anthropological ethnographies and in word lists compiled by linguists. Some names are still in use today.

Religious Observances Shown on Baskets

Perhaps the most apparent example occurs on some Pomo twined baskets. These include the occasional addition on Pomo baskets of orange flicker feather shafts and the use of a break in the design called a "dau." These are discussed in the Pomo chapter.

The Most Common Types of California Indian Twining

Plain Twining

Plain twining involves weaving two weft strands around warps. It is the most common twining technique in California. Plain twining is most often used to form the main body of the basket. It was used virtually statewide.

Diagonal (Twill) Twining

Diagonal twining gets its name from the step-like diagonal appearance of the wefts. While the wefts look like they are woven diagonally, the weaving process is actually horizontal. We still prefer the term "diagonal twining" to "twill" because it is easy to remember what to look for when seeing this twining technique.

In diagonal twining, the wefts in each adjoining row are wrapped around two or more different warps. If, for example, in row 1 the wefts are wrapped around warps A and B, then in row 2 the wefts will be wrapped around warps B and C. The result is that basket's wefts are arranged like layered bricks. Each space between the wefts is the mid-point of the weft above and the weft below. Diagonal twining is easy to spot if you look for wefts woven in a pattern like brickwork. Even though woven horizontally, the wefts appear to rise diagonally across the side of the basket. Diagonal twining is most often used to form the main body of the basket. Diagonal twining was most often used in Central and Southeastern California.

Three-Strand Twining

Three-strand twining involves weaving three weft strands around warps. It was used most often as a strengthening feature at critical points on predominantly plain twined baskets. Baskets made mostly of three-strand twining were almost unheard of.

Three-strand twining can be easily identified on a field of plain twining, its usual location. The three strand twining will be wider and narrower than the plain twining. Visually, three-strand twining can be seen going across two warps, whereas plain-twining looks wrapped around one warp. Three-strand twining will also rise slightly above the general surface than plain twining. This type of twining is most often found on the base surrounding the starting knot, at the curve from the bottom to the sides or near the rim. All these are critical places requiring a sturdy weave. **Three-strand braiding** is similar to three-strand twining, except that its wefts are interlaced with one another as they pass around the warps.

Lattice Twining

Lattice twining is easily identified by the fact that on the basket's exterior it looks like finely made single rod coiling, but on the basket's interior it looks like plain twining. This is especially apparent on baskets using plain twining with lattice twining reinforcing bands, such is found on Pomo winnowing trays. For baskets where both weaves are used, the lattice twining is clearly seen on the convex (rounded) side as raised above the surface of the plain twining. While lattice twining was most often used as a reinforcing weave for strength, the Pomo people made entire baskets using lattice twining.

Lattice twining is easy to remember because it has two crossed sticks looking somewhat like latticework. Actually, lattice twining involves a vertical warp and two wefts. What is distinctive is that one weft stays entirely on the basket's exterior. It looks like a rod running around the outside. The second weft winds between the basket's interior and exterior, wrapping around the horizontal exterior weft and the vertical warp. As mentioned, this results in an interior that looks like plain twining and an exterior that looks (but is not) coiled.

Reinforcing supports are often found on twined baskets. Some baskets were destined for such hard use that very strong rods had to be placed at the rim or along the sides for strength. Most burden baskets had a reinforcing rod at the rim. Mortar hoppers often had reinforcing rods attached to their sides. Three-strand twining or lattice twining or both could also be used to provide added reinforcing support.

Main Construction Weave or the Basket Wall

This is simply the type of twining used for most of the basket. Some types of weaves, such as plain twining and diagonal twining, are regularly used for most or all of a basket. Other types of twining, such as three-strand twining, are almost never used for an entire basket. Lattice twining, however, can be used for virtually all or merely a tiny part of a basket.

WICKERWORK BASKETS

In wickerwork, the weft passes alternately over and under one or more warps. Wickerwork was rare in California. Its best-known survival is as seed beaters among the Pomo people and some of their neighbors. Wickerwork is more common in ancient archeological sites in western Nevada and California than in cultures at the time of European arrival. This suggests that wickerwork was a technique already on its way out prior to European contact.

BOUND WEAVE BASKETS

Bound weaves are a distinctive type of weaving that is neither coiling nor twining. A distinctive feature of bound weaves is that they have a moving element and a passive element that binds the basket. In North Central California these elements are made of string. Bound weaves of string were used in Pomo, Wappo and Lake Miwok cradles to secure the willow, hazel or dogwood warps that make up the body of the cradle. Either Native or commercial string might be used in bound weaves.

STRING BASKETS

Some Sierra Miwok, Yokuts and Western Mono made string baskets using many pairs of strings radiating out from the basket's center to hold a coil foundation together. In the case of each pair of strings, a passive string lays perpendicular to the coil rows on one side of the basket. The other string actively loops around the foundation coil and the passive string to hold the basket together. Although looking somewhat like coiling, string baskets are a distinctive technique.

String baskets also should not to be confused with coiled baskets sewn using a needle and string. These needle and string coiled baskets were circa 1900 innovations. While looking much like old string baskets and inspired by them, they are actually a very different technique (see: Tulloch and Polanich 1999).

Materials

Most tribes used less than ten basketry materials (Merrill 1923, 216). If we look at the truly common materials, the number is even fewer. The following are all major materials. Less common materials are found in the chapters on individual cultures.

Some Tips on Identifying Major Materials

While there is no substitute for seeing the actual material on the basket itself, we can offer some helpful hints to assist in recognizing these materials. Please note that we mention the major regions where these materials were most often found. The materials were also sometimes found elsewhere. When this occurs, details are given in the tribal chapters.

Beargrass (*Xerophyllum tenax*) is used primarily as an overlay material in Northwestern and Northeastern California. Beargrass was used in both regions for designs, but in Northeastern California it was also used as a background material. It has an off-white color when new that turns a rich yellow with age. If you look beneath the beargrass overlay, you can see the brown conifer root weft.

Bracken fern root (*Pteridium*) was used for black designs. Light brown in color when gathered, it is commonly boiled for a short time when dying it to produce a black color. Sometimes the bracken fern still retains brown shades with the black (Barrett 1996, 139). Bracken fern root was an especially popular black weft material among the Western Mono and Yokuts, but was also often used by the Maidu, Sierra Miwok and Coastal Pomo in North Central California. Bracken fern root wefts are characteristically flat looking with a slightly dull black color.

Bulrush Root (*Scirpus*) is a common material used for black designs among the Pomo, Patwin, Wappo, Lake Miwok and others. Bulrush root is pink before it is dyed black. When you look at baskets using bullrush root, usually some wefts will show pink, pinkish-black or deep brown tones where the dye did not turn some wefts completely black. Bulrush root also tends to be used as very narrow wefts. It has tiny, but fairly prominent ridged striations.

Cattail (*Typha*) is lighter colored than tule. Cattail tends to be off-white or very light brown. Cattail was used for wefts. **Tule** (*Scirpus*) was used for wefts, warps and cordage warps. Tule is darker than cattail and is distinctively brown rather than the off-white color of cattail. Tule was used in Central California for utility baskets. Finely made cattail and tule weft baskets were made by the Klamath, Modoc and others using tule cordage wefts. Both tule and cattails are rushes.

Conifer Roots from trees such as pine (*Pinus*), redwood (*Sequoia*) and spruce (*Picea*) were made into thin, pliable weft strands. Conifer roots were the primary weft material for twining in Northwestern California, Northeastern California, and among the Southern Humboldt Athapaskans. In North Central California the Pomo, Yuki, Mountain

Maidu and Sierra Miwok also used conifer root wefts in certain types of twined baskets. Conifer roots range in color from deep chocolate brown to tan. It is usually a dull color and most often serves as background and structural support for overlay designs.

Deergrass (*Muhlenbergia rigens*) served as the main foundation material for coiled baskets among the Yokuts, Western Mono and many Southern California cultures. Deergrass bundle foundation facilitates making fine, thin walled baskets. In North Central California, the Sierra Miwok often used it for foundations in their winnowers.

Devil's Claw pods (*Proboscidea*) were used for black designs in Southeastern California. The pods were cut into thin strips and used for weft material. Because they are naturally black, Devil's claw pods did not have to be dyed. The pods were split into thin strips for use as wefts. If you hold the basket and look closely along the side you can see that some black wefts have white or brown sides where they were cut into weft strips. You can see these white or brown sides only if you look carefully as they tend to be toward the inside of the weft below the black surface and can be difficult to see. The Chemehuevi and other Southeastern California desert cultures used devil's claw for their black designs.

Hazel (*Corylus*) shoots serve as warps in Northern California twining. With age, hazel looks very smooth and has a brown sheen. Hazel provides thin, strong warps useful in making fine twined baskets.

Joshua Tree Root (*Yucca brevifolia*) is identified by its orange-red color. It is much more orange-red, or at least a lighter red, than redbud. Unlike most other materials, the red yucca bark sometimes chips off the weft so that little pieces of red are missing from the weft, a characteristic other materials rarely have. Joshua tree root tends to be used as thin wefts. Southern California desert cultures such as the Kawaiisu, Tubatulabal, Panamint and others used it often in their coiled baskets. Other species of yucca were occasionally used as well.

Juncus (*Juncus*) is a rush used for wefts and warps over much of coastal Southern California inland to the desert. It is distinctive because of its golden mottled color, which provides many rich tones that can range from light tan to a golden orange. Juncus was also dyed black for use in designs. The Chumash, Gabrieliño and the Southwestern Californians used juncus extensively for both coiling and twining. Juncus was also used in north central Oregon by the Kalapuya and Upper Umpqua.

Maidenhair fern (*Adiantum*) stems are a shiny, rich black color. Maidenhair fern stems were most often used for black overlay designs in Northwestern California, Northeastern California and Southwestern Oregon.

Redbud (*Cercis occidentalis*) bark of young redbud shoots is a rich, dark red. A useful feature in identifying redbud wefts is that they often have very tiny white dots on them. These dots are not much bigger than a pinpoint. Redbud was used over most of Central California and Northeastern California for wefts. It was used on both coiled and twined baskets. Sometimes the bark was peeled and used for background wefts, as among the Yuki and Cahto.

Occasionally old redbud wefts get a fine white powdery coating of naturally occurring wax on the material. If this occurs, it is usually found around the edges of the wefts where they curve in toward the foundation. Reportedly, a clean, very soft white cloth may be used to clean it, but the wax is harmless (Turnbaugh and Turnbaugh 1997, 93).

Sedge Root (*Carex*) has subtly rounded edges. It is white when new but darkens to a rich buff color with age. Sedge root wefts often have a slightly dusty look, when viewed very closely. The Pomo, Patwin, Valley Maidu, Wappo, Ohlone (Costanoan), Coast Miwok, Yokuts, Western Mono and others commonly used sedge root for coiled background wefts. Sedge root was also used in twining for wefts.

Sumac or Sourberry (*Rhus trilobata*) is a rugged material very useful for wefts where durability is important. It was common in the coiled baskets of the Chumash, Gabrielino, Southwestern California and others. Sumac wefts were often used on the same baskets as juncus wefts. The sumac is stronger and therefore often found on the bottoms of such baskets since it holds up to wear better than juncus. Sumac is lighter colored than juncus and not as shiny. When new, sumac is white but as it ages it turns a light gray or tan.

Willow (*Salix*) was one of the most widely used materials in California. It can be very white, buff colored or brown. Willow wefts often have a shine to them. Willow served as wefts and warps and in both twining and coiling. It was a very common foundation material among Central California coiled baskets. Willow was very often used to make openwork utility baskets. Willow is a versatile material. It could be used peeled, unpeeled and even purposely colored by exposure to the sun (often called "sunburned willow").

Woodwardia Fern or Giant Chain Fern (*Woodwardia*) stems contain strong inner fibers useful as weft strands. The natural color of these strands is white, but in Northwestern

California and among the Wintu they were dyed an orangey-red using alder bark (Alnus). Red dyed alder bark wefts are a much lighter red color than the deep red of redbud wefts. Woodwardia was used only in the northern part of California.

Feathers, beads, porcupine quills and commercial fabric

Non-plant materials were also used to decorate some finely made fancy baskets. Clamshell disc beads, olivella shell disc beads and abalone and magnesite pendants were used. Quail topknots, red woodpecker feathers and many other kinds of bird feathers and quills were added to the baskets of some cultures. Additionally, European-made trade beads and fabric were occasionally used as decorative elements. All these materials are discussed in the individual chapters as they occur.

The History of Twining and Coiling: Two Distinct Traditions

The Four Major Types of California Twined Basketry

The vast majority of California Indian baskets were done in twining or coiling. These two traditions have existed side by side in Central California for many centuries, yet they have different origins, histories, technical weaving features, and are quite different in appearance. They frequently serve different purposes and often have different design concepts.

Twined basketry predates coiling in California (Dawson 1988, 1-4). Twined baskets, bags and mats were probably brought into California with the first Native people. The distribution of specific twining techniques and certain types of twined baskets suggest early migrations both along the coast and via inland valleys.

California twined basketry was partly of northern origin and partly the result of local innovation within the state. **Plain twining** and **three-strand twining** are northern techniques found from Alaska south through Oregon to California. Plain twined basketry probably developed in the Northwest Coast and moved south along the Pacific Coast and through inland valleys to California. One variation of plain twining particularly significant in California, that having overlay-type designs, is found from Alaska southward to northern California. Three-strand twining likely has a similar history of a north to south spread. Interestingly, some northern twining techniques, such as false embroidery, never reached California.

Lattice twining and **diagonal twining** were probably California innovations. Lattice twining reached its highest development among the Pomo and their Wappo and Lake Miwok neighbors. These cultures

All twined baskets begin with a starting knot which secures the warp sticks. The starting knot is at the very center of the bottom on most California Indian twined baskets. In this photo, the warp sticks that radiate out from the starting knot can be seen beneath the wefts that are woven to hold the basket together. (Private Collection)

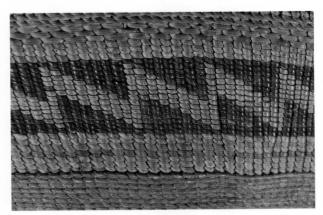

Note the rich variations in twining that can be seen in this small detail of a Pomo twined basket. At the bottom are rows of lattice twining with a rod running horizontally beneath the wefts. In the middle section with the redbud design, plain twining over a single vertical warp stick is used. Above this are three rows of diagonal twining. Note, too, that all three types of twining in this basket have wefts that slant down-to-the-right. Slant of weft twist is one of many important identifying factors in attributing twined baskets. (Private Collection)

Coiled basketry was sewn in ever-widening spirals beginning at the starting knot at the center of the basket's bottom. The corrugated look of coiled basketry is evident on this coiled basket. Note, too, the slightly larger and stronger top coil at the rim. This is a Yuki basket from Mendocino County made prior to 1904. D: 20", H: 6" (Maryhill Museum of Art, Goldendale, Washington, #98-104)

made entire baskets using lattice twining. Lattice twining spread from the Pomo area to many cultures, but it was never used as extensively elsewhere. Other cultures primarily used lattice twining minimally to strengthen baskets at points where they were subject to wear or breakage.

Diagonal twining probably began among the Pomo and the Esselen (see the Esselen and Pomo chapters). Diagonal twining spread from coastal California inland across the state. The spread of diagonal twining continued eastward as the Paiute and Shoshone carried diagonal twining with them as they expanded across the Great Basin in Nevada and beyond.

Thus, some twining reached California from the north. Once here, twining flowered into an unsurpassed art and innovative forms of twining developed. Virtually entire baskets were made in plain twining, diagonal twining and lattice twining. Three-strand twining and various other minor kinds of twining were used only for strengthening and for artistic effect.

The Five Major Types of California Coiled Basketry

Coiled basketry came into California thousands of years after twining. Coiling seems to be older in western Nevada than in California and to have spread from the interior toward the coast. Coiled basketry is less widespread in California than twining, has a more limited number of uses and shows innovative variations all of which suggest a more recent adoption (Dawson 1988, 1-4; see also the Sierra Miwok, Maidu and Yuki chapters in this volume). Although coiling spread west and south within California, it did not spread to northwestern or northeastern California. There was a critical difference between coiling and twining. Many California cultures lived well with only twined baskets; none could survive with only coiled baskets.

But coiled basketry had great aesthetic and functional appeal and it came into use among all or nearly all Central and Southern California people.

Coiled baskets have obvious advantages for certain culinary functions and when well made possesses great beauty. The spread of coiled basketry was probably the greatest single artistic movement in Native California art history.

While coiled basketry did spread along with some population movements, it more often spread by diffusion from one people to the next. Coiling spread in clear paths across Central and Southern California.

Coiling came into North Central California with several different groups and at different times. All, or nearly all, the coiled basketry discussed in this volume seems to have ancient ancestral roots in western Nevada and to have come in over the Sierra Nevada Mountains into North Central California. The Maidu may have been the first people to bring coiled basketry in North Central California. This Maidu derived coiling spread widely. It came to be made by the Maidu, Pomo, Patwin, Wappo, Coast Miwok, Lake Miwok, Nomlaki, Ohlone (Costanoan) and Huchnom, We call this tradition **Maidu-Patwin-Pomo type coiling**. It is described in the chapters of each of these cultures.

A second type of coiling made by early western Nevadans was also the forerunner of the coiled basketry of the Sierra Miwok and the Washoe, the latter people a Great Basin tribe. We call this tradition **Sierra Miwok-Washoe type coiling**. This coiled basketry did not spread widely in California and was made only in the Sierras and adjacent Great Basin. For details on the introduction of coiled basketry into California, please see the Sierra Miwok and Maidu chapters.

A third type of North Central California coiling, Yuki coiled basketry, likely developed locally, but with influences from other traditions. We call this **Yuki-type coiling**. Yuki coiling was the prototype for the coiled basketry of the Wailaki, Cahto and several Southern Humboldt Athapaskan groups. The coiling of these Yuki neighbors is discussed in the side bar in the Yuki chapter.

In this volume we explore in detail these three North Central California coiling traditions and the unique variations found in each culture. In Volume II of this series, we will discuss other major types of California coiled basketry found in South Central California and Southern California. One is **Yokuts-Southwestern California type coiling**, which was influenced by string basketry. String basketry looks rather like coiled basketry, but is a very different weave. String basketry is old and carbonized archeological fragments have been found in the San Joaquin Valley (see Dawson 1988, 2-3; Pritchard, 1970, which also includes Lawrence Dawson's

comments on string basketry). String basketry was important among the Yokuts and was at least in part the likely inspiration for the grass bundle foundation and rightward work direction found in Yokuts coiled basketry. This Yokuts-Southwestern California-type coiled basketry with its distinctive work direction, grass bundle foundation, interior work face on flaring bowls, weft spacing and the presence of certain designs came to be made by the Yokuts, Western Mono, Salinan, Tubatulabal, Kawaiisu, Southwestern Californians ("Mission" tribes), Kitanemuk and to a limited extent by the Chumash, Gabrielino and Panamint. This kind of coiling did not come from western Nevada for there is a lack of anything like Yokuts-Southern California coiled work in western Nevada archeological basketry. Yokuts-Southwestern California coiling is almost certainly a California invention.

The final California coiling tradition is the **Chemehuevi-Early Puebloan (Anasazi) type**. The Chemehuevi made this type of basketry in California, although similar (but not identical) coiled basketry was found eastward as far as New Mexico. Chemehuevi-Puebloan coiling was late coming into California, yet developed distinctive features and flowered among the Chemehuevi. Both Yokuts-Southwestern California and Chemehuevi-Early Puebloan coiling are discussed in Volume II since they are not the North Central California coiled basketry.

California Coiling Connections to the Great Basin and Southwest

Coiling appears to have spread westward from the Great Basin into California by several routes. There are close coiled basketry connections between California and western Nevada. These ancient connections also extended beyond California and Nevada eastward as far as Utah, New Mexico, west Texas and northern Mexico (see the Sierra Miwok and Maidu chapter for discussions and archeological citations).

Comments

Despite sharing its roots with other Indian people, every California culture's basketry shows unique innovations and unsurpassed artistry. Native California created the widest array of basketry types, the most amazingly decorated baskets, and invented baskets for more purposes than any other region in North America and perhaps the world. The art, function, and history of Native California's coiled and twined basketry is a unique world-class treasure.

This Ohlone/Costanoan coiled basket is from Santa Clara near San Jose. It is decorated with olivella shell disc beads. There are remnants of red woodpecker feathers and quail topknot feathers on a background of sedge root wefts. Note the split triangle designs and absence of pendants. D: 14", H: 5" (Smithsonian Institution, #E 313234)

The high art of San Francisco Bay Native Americans. This Ohlone/Costanoan coiled basket has lavish designs of intricate diamonds and zigzags formed by olivella shell disc beads. Use of olivella shell disc beads on coiled baskets was a San Francisco Bay art form. (Peabody Museum, Harvard University, #32-54-10/176)

OHLONE / COSTANOAN BASKETRY

The Ohlone or Costanoan homeland consists of the Pacific Coast from the city of San Francisco south to Monterey Bay and beyond, almost to Point Sur. Inland, Ohlone country includes the East Bay from Carquinez Strait south through the present day cities of Berkeley, Oakland, San Jose and Gilroy southward beyond San Juan Bautista and Salinas. All or part of San Francisco, San Mateo, Contra Costa, Alameda, Santa Clara, Santa Cruz, San Benito and Monterey counties are in Ohlone territory. [1]

This land is rich in coastal and estuary food resources, oak woodlands, chaparral and freshwater streams. It varies from hilly to mountainous and contains many fertile valleys. Year round the climate is generally moderate.

Ancestral Ohlone probably came from California's Great Central Valley to the San Francisco Bay Area. The Ohlone people probably entered the Bay Area from the Sacramento-San Joaquin River Delta, perhaps traveling along the south shore of Suisun Bay and Carquinez Strait. The Ohlone first settled in western Contra Costa County and in Alameda County. Then they spread rapidly southward as far as the Monterey Bay area. San Francisco and coastal San Mateo County were probably settled later as archeological evidence suggests that the Ohlone moved around the south bay via Santa Clara County to reach the San Francisco-San Mateo Peninsula. The coastal side of San Mateo County and the San Francisco area were probably the last area settled by the Ohlone (Moratto 1984, 266, 279-280, 555; Breschini 1983, 71; Foster 1994, 89; Eshleman 2002, 74-76; Breschini and Haversat 2004, 189-198).

The Ohlone almost certainly encountered Esselen-speaking people already present around San Francisco Bay and Monterey Bay (Beeler 1961, 197 and 1978, 35; Whistler 1977, 169; Breschini and Haversat 2004, 189-198). Linguistic, archeological and basketry research suggest that the Esselen occupied the San Francisco and Monterey Bay areas prior to the arrival of the Ohlone. Over the centuries, most of the Esselen were gradually absorbed into the Ohlone population (Breschini 1983; Breschini and Haversat 2004, 64-65, 191-194). By the time of European arrival, the Esselen people held only a small remnant of their southern territory, a remote section of coastal Monterey County.

Yet, the Esselen seem to have had a major impact on Ohlone twined basketry. In fact, Ohlone twined basketry seems largely adopted from the Esselen. The history of this unique type of twined basketry is related both in this chapter and the Esselen chapter.

In contrast to twining, the Esselen had little or no impact on Ohlone coiled basketry. The Esselen apparently did little coiling, while some Ohlone groups made spectacular and distinctive coiled baskets. Ohlone coiled baskets were often lavishly decorated with thin, round olivella shell disc beads and feathers. They are some of the finest coiled baskets in California.

Ohlone Coiled Basketry

Most early California baskets were collected during voyages when ships put into various California seaports. Since few mariners ventured inland, basketry from the coast was largely what they collected. Among the early coiled baskets collected were highly distinctive baskets from the San Francisco Bay Area.

The unique features of the San Francisco Bay Area baskets, combined with our knowledge of surrounding coastal cultures' basketry (Pomo, Wappo, Patwin, Plains Miwok and Yokuts), allow us to rule out these neighboring tribes as the source of the distinctive San Francisco Bay coiled baskets. The San Francisco Bay baskets we will describe could only have come from the Ohlone or the Coast Miwok. Some of these baskets are documented as being Ohlone, so we have a documented sample to serve as a basis for identifying additional baskets as Ohlone.

Surviving documented baskets also allow us to distinguish Ohlone baskets from probable Coast Miwok ones. Similar, but not identical, baskets that we believe to be Coast Miwok are described in the Coast Miwok chapter. There are also a

---

[1] The names Costanoan and Ohlone are synonyms for eight very similar cultures speaking related languages. The name Costanoan, long the standard in scholarly literature, is from the Spanish word Costanos, meaning Coast People. It has the advantage of having always referred to all the people of this culture. The term also recognizes the important maritime heritage of the people. Ohlone was originally the name of a cluster of villages located along San Gregorio Creek in San Mateo County (Levy 1978, 485, 494-495). The term Ohlone has the advantage of being a Native word and being more widely recognized by the general public. Today, some Costanoan/Ohlone people use one term and some the other. Most anthropologists seem to use Costanoan; museum professionals seem evenly divided. Both names honor Native people in different ways.

Intricate designs of olivella shell disc beads on a sedge root weft background decorate this Ohlone coiled basket. Once erroneously referred to in a publication as a Wappo basket, it is actually a classic Ohlone coiled basket. The Wappo did not use olivella shell disc beads on their baskets. (American Museum of Natural History, #50.1-6059)

few baskets that are intermediate between the Ohlone and Coast Miwok types, yet even some of these can be tentatively attributed.

Key criteria for determining which baskets are Ohlone include: (1) baskets having a cluster of technical features and a style distinct from neighboring tribes, (2) baskets with a documented history of being made in the San Francisco Bay area, (3) baskets with early known collection dates, and (4) baskets handed down in old local families, often of Spanish or Indian heritage (Dawson and Shanks research).

Technical Features of Ohlone Coiled Baskets

Nearly all Ohlone coiled baskets used three-rod **foundations**. Two-rod coiling foundations were also present, but only to a very limited extent. There are just two Ohlone baskets known to employ two-rod foundations. One basket, at the Pacific Grove Museum of Natural History, has a two-rod foundation in all or part. The other is an oval basket at the Musee de l'Homme in Paris, which has a two-rod rim (see: Heizer, April-June 1968, 72). Single-rod foundations seem to be absent (Dawson p.c.).

Ohlone coiled **work direction** was uniformly to the left. **Starting knots** were either a very tight spiral or a more open spiral which leaves a small hole that is stitched over. **Weft fag ends** were handled in three ways: (1) concealed in the bundle, (2) bound down and under other wefts, or (3) trimmed on the basket's work face. **Weft moving ends** were either: (1) bound under successive stitches on the back face, or (2) trimmed flush on the back face (Dawson p.c.). The weft moving ends were sometimes covered by successive stitches. If **weft stitches** were split, it was on the basket's back face (the side held away from the weaver, normally the interior on Ohlone pieces). Some baskets have, in addition to split

stitches, many interlocking stitches as well. Ohlone weft stitches are not as fine as those of the Pomo but were quite beautiful. **Rims** were plain wrapped (self rims) with none of the rim over-stitching the Miwok often did. **Coil endings** were tapered.

The variations in handling weft fag ends and moving ends probably indicate differences in the histories of the eight Ohlone (Costanoan) language groups. Some of the branches of the culture may have arrived in the San Francisco-Monterey Bay Area at different times or have had contact with different cultures. Such experiences would help explain some variations we see in the technical features of the baskets.

The technical features of Ohlone coiling show that there are clear ties to the cultures to their north and northeast. Ohlone coiled basketry is most closely related to Coast Miwok, Patwin, Wappo and Pomo coiling, in that order. It also shows some relationship to Plains Miwok coiling (Bates p.c.; Bates 1983, 36-40). These are all North Central California tribes.

The Yokuts of South Central California played a limited part in the history of Ohlone basketry, although Yokuts influence may only date from the Spanish mission period. Several Ohlone coiled baskets use trimmed weft fag ends, which suggests a relationship to Yokuts work. Yokuts influence probably occurred when many Ohlone and Yokuts people were living at the same Spanish missions and intermarrying. The ties of Ohlone coiled basketry are much older and far stronger to North Central Californians such as

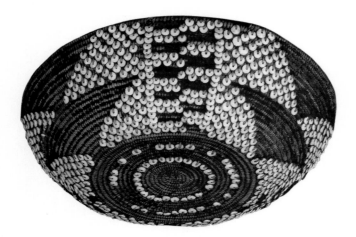

Olivella shell disc beads on a background of red woodpecker feathers highlight this stunning Ohlone/Costanoan basket. This is a very ornate basket with designs extending across its bottom. (Copyright © The British Museum, #6222. Used with permission)

the Coast Miwok, Patwin, Wappo, Pomo and Plains Miwok, than to the Yokuts.

Forms of Coiled Ohlone Baskets

Ohlone fancy baskets were made in four main shapes. Three were round bowls: (1) flaring bowls, (2) fairly low, broad globular bowls, or (3) fairly low, broad bowls incurving at both top and bottom, but less rounded then the globular type. The first two types, flaring bowls and globular bowls, were the kind most commonly decorated with shell beads. There was also (4) an oval bowl that curved inward toward the mouth. Feathers and beads could occur on all four forms.

Olivella Shell Disc Beads

The Ohlone use of olivella shell disc beads and red woodpecker feathers on their coiled baskets resulted in some of the most beautiful baskets made in California. These distinctive and spectacular baskets were extensively decorated with thin, round or nearly round, slightly convex olivella shell disc beads with a hole drilled in the center. Olivella shell disc beads were similar in diameter to the round clam shell beads regularly used by the Pomo and Wappo, but were thinner and slightly convex, unlike flat clamshell disc beads.

Ohlone olivella disc beads are not to be confused with whole olivella shell beads. The whole olivella shell was not used to decorate baskets. The Ohlone made their olivella shell disc beads using only a small part of the side of an olivella shell.

This is the oval form of ornate Ohlone/Costanoan coiled baskets. Note the olivella shell disc beads attached using weft strands arising from below the beads, an unusual feature for the Ohlone. (Musee de l'Homme, Paris #81-108-1)

The Ohlone often used patterns formed by olivella shell disc beads as the main design on the basket. Some Ohlone baskets are almost entirely covered with olivella disc beads and tufts of red woodpecker feathers. In contrast, the Pomo and Wappo usually used clamshell disc beads only to accent designs.

The Ohlone used olivella shell disc beads for money, while the Pomo used clamshell disc beads for money (Harrington 1942, 1, 27). This could have been a deciding factor in the Ohlone preference for decorating their baskets with olivella shell disc beads and the Pomo choice of clamshell disc beads to ornament their baskets. The Ohlone did use clamshell disc beads on their baskets, but these were always a small percentage compared to the olivella disc beads present. The Pomo are not known to have used olivella disc beads on baskets.

The olivella shell disc beads on both Ohlone and Coast Miwok baskets were attached using sedge root wefts. Weavers normally attached the bead from above the bead hole so the bead hung down. But in at least two cases beads were attached from below the bead, giving the basket a shingled effect. In contrast, the Pomo and Wappo normally sewed their clamshell disc beads on using Native or non-native string.

A few baskets in European museums have both olivella and clam shell disc beads on them. Their identification is less certain, but if they lack abalone pendants and have plain wrapped rims, they are probably Ohlone. Those with pendants and over-stitched rims are likely Coast Miwok.

Most Ohlone baskets have olivella shell disc beads with edges that were very finely finished. On any one basket the beads usually have consistent degrees of smoothness

Open diamond-shaped designs such as these are very frequently found on both Ohlone coiled and twined baskets. This view nicely shows the bottom of a fancy coiled Ohlone/Costanoan basket. The three-rod foundation is probably of willow, wrapped with sedge root wefts. D: 9", H: 4.5" (Smithsonian Institution, #E313260)

This Ohlone/Costanoan coiled basket has roughly shaped olivella disc beads, black dyed bulrush root designs and remnants of woodpecker feather decoration on a background of sedge root wefts. Known as "the Breen basket" after the family that once owned it, this basket dates from the 1840s. D: 10", H: 5" (Monterey Museum of the American Indian, Monterey State Historic Park, #411-162-1)

at their edges. This is probably due to the baskets coming from the same bead maker since a group of beads were usually smoothed at the same time. But interestingly, there is a gradation in degree of bead finishing from one basket to another. At least two baskets have olivella disc beads with very roughly finished edges. These beads were chipped out in a roughly circular form and never smoothed. The next higher degree of refinement consists of beads that are smooth, but not quite as perfectly circular as usual. Such beads seem not quite completely finished (Heizer, April-June 1968, 71). Finally, completely finished, smooth edged beads appear on most Ohlone olivella shell disc beaded baskets.

The Pomo and Coast Miwok often used abalone shell pendants on their fancy coiled baskets. The Ohlone did not use abalone shell pendants on any documented coiled baskets, although abalone pendants were reportedly used on two types of twined baskets. Abalone pendants and European trade bead pendants do appear on several undocumented coiled baskets that may be Ohlone. The Ohlone definitely did use European trade beads individually attached to the basket.

The distinctions between Coast Miwok and Ohlone coiled baskets are discussed in the Coast Miwok chapter. But it needs to be mentioned that their rim finishes and use of beads were different. The Ohlone simply used a plain wrapped rim while the Coast Miwok used over-stitching atop the rim, at least on fancy baskets. Both the Ohlone and Coast Miwok often used olivella shell disc beads to create their main designs. In contrast, the Pomo and Wappo only used clamshell disc beads and then primarily as accents to designs done using weft material.

European trade beads appear occasionally on Ohlone coiled baskets, typically individually sewn on rather than as pendants. A fine example is in the collection of the Santa Cruz Museum of Natural History (basket #2250). This basket has early white trade beads, probably from the Gold Rush era or earlier. Trade beads also appear on several attributed Ohlone baskets.

Materials

Coiled Ohlone baskets had foundations of peeled shoots, probably willow and hazel (Mathewson 1998, 148). Wefts were made of sedge root (*Carex*). Black designs were of dyed bulrush root (*Scirpus*) and occasionally bracken fern root (*Pteridium*) (Bocek 1984, 247; Dawson p.c.). Attached olivella shell disc beads and red woodpecker feathers often served as decoration. Quail plumes were occasionally used. Clamshell disc beads may have been occasionally used at the rim.

No reliably documented Ohlone basket used redbud, probably because redbud did not grow in Ohlone country (McMinn 1970, 233). There are two baskets said to be Ohlone that have redbud designs, but the technical features of these baskets show them to be Yokuts in one case and Sierra Miwok in the other. Both have poor documentation.

Design Layouts
When Using Olivella Shell Beads and Feathers

Designs commonly appear on both the sides and bottoms of Ohlone baskets. Downward pointing triangles typically split by vertical designs are a hallmark of Ohlone olivella beaded designs. Diamonds and inverted "V" or "W" patterns done in olivella disc beads also appear. The "W" shaped designs sometimes serve as independent filler elements.

The Ohlone/Costanoan used European glass trade beads on some coiled baskets. White beads were preferred, although other colors such as red occasionally occur. (Santa Cruz Museum of Natural History, #2250)

Simple narrow linear lines of designs were often part of the overall layout.

The diamonds and narrow linear designs of the coiled baskets were also used on Ohlone twined baskets. Some twined winnowers had fairly complex diamond designs like those found on some of the coiled baskets. Thus, Ohlone design concepts were shared on coiled and twined baskets. This is not surprising since designs were the most easily transferred of all basketry features.

The Early Demise of Ohlone Olivella Shell Disc Beaded Baskets

The production of baskets decorated with olivella shell disc beads must have ceased very early. Surviving examples with dates place them primarily from about the 1790s through the 1840s. The missionization of the Ohlone people and early suppression of the culture brought the weaving of these exquisite coiled works of art to an early end. Twining seems to have lasted longer. This was probably because one vitally needed utilitarian form, a scoop-shaped winnower, had no counterpart in European culture and could not be replaced.

Ohlone Coiled Baskets without Olivella Shell Beads

Some Ohlone coiled baskets did not have any olivella shell beads at all. Baskets without olivella shell beads had designs using: (1) black dyed bulrush root and less commonly bracken fern root, (2) feathers, or (3) European trade beads. The trade beads were overwhelmingly white, but red beads or black beads also appear. Feather decoration was combined with either black weft designs or trade beads, or both.

This coiled winnowing basket was said to be Ohlone by scholar C. Hart Merriam, but it may be Northern Valley Yokuts. Although this basket was collected from Barbara Salorsano, an Ohlone, at San Juan Bautista in 1902, there is scholarly debate as to whether any Ohlone made coiled winnowers in addition to their twined ones. D: 16" (C. Hart Merriam collection, University of California at Davis, #336)

Most commonly these designs were arranged in horizontal bands. Narrow rows of beads typically alternated with narrow rows of feathers. In the case of black weft designs, sometimes the design layout was a horizontal band of connected downward pointing "V"s. Ohlone designs on non-beaded baskets tended to be narrow, with ample background area. Designs appeared on the sides and usually the bottom of Ohlone coiled baskets.

Other Coiled Basketry: Possible Flat Coiled Trays and Coiled Cooking Pots

The ethnographic information on coiled trays is contradictory. At least three large flat, round winnowing trays were collected from the Ohlone (C. Hart Merriam, University of California at Davis; Mason 1912, 232, plate 33; J.P. Harrington notes; and a basket in a private collection). However, Harrington's Ohlone consultants did not recall whether or not coiled winnowers were actually made by Ohlone weavers (Harrington 1942, 21). Lawrence Dawson suggested that Northern Valley Yokuts weavers brought to the missions during the Spanish period could actually have made these coiled winnowers. The well-documented existence of close-twined winnowers among the Ohlone suggests that there would have been little need for a coiled

An Ohlone/Costanoan coiled basket from Santa Clara, said to have been in the family of Mexican California Gov. Juan Bautista Alvarado since 1796. It lacks beads, but has three rows of remnant feather decorations. The black designs are in bulrush root on a sedge root background with a three-rod foundation. The designs extend to the bottom. D: 13", H: 7" (C. Hart Merriam collection, University of California at Davis, #337)

winnower. The best that can be said is that the Ohlone may have made coiled winnowers as well. The answer could be as simple as some groups made them and others did not.

It has been suggested that there may also have been coiled cooking pots among the most northern Costanoans where coiling influence was the strongest (Dawson p.c.). The Ohlone did make twined cooking pots, but there is as yet no record of coiled ones.

Ohlone Twined Baskets

Ohlone twining is one of the most unique and interesting basketry traditions in California. Its origins and relationships are entirely different from coiling. Ohlone coiling was closely related to Coast Miwok, Patwin, Wappo, Pomo, Valley Maidu and Plains Miwok coiled basketry. All these cultures lived north and northeast of the Ohlone.

A walaheen, the unique U-shaped twined winnower of the Ohlone/ Costanoan people. These modest appearing baskets were the most technologically complex and unusual baskets in North America. The black designs are apparently equisetum (horsetail) root and the background is sedge root. Note the subtle diamond patterns done in sedge root with no color change. This basket is believed to have been made by the Mutsun branch of the Costanoan in the San Juan Bautista and Gilroy area. L: 13.5", W: 11.5" (Southwest Museum of the American Indian, Autry National Center, Los Angeles, #811-G-984)

In contrast, Ohlone twining was related to their southern neighbors, the Esselen (Dawson and Shanks research; Mathewson 1998, 11; Breschini and Haversat 2004, 131-139). It is reasonably certain that the Ohlone learned Esselen-style twining when they moved into northern Esselen territory. As noted in the opening section of this chapter, linguistic and archeological research support the conclusion that the Ohlone displaced and/or absorbed Esselen living around San Francisco Bay and Monterey Bay. A rich and fascinating twining tradition resulted.

While all Ohlone groups made twined baskets, not all Ohlone groups made coiled baskets. Surviving coiled baskets come from the San Francisco Bay Area and perhaps as far south as San Juan Bautista. Ohlone coiling apparently became less important the farther south you went in Ohlone country. The Rumsen, a southern Ohlone group, only made twined baskets (Merriam 1967, 372; Broadbent 1972, 63). It is significant that the Rumsen Ohlone, who lived around Monterey and southward, were neighbors of the Esselen at the time of European contact. The nearer the Ohlone were to the Esselen, the more important twining became. This supports the view that the Esselen introduced the Ohlone to a strong, well developed twining tradition but not to coiling.

For all Ohlone groups, twining was the most important basketry technique. All or nearly all Ohlone baskets made for every day utilitarian purposes were twined. This Ohlone-Esselen twining was not only culturally important, it was also one of the oldest basketry traditions in all California (Dawson p.c.). Its history is discussed in the Esselen chapter.

Ohlone Twined Design Techniques:
Designs Created by Changes in Texture and Weave

In Ohlone and Esselen twining we find an unparalleled use of designs created, not by color change, but by varying weft texture and twining technique. Texture variations were produced by three methods: (1) using varying slants of weft twists, (2) changing the exposed side of split shoots to contrast the round side of the shoot with the flat side of the shoot, and (3) using contrasting types of twining to produce changes in texture so as to create designs. In all three methods there is no color change, just a change in texture or type of twining. Diamond-shaped and narrow linear patterns were produced in these ways. Such designs are very subtle and easily overlooked at first glance.

Designs were made using the contrasting texture of plain twining with diagonal twining. Lattice twining and three-strand twining were not used by the Ohlone to create designs (Dawson p.c.).

Designs Created by Color Change

Weft substitution was the most common technique for making designs throughout Central California. Weft substitution involves switching from one weft material to another material of a different color to produce a design. Although Ohlone weavers did use weft substitution, they used it only sparingly in their twined baskets. The most common designs made using weft substitution were narrow black bands extending either partially or entirely across the basket face. These horizontal bands often had diagonal lines extending downward for a short distance. Designs were done in black using what is believed to be equisetum root, commonly called horsetail or Indian scouring rush.

Ohlone Twining Materials

Sedge root was the most important Ohlone basketry weft material (Merriam 1967, 381). For warps, the preferred materials were willow and hazel (Mathewson 1998, 148, 167, 179). Dogwood (*Corylus*) and chamise (*Adenostoma fasciculatum*) were also said to have been used as warp materials (Bocek 1984, 252, 249). As mentioned, horsetail and Indian scouring rush (*Equisetum*) were apparently used for black designs in twined baskets. Juncus rush (*Juncus*) was used on one winnowing basket for designs.

TYPES OF OHLONE TWINED BASKETS

The Ohlone Twined U-Shaped Winnower: The Remarkable Walaheen

The Ohlone made one of the most remarkable twined baskets in all North America. This was a truly unique basket. It is also one of the most subtle artistic creations ever made. That such statements can be made about a rather small, plain looking winnowing basket makes this all the more impressive.

The distinctive twined Ohlone basket was a very shallow, U-shaped winnower. It was typically around a foot wide and just under a foot and a half in length. Its color was buff or gray with a few modest black designs. Its Ohlone name has been spelled walexin, walaheen and various other ways. We use the spelling walaheen, the most common and clearest spelling. The name is pronounced "wah-la-heen," with the accent on the last syllable.

Walaheens were used for winnowing seeds and other related food processing tasks. These U-shaped baskets had an attached reinforcing rod, which was attached in an unusual and innovative manner. While a reinforcing rod is wrapped along its length, it is only attached at periodic points around the edge of the basket. This clever feature makes replacing a worn out reinforcing rod easy.

Although simple linear designs done in black were used, most designs were created without any color change. This was done by: (1) contrasting plain twining with diagonal twining, (2) contrasting the flat side of a split shoot with its round side, or (3) contrasting aligned weft rows having an up-to-the-right slant of weft twist with an adjacent weft row having an up-to-the-left slant of weft twist.

Nearly all other California baskets begin with a relatively small round or oval starting knot. In contrast, the walaheen begins with a very long, narrow starting row. This starting row extended across the flat end of the walaheen.

Because the walaheen is so unique, complex and fascinating, its technical features and unusual design techniques are discussed in detail in the special sidebar at the end this chapter.

The Ohlone Homron

A second type of Ohlone winnower was oval. It was called a homron, a Mutsun Ohlone word for a shallow bowl-shaped basket with flaring sides. Anthropologist J.P. Harrington described this as "a basket shaped like a dish pan." (Harrington, in Heizer 1967, part III, 393). This basket was used for winnowing seeds and perhaps other purposes.

The homron's wefts were made of sedge root and possibly willow. Mud-dyed sedge root wefts were reportedly used for black designs. Although tightly woven, the wefts were arranged in rows with spaces between the rows where the warps are visible. The warp was made of peeled shoots, probably willow or hazel. The homron seems to have been used for parching as well as winnowing. It was largely diagonally twined with an alternating slant of weft in each

The oval twined winnower called a homron. The Ohlone/Costanoan peoples made several types of twined winnowers: the oval homron and the U-shaped walaheen. L: 17.5", W: 14" (State Museum Research Center, California State Department of Parks and Recreation, #082-X-1509)

successive row. Plain twining over parallel warps occurred at the end of the basket farthest from the starting knot. The start was a cluster of warps gathered together; the same type start typically used on many California seedbeaters.

There are interesting links between homron and walaheen winnowers. Both have a rim hoop. Decoration on both consists of narrow black bands. Like the walaheen, the homron uses alternating weft rows with opposite slant of twists. The same splices for the weft ends are used where possible. Another common feature, plain twining over paired warps, occurs on the homron and on one or more of the walaheens.

There is a superficial resemblance to at least one southern Sierra Miwok winnower in that both had similar banded designs. But the baskets were woven differently and the homron is clearly not a Sierra Miwok-type basket (Dawson, Bancroft notes).

Openwork Winnowers

There was also an openwork winnower. It was called "see-wen" in Rumsen Ohlone.

The Wide Variety of Ohlone Winnowers

We have mentioned three types of Ohlone winnowers: (1) the close twined walaheen winnower, (2) the semi-openwork homron winnower, and (3) the openwork see-wen winnower. Additionally, there was a Rumsen Ohlone term which applies to yet a fourth type of twined winnower called a wahr-sahn and a fifth type called a tip-rin (J.P. Harrington 1967, 393-394). As discussed in the section on coiled basketry types in this chapter, there may also have been a coiled winnower. Thus, there may have been five types of twined Ohlone winnowing trays, possibly a coiled winnower and perhaps other types that were never recorded. Only the Paiute and perhaps some of their neighbors had such a diversity of winnowers. This illustrates how important seed processing was in Ohlone culture.

Cooking Pots

The Ohlone made twined cooking pots (Harrington 1942, 2). Twined cooking pots tended to be used by people who made twined winnowers, as in the case of the Ohlone and the Pomo. At Monterey in 1791, artist Jose Cordero drew an illustration of a beautiful Rumsen Ohlone woman holding what may be a cooking pot. This basket seems to use both weft substitution and changes in weft texture to form the narrow band designs (Smithsonian collection, illustrated in Bibby 1996, 1).

Small Mush or Soup Bowl

A small bowl was used for dipping from the cooking pot to serve acorn soup and mush (Merriam 1967, 372; Broadbent 1972, 61).

Mortar Hoppers

A mortar hopper fragment was found in Ohlone territory south of Carmel at the Smith site (MNT-463) in Las Piedras Canyon. This fragment consists of badly decomposed remnants of a diagonally twined mortar hopper asphalted to a shallow sandstone mortar. The slant of twist was probably up-to-the-right (Howard 1973, 8-9).

The fact that diagonal twining was used at the basket's bottom does not necessarily mean the entire mortar hopper was diagonally twined. It is possible that above the diagonal twining, plain twining could have prevailed. But the Ohlone and Esselen used diagonal twining extensively and if anyone in Central California made a diagonally twined mortar hopper it was these two cultures.

The Ohlone are known to have attached their mortar hoppers to stone mortars using asphaltum (Broadbent 1972, 60). They were the northern-most group to do this. To the south, the Esselen, Salinan, Chumash, Gabrielino (Tongva) and some Yokuts weavers also attached their mortar hoppers to mortars using asphaltum (Harrington 1942; Breschini and Haversat 2004, 131). This is another connection between Ohlone twining and the tribes to the south.

Berry Basket

A small, roughly made conical berry basket was made, probably for gathering. It was made of tule and lined with sycamore leaves (*Platanus racemosa*) to prevent the berries from falling between the warps. This basket was plain twined with a down-to-the-right slant of twist (Harrington 1967, 393). An example is Smithsonian Institution basket, #345-441.

Burden Baskets

Ohlone close-twined burden baskets were conical. There was probably an openwork burden basket as well. A pack strap was used when carrying burden baskets (Harrington 1942, 2, 20, 22; Harrington 1967, 393). Burden baskets were normally used for carrying articles; however, they are reported as being occasionally used as cooking pots. Merriam disputed this, stating that only cooking pots were used for cooking (Broadbent 1972, 61).

The use of burden baskets as occasional cooking pots was also reported from the Coast Miwok. Burden baskets were supposedly sometimes used as leaching baskets as well. Most likely the multiple use of burden baskets occurred only after the severe disruption of a culture by Europeans when baskets became scarce.

Acorn Storage Baskets

Large, three to four foot high openwork storage baskets were made. These were made of peeled willow warps and were coarse utilitarian baskets wrapped with willow bark. The bottom was covered with cattail (*Typha*) leaves and the top with madrone (*Arbutus menziesii*) leaves. These baskets were used to store acorns inside the home.

Leaching Baskets

After acorns were pounded and sifted, the Ohlone used an openwork basket to leach acorn flour to remove the bitter tannic acid (Harrington 1942, 21; Harrington 1967, 400). The leaching basket was said to have "a pointed bottom," indicating a conical shape. If the Ohlone version was truly openwork, leaves probably were used to help prevent the acorn meal from being washed out through the spaces between the warps when water was poured on the acorn meal. It may have been similar in form to the shallow, cone-shaped Kitanemuk leaching basket (illustrated in Hudson and Blackburn 1981, 160). Cone-shaped leaching baskets were a southern California type basket found among the Chumash, Kitanemuk and others. This is one more tie between Ohlone twining and coastal tribes to their south.

Seedbeaters

A round or oval seedbeater with a handle was made. Based on a drawing by the artist Alphonse Pinart in 1878, the seedbeater handle passed through the twined round portion and protruded a little beyond (Heizer 1952, 35; also see Harrington 1942, 21).

There was said to be a second type of seedbeater without a handle and with a rounded end (Broadbent 1974, 63). This description sounds like a winnower rather than a seedbeater.

Water Bottles

Ohlone water bottles were caulked with asphaltum and were used to carry water (Harrington 1967, 393; Dawson p.c.). In 1878, Alphonse Pinart drew a sketch of an olla-shaped basket with a narrow neck, which may be a water bottle. Water bottles were not a Central California basketry type but were widespread in southern California and the Great Basin. These water bottles were yet another feature linking Ohlone twining to tribes to the south.

Twined Fancy Baskets

The Ohlone are known for their exquisite coiled fancy baskets. But they also made a nearly globular, twined fancy basket. This basket had a rounded shoulder and woven decorations (Harrington 1942, 22). There were apparently two sizes of this kind of basket. These twined baskets were ornamented with abalone shell pendants, quail plumes and red woodpecker feathers (Merriam 1967, 372-374; Harrington 1967, 393). It is interesting that abalone pendants have been reported on Ohlone twined baskets, but not on coiled ones.

Weavers' Baskets

These twined baskets were reportedly decorated with quail plumes, other feathers and abalone pendants. They held sewing materials for weavers and were destroyed when a person died (Broadbent 1974, 63). Again, the suggestion of pendants is interesting since they may have been solely or primarily used on twined Ohlone baskets.

Cradles

Cradles made with a Y-shaped stick frame are known, but none have been preserved. They may have had a hood to protect the baby. There probably was also a soft tule cradle made for young infants (Harrington 1942, 24).

Hats

Although the early traveler Laperouse reported basketry men's hats, this seems improbable. In fact, based on his early research, C. Hart Merriam stated that it was incorrect. Harrington's Ohlone consultants also did not recall hats being used.

Comments

There is a fascinating contrast in Ohlone basketry. Ohlone coiled work was largely limited to fancy baskets, often lavishly decorated with shell beads and feathers. Thus, coiling was used solely or primarily for the most ornate baskets.

Ohlone coiled basketry is related to people to the north and northeast. It is most like Coast Miwok and Patwin coiling. Along with the Coast Miwok and Patwin, Ohlone coiled basketry shares a common ancestry with Wappo, Pomo, Lake Miwok, Plains Miwok and Valley Maidu coiled work. All these traditions probably developed from coiled basketry brought into California by ancestral Maidu.

It is interesting that Ohlone coiled basketry is not closely related to Sierra Miwok basketry, even though there are linguistic ties between these two peoples (Callaghan p.c., 2005). This suggests that Ohlone adopted Maidu-Patwin-

Pomo style coiled basketry after they arrived in the San Francisco Bay Area. The fact that the southwestern-most Ohlone did little or no coiling supports the view that coiled basketry was adopted from one or more of these northern cultures.

Ohlone twined basketry is related to the south to the Esselen. Ohlone twining was at least in part adopted from the Esselen. If the archeological basket fragments found in Esselen territory are truly Esselen, as they are believed to be, then Ohlone and Esselen twined basketry are nearly identical. Over the centuries the Ohlone would have added to the development of this unique twining tradition.

The result of this merging of coiling influences from the north and twining influences from the south was that Ohlone (Costanoan) basketry ranked among the most spectacular and distinctive in the world.

TECHNICAL FEATURES AND DESIGN TECHNIQUE OF WALAHEEN WINNOWERS

In terms of complexity, creative technical features and design techniques, the U-shaped Ohlone/Costanoan walaheen winnower is perhaps the most amazing basket in California. Most surviving walaheens are definitely Ohlone. One walaheen could be either Esselen or Ohlone. The following information on walaheen technical features and design methods is taken from a study conducted by Lawrence Dawson and Ralph Shanks. Many features make the U-shaped walaheen winnower unique and deserve detailed coverage. For those interested in the technical aspects of walaheen construction we offer this section.

The Walaheen Starting Row

Remarkably, the walaheen did not have a conventional starting knot, but rather had a starting row. This was done with a bound weave somewhat similar to the way some mats were started.

A somewhat similar concept was used on Pomo baby cradles, which also begin with a variation of a bound weave and were U-shaped. But there were major differences between the two basket types. The Pomo cradle was an openwork basket that was deep, usually without designs and simpler in construction. The Ohlone walaheen, in contrast, was closely woven and had numerous subtle designs and intricate weaving variations on each basket. There is no known counterpart to the walaheen winnower among the baskets of any other tribe except the Esselen.

The walaheen began with a starting row of two-strand herringbone bound weave, which was essentially the starting knot. Not all walaheens had the same type of starting row for there were two kinds of starting rows. In one variation both strands of the starting row perform the same operation: they go over three warps and back around one warp. In the other kind of starting row, the weft strands act differently. One weft strand goes over three warps and back around two warps, while the other weft strand goes ahead over two warps and back around one warp (Dawson p.c.). These may be regional variations, since walaheens were made from Monterey Bay north to San Francisco Bay.

In forming the starting row the butt ends of the warp are held upwards by the weaver and one warp at a time is added. The warp ends were allowed to project

Twined walaheen winnowing trays were probably the last type of Ohlone basket to be made. The survival of this food processing basket probably occurred because European society offered no substitute for a good winnower. Today, contemporary Ohlone weavers and others have revived the art of making walaheens. (Carmel Mission Museum)

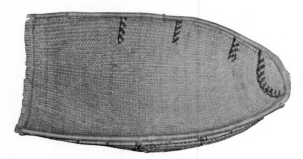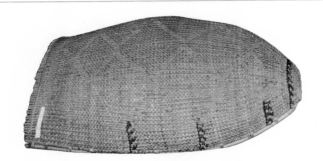

Views of both sides of a walaheen winnower. The black designs done using weft substitution extend out from the sides and across the bottom, a typical walaheen pattern. Subtle diamond patterns done by changing twining techniques are visible in the buff colored central section of the basket. (Private collection. Photo by Lawrence Dawson)

about a centimeter above the starting row. The starting row was woven from left to right. A herringbone pattern occurs in this type of weave and it points in the direction the work progressed.

Walaheens were thus begun at the broad flat end using the starting row technique described above. This was another interesting walaheen feature, since baskets of somewhat similar shape from other tribes were usually begun at the small end.

The Main Body of the Walaheen

The starting row ended at the right margin of the basket. The wefts were then woven back across the basket beside the starting row in either plain twining or diagonal twining. If plain twining was used, it was done only for a row or two. After that the walaheen continued to be woven primarily in diagonal twining.

The basket was then turned over so that the convex side (the back side) of the basket was now the work face; that is, the side of the basket facing the weaver. The walaheen continued to be woven in this position.

However, since the weaver no longer turned the basket over each time the weft row reached the basket edge, this resulted in every other row being woven in the opposite direction as she wove back and forth across the basket. This reversal of twining direction gave each row an alternating slant of twist. One row would have up-to-the-right slant of wefts, the next row would have down-to-the-right slant of wefts. This alternating slant of weft rows results in an unusual look to the basket, since most twined baskets have every weft row woven in the same slant. Weft rows with alternating slants are a feature nearly unique to walaheens.

Ohlone weavers spliced new weft elements into walaheens in the following manner: the weft's moving end was brought to the work face, below the alternate weft and then trimmed flush with the surface. The next weft strand's fag end was then inserted one warp ahead of the first weft twining turn. The weft stub now projected on the basket's work face. It was then wound back over onto the back face. The result was that the new replacement strand emerged beside the trimmed moving end. The stub of the weft fag end thus appears one warp space ahead of the moving end. It was now on the underside of the twining weft row and held in place by it. This type of weft splice procedure was particularly effective because the weft fag ends were held firmly in place and tension maintained on the weft strands without pulling them out of place. The stub ends of these weft splices can be seen on the convex side of the basket.

How the Walaheen was Formed

Usually the thick end of each warp stick was sharpened prior to inserting it into the basket. As the walaheen moved toward completion, the sharpened ends of the added warps were inserted so that they projected across one or two completed weft rows, thus telling us the direction the basket was woven. The small, rounded end of the walaheen was where the weaving was terminated. The broad end with its starting row was where the basket started.

The first warps were added at the second row of twining in about half the known walaheens. These additions followed a formula on three of the baskets. Two existing warps are followed by a new warp, then two existing warps occur and then again a new warp is added, and so on. No further warps were added until many weft rows later, typically about five inches down the basket. At this point, a new row of inserts appears in which the added elements were somewhat under an inch apart. Thereafter, inserts were only sporadically added as needed. Those walaheens that carefully follow the formula described above have an especially well defined shape. They probably represent the original concept of a proper walaheen. Those walaheens that do

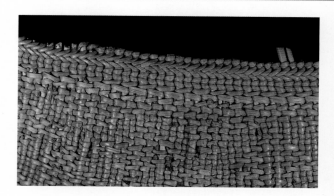

Even the starting knot on an Ohlone walaheen winnower was amazing. The horizontal herringbone-shaped weaving at the rim is the starting knot, best described as a long, narrow starting row. Below the starting row, plain twining is used for two rows and then is followed by diagonal twining for two rows. Note the varying slant from one weft row to the next. (Southwest Museum of the American Indian, Los Angeles, Autry National Center, #811-G-984)

not follow this pattern are less regular in their weaving and may represent a decline in the art.

The Hoop

Ohlone walaheen winnowers have a U-shaped stick hoop attached to the basket. As is so amazing about the walaheen, even the hoop lashing was unusual. A strand of sedge root material was closely wound around the hoop stick, which provided a neat, finished appearance. At intervals of an inch or more, the hoop was lashed with two turns of this sedge root strand to the basket's outermost warp stick. The only edge not reinforced with the hoop was the basket's top where the sturdy starting row was located. Less stress occurred at the top because the woman using the winnower held the basket by its sides rather than at the top.

The hoop provided additional strength, helped preserve the basket's shape, and served as a convenient and comfortable handhold. Should the warp stick eventually loosen, break or wear away, the technique of placing lashings only every inch or so allowed easy replacement of the hoop. If the hoop had been attached at every turn of the sedge root wrapping, replacement would have been far more difficult. The ingenuity of Ohlone master weavers appears again in the walaheen.

Walaheen Materials

The materials used on walaheens were buff colored sedge root wefts (*Carex*) and peeled shoot warps usually of willow or hazel. On two walaheens it was difficult to determine the weft material due to weathering. However,

these wefts were probably weathered sedge root. Black designs apparently using the roots of Equisetum (commonly called horsetail or Indian scouring rush) were found on all full size walaheens, except one. Equisetum was used elsewhere in California basketry. For example, the Wiyot and Whilkut of Northwestern California used this root. Equisetum was also used in other states, such as in western Washington in some Salish basketry (Suquamish Tribe 1985, 23).

The hollow juncus rush (*Juncus*) was used as a decoration on one walaheen. This winnower is at Carmel Mission in the Munras collection. It should be noted that the Carmel Mission collection contains at least one very old Chumash basket and the use of juncus could have been introduced to weavers at Carmel by a Chumash basket weaver visiting or relocating there.

Walaheen Designs

Walaheen decoration was unique. In most California basketry, bold red or black colors were used to create striking designs. In contrast, decoration on Ohlone and Esselen twining was remarkably subtle. Four types of decoration methods were used on walaheens.

1) Black designs were woven using strands of equisetum roots. Equisetum root was added by weft substitution; that is, black equisetum root weft replaced brown sedge root weft whenever a colored design was desired. These black designs often consisted of short segments of simple patterns extending horizontally out from the basket's sides. Sometimes a band near the round end of the basket would run completely across the basket. One basket had five rows of narrow bands extending horizontally all the way across the basket (Bernstein 2003, 54, fig. 5/786). Some bands had a series of short diagonal rows extending downward. Another walaheen (Hearst Museum 1-14988) has a design similar to the letter "H" on it (Mason 1912, plate 36). All full size walaheens have black designs, except the walaheen in the Monterey County Historical Society's collection (#60.1.MC2). As discussed in the Esselen chapter, this particular basket could be Esselen rather than Ohlone. It at least has design influences that are Esselen.

2) Two contrasting types of weaves were used to create diamond patterns. This technique was used on roughly half of the walaheens studied. Plain twining was used to create the diamond patterns on a background of diagonal twining. The plain twining design rows were typically four wefts rows wide. The diamonds formed an even net-like pattern across the basket's face. To create the diamond patterns, the weaver merely switched from diagonal twining to plain twining at the appropriate places. The color remained the same; only the change in twining technique provides the design. The diamond patterns are so subtle that when first noticed it is often puzzling to see them appear. Once again, the walaheen amazes the viewer.

3) A change in weft face from the rounded side to the flat side of split shoots was a very creative form of walaheen decoration. This technique involved varying which side of a split weft strand faced outward and was thus visible. Throughout California the round face of split weft strands was normally kept outward where they could be seen. On the walaheen this is the predominant case, too. However, what is exceptional is that on at least five walaheens sometimes the flat side of the split weft was turned outward. The flat weft face was used to form very subtle patterns amidst the round shoot faces that form the background. This technique has also been found in archeological fragments from Isabella Meadows Cave in Monterey County, deep in Esselen territory.

4) Horizontally aligned weft rows contrasting with a background of weft rows with alternating down-to-the-right, up-to-the-right slant of weft turns was the subtlest of all basket design techniques. The design technique of aligned slant of turns contrasting with a background of alternating slant of turns design style was found on only one walaheen, the Monterey County Historical Society basket (#60.1.MC 2). It takes careful inspection to see it, but the technique is clearly there. Typically, about three weft rows are carefully woven horizontally with almost no slant of twist. Some of

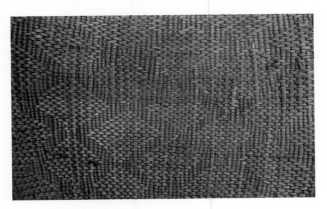

Detail of the subtle designs on an Ohlone walaheen winnowing basket. The diamond patterns are done in diagonal twining with rows of alternating down-to-the-right, up-to-the-right slant of weft twists. The diamonds are outlined using plain twining amid a background of diagonal twining. Notice that no change in color is used; changes in twining technique alone produce the designs. (Southwest Museum of the American Indian, Los Angeles, Autry National Center, #811-G-984)

these rows run only part way out from the edge of the basket, while others run all the way across the basket. In both cases, entire weft rows slanting either up-to-the-right or down-to-the-right provide a contrasting background to offset the carefully aligned horizontal weft rows that form the designs (see also: Breschini and Haversat 131-139).

On the Monterey County Historical Society walaheen, four bands of three to five courses of horizontally arranged, non-slanting wefts were arranged in rows about half an inch wide. Most sections of aligned weft rows were spaced approximately an inch from the next section of aligned weft rows. The slant in some places was unclear, and where this happens there may be a space of up to three and a half inches between aligned weft rows (Lisa Woo Shanks p.c., 2004). This basket also has two rows of tightly done plain twining design placed two rows below the long horizontal starting row. This walaheen is unusual in that it is the only full size walaheen that lacks any black designs.

The Richness of Walaheen Designs

We have studied eight of the nine known surviving historic walaheens (the ninth is a miniature version). Most of the eight full-size walaheens studied have three of the four design techniques described above. Three different design techniques can sometimes be found in an area as small as two square inches!

This density of pattern and technical variation in a single basket is unparalleled in all of North America (Dawson p.c.). Changes in twining techniques were used in designs by many other Native American groups. But nowhere else were they as varied on an individual basket to the extent found in Ohlone and Esselen twined baskets. This degree of emphasis on textural effects is highly divergent from other California cultures. Elsewhere in California designs were made primarily by color changes done by substitution of different weft materials.

Use of the Walaheen

Being a winnower, the walaheen was used to process seeds. Parching may also have been done using walaheens. We know that the walaheen was used during the serving of roasted islay (*Prunus ilicifolia*) (Bocek 1984, 244-245). Ohlone elders at Carmel Mission reportedly stated that the basket was held with the open end away from the body (Harry Downie p.c.). This winnower probably survived longer than any other Ohlone basket because European culture never produced anything that could equal a good walaheen for seed processing.

Esselen land in the Santa Lucia Mountains is isolated and much of it seldom visited to this day. In this rugged country a specialized type of twining was found. Illustrated here is the only known surviving Esselen-style basket. This twined winnowing basket has Esselen-style designs done by: (1) changing the twining technique, and (2) changing the side of the weft so that either the flat side or the round side faces outward. This winnowing tray lacks the black designs done using weft substitution found in similar Ohlone/Costanoan winnowers. It also uses a specialized decorative technique only known from Esselen archeological basket fragments. This basket was made by a weaver who was likely either Esselen or of mixed Esselen-Ohlone heritage. (Courtesy of the Monterey County Historical Society, #60.1.MC2)

ESSELEN BASKETRY

Esselen territory extended along Monterey County's spectacular Big Sur coast from the Little Sur River southward for approximately twenty-five miles. The Esselen Coast included Point Sur, the Big Sur River and the present day town of Big Sur. Inland from the shore, Esselen country ran eastward over the steep Santa Lucia Mountains and into the portion of the Salinas Valley where the communities of Soledad and Greenfield are located today (Breschini and Haversat 2004, 6). Thus, the Esselen held one of the smaller territories among California Native people. This was not always so.

Esselen Influence in a Once Great Territory

The Esselen once held a vast land. About 4,000 years ago Esselen speaking people lived from San Francisco Bay and Carquinez Strait south to Monterey County. The Ohlone expansion into Esselen territory was quite gradual, taking perhaps 1,500 years to accomplish. Archeological findings suggest that the Esselen held the San Francisco Peninsula until at least 1000 B.C.

Linguistic studies show that Esselen loan words are found in Ohlone (Costanoan), even in Karkin the northern-most Ohlone language. The Ohlone borrowed words related to the ocean from the Esselen. This supports an inland origin for the Ohlone and an arrival on the coast after Esselen people were already present. Basketry studies point toward Esselen territory as having once been much larger. (Kroeber 1925, 544-545; Whistler 1977, 169; Levy 1978, 3-38; Breschini 1983, 72; Moratto 1984, 246-247, 266; Foster 1996, 89; Breschini and Haversat 2004, 58, 63-66, 192-193, 196; Breschini p.c., 2005).

The Ohlone's northeastern neighbors, the Bay Miwok of the Mount Diablo region in Contra Costa County, were also almost surely influenced by the Esselen. The Bay Miwok had moved into the San Francisco Bay around the same period as the Ohlone did (Foster 1996, 89). Archeological basketry awls necessary to make coiled baskets are rare in Bay Miwok archeological sites. In contrast, neighboring Miwok sites to the east commonly yielded basketry awls (Bennyhoff 1977, 49). This indicates that, unlike Plains and Sierra Miwok, the Bay Miwok were probably more a twining people than a coiling culture.

Why were the Bay Miwok different from other Miwok? It is probable that they had adopted the Esselen practice of using twined baskets more extensively than coiled baskets. Like the Ohlone, the Bay Miwok almost certainly displaced Esselen people upon arriving in the East Bay area of the San Francisco Bay region.

Based on archeological basketry evidence, there is even the possibility that Esselen rather than Yukian speakers may have lived in Marin County prior to Coast Miwok arrival (see the Coast Miwok chapter in this volume).

Esselen territory may once have been even larger than part or all of the San Francisco Bay and Monterey Bay areas. There was a strong twining tradition among the southern San Joaquin Valley Yokuts. Southern San Joaquin Yokuts elders stated that coiling was absent in pre-European times, at least in some Valley Yokuts tribes. For example, the Tachi Yokuts, the best-known Southern Valley Yokuts tribe, only did twining prior to European arrival (Gayton 1948, 17; Dawson p.c.).

It is possible that Esselen territory once extended southeast into the San Joaquin Valley, perhaps as late as 2000 B.C. Linguistic studies have suggested that an Esselen language was once spoken in the San Joaquin Valley (Breschini and Haversat 2004, 64). The Southern San Joaquin Valley Yokuts emphasis on twined basketry, including the presence of diagonally twined cooking pots, supports this view. The former presence of ancestral Esselen in the San Joaquin Valley would explain how the Tachi Yokuts and Esselen came to have some important shared basketry traditions.

A similar well-developed diagonal twining tradition existed among the Numic speaking people of eastern California and the Great Basin. These Numic cultures included the Paiute, Western Mono, Kawaiisu, Panamint and others. While these cultures also made excellent coiled basketry, most Numic baskets made for daily use were twined. Burden baskets, winnowers, water bottles and other forms were diagonally twined.

A diagonal twining tradition extended eastward from the Esselen. It spread through the southern San Joaquin Valley Yokuts, the Kawaiisu, Tubatulabal and on to the Numic-speaking people of eastern California and the Great Basin. The Numic speaking peoples are believed to have originated in California and to have spread northeast across the Great

Basin to Nevada, eastern Oregon and beyond (Bettinger and Baumhoff 1982; see also: Polanich 1994 for a discussion of the Western Mono basketry history). Some Numic speakers almost certainly were once neighbors of the Esselen. There are, in fact, linguistic borrowings of Esselen words in Numic languages indicating contact between these cultures (Moratto 1984, 560).

It is believed that Esselen twining is related to the twined basketry of these Numic speaking peoples (Dawson p.c.). This was a parallel development to the other great band of diagonal twining that spread across North Central California from the Pomo east, Patwin, Valley Maidu, and Sierra Miwok to the Washoe and Paiute. The spread of diagonal twining must have followed both paths. Esselen weavers were surely among the originators of diagonal twining.

THE CONTRACTION OF ESSELEN TERRITORY

Why did the Esselen survive only in the rugged Santa Lucia Mountains and vicinity? The expansion of ancestral Ohlone mainly followed marshes and oak woodlands. The Ohlone are believed to have had a more tightly integrated social organization that allowed them to out-compete the less populous Esselen. The Bay Miwok, Coast Miwok and Valley Yokuts probably had the same advantages.

But a larger population extensively utilizing oak woodlands and marshland resources lost its advantage in the Santa Lucia Mountains where resources were less plentiful and survival required a very flexible social organization. Thus, the Esselen people were at an advantage in the mountains and small valleys. It was an advantage they never lost. However, there was one great disadvantage: only a small population could be sustained in this demanding environment. The Esselen population was small and proved vulnerable when Europeans arrived (see: Breschini and Haversat 2004, 191-194).

ESSELEN BASKETRY
THE ARCHEOLOGICAL EVIDENCE

The Esselen, no longer a numerous people by 1769, were taken to the Spanish missions where survivors intermarried with the Ohlone and with non-Indians. As a result, no documented ethnographic Esselen baskets exist in museum collections. There is, however, one known basket that clearly has Esselen characteristics. It is an undocumented walaheen winnowing basket in the Monterey County Historical Society collection in Salinas (cat. no. 60.1, MC 2). This type of basket is discussed in detail in the Ohlone chapter.

There are significant archeological basketry fragments found at Isabella Meadows Cave (Site MNT-250) in Monterey County. Named in honor of an Esselen-Ohlone elder whose grandfather had taught her about Esselen culture, this cave is located in the Santa Lucia Mountains near the very center of Esselen country (Meighan 1955, 1).

The presence of the remains of a sheep indicates European contact, and archeological dating has placed this site in the Spanish mission period. An Esselen fleeing the missions may have brought the sheep with him as a gift to his kin (Meighan 1955, 7). It is probable that the Esselen people were making a last valiant stand against Spanish domination at this site. By about 1825 the cave was abandoned (Meighan 1955, 23).

A variety of artifacts from Isabella Meadows Cave were found, but the most significant were 91 basketry fragments. These fragments are nearly the sole surviving examples

These two photos compare an Esselen archeological walaheen winnower basketry fragment (at left) with the lone surviving Esselen-style walaheen winnower's designs (at right). Note that on both baskets, subtle designs are created by contrasting areas of aligned slant of wefts (outlined with rectangles) against a background of alternating up-to-the right, down-to-the-right slant of wefts outlined with circles. Perhaps no other cultures produced as subtle basketry designs as the Esselen and Ohlone. (Left photo: Courtesy of the Phoebe Apperson Hearst Museum of Anthropology and the Regents of the University of California, #1-132785. Photo by Therese Babineau. Right photo: Courtesy of Gary Breschini and Trudy Haversat. Copyright 2004 by Coyote Press; all rights reserved.)

of Esselen basketry. Except for a rough, single-rod, non-interlocking coiled patch, all the Isabella Meadows Cave fragments are of twined basketry (Meighan 1955, 12).

An archeological basket fragment from a rock shelter (MNT-838) in Reliz Canyon, west of King City, Monterey County, provides additional supporting information. This diagonally twined fragment corresponds in every way to Esselen or Ohlone walaheen winnowers.

Reliz Canyon is in Esselen territory. Interestingly, however, rock art found in the Reliz Canyon area is Salinan. It is probable that the Native people in Reliz Canyon were Esselen and Salinan, not Ohlone. Since Salinan twined basketry is very different from Esselen-Ohlone twining, Salinan weavers did not make this fragment. This leaves the Esselen as the probable weavers of this basketry fragment (Dawson, Bancroft notes 1977; Breschini and Haversat 2004, 6, 134).

In sum, both the Isabella Meadows Cave and Reliz Canyon basketry fragments are almost certainly Esselen (Meighan 1955, 24; Hester 1978, 498; Dawson p.c.; Dawson, Bancroft notes; Breschini and Haversat 2004, 131-139). None of these fragments are similar to Salinan basketry. The fragments are very close to Ohlone twining. Yet there are distinctions that suggest that they are more likely Esselen.

ESSELEN TWINING RELATIONS TO COSTANOAN/OHLONE TWINING

The Isabella Meadows Cave and Reliz Canyon Esselen basket fragments have a number of differences that distinguish them from Ohlone work. No colored equisetum weft designs were present, unlike twined Ohlone baskets that regularly used black weft designs. Neither does plain twining occcur in horizontal rows such as the Ohlone used near the flat end of their walaheens. The Isabella Meadows Cave walaheen-type of U-shaped winnowers did, however use diamond pattern designs woven in plain twining. The Isabella Meadows Cave Esselen mortar hopper fragment, also used this type of plain twined diamond pattern.

Surprisingly, no openwork twining was found among the Isabella Meadows Cave Esselen fragments. In contrast, the Ohlone are known to have made a number of openwork baskets. The Esselen probably did openwork weaving, but it may not have been as important as among the Ohlone. The use of a crude, single rod coiled patch is also in stark contrast with the very finely coiled baskets the Ohlone made using three-rod foundations.

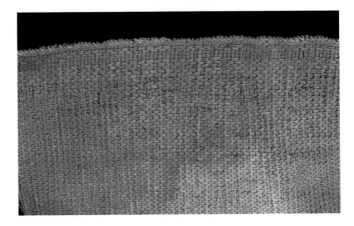

This is the long, narrow starting knot extending all the way across the top of an Esselen-style walaheen winnowing basket. Note the contrasting two rows of diagonal twining just below the starting knot followed by three rows of plain twining. After that, diagonal twining resumes. (Courtesy of the Monterey County Historical Society, #60.1.MC2)

Still, there were close relationships between Esselen and Ohlone twining. Both cultures primarily used changes in twining techniques to create designs, while all other California cultures primarily used changes in weft color to produce designs. The Esselen and Ohlone used shared design layouts, usually involving plain twined designs on a background of diagonal twining. The design technique of using the round side of a split shoot's weft face to contrast with its flat side also links Esselen twining closely to Ohlone twining. The presence of the U-shaped walaheen winnowers among both peoples is very significant, too (see the Ohlone chapter for a detailed description of walaheen winnowers). Esselen twining was nearly identical to Ohlone twining. Esselen twining was very different from that of their Salinan neighbors.

ESSELEN BASKETRY DESIGN TECHNIQUES

Esselen twining designs used changes in twining technique rather than color changes to produce designs. This was done in four ways: (1) by varying which side of a split shoot weft was shown (the rounded side versus flat side), (2) by changing the slant of weft twist (up-to-the-right slant of weft versus down-to-the-right weft slant), and (3) by using plain twining designs on a background of diagonal twining. Where plain twining was used to create designs, Esselen basketry fragments only used it when creating diamond or narrow horizontal band patterns. Finally, (4) a type of texture contrast design technique was found on a single Esselen fragment using three-strand twining to provide

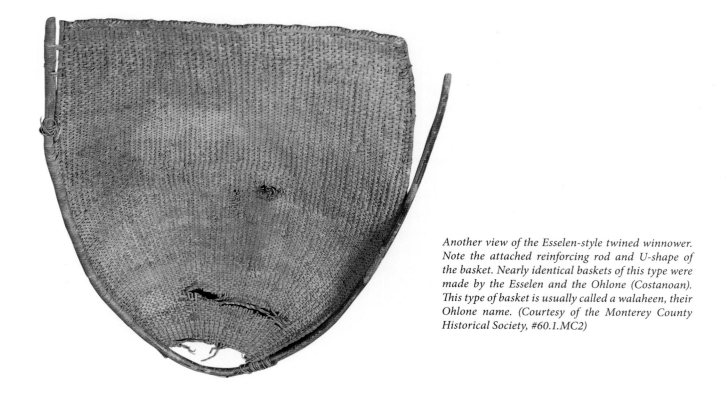

Another view of the Esselen-style twined winnower. Note the attached reinforcing rod and U-shape of the basket. Nearly identical baskets of this type were made by the Esselen and the Ohlone (Costanoan). This type of basket is usually called a walaheen, their Ohlone name. (Courtesy of the Monterey County Historical Society, #60.1.MC2)

a texture contrast design, a feature absent from all known Ohlone walaheens. Human hair was also used as a design weft material in one fragment.

Nearly every basketry fragment found at Isabella Meadows Cave shows some decoration, even pieces as small two inches square. This is a remarkable density of decoration rarely, if ever, found in archeological basketry elsewhere. This density of decorations is at least comparable to and may even exceed that found in surviving Ohlone baskets. What is absent among the Esselen work is the use of designs made using weft substitution. The Ohlone used horsetail or Indian scouring rush (*Equisetum*) root for black designs, a black design material found on all full-size Ohlone walaheens. The Esselen are not known to use any color designs (Dawson and Shanks research).

ESSELEN MATERIALS

Some materials are identifiable from the archeological fragments. Materials used in the Esselen Isabella Meadows Cave fragments include wefts of sedge root. The sedge roots were split in half, providing a round side and a flat side of the weft element. By selectively using either the round side or the flat side of the weft, designs could be created. The Esselen contrasted the round face with the flat face of the split sedge to create designs in the same manner as the Ohlone did. Remarkably subtle designs could be created this way.

Split juncus appears to have been used on two pieces. Tule is reported to have been used in Esselen basketry as well (Hester 1984, 497-498).

Equisetum root, commonly known as horsetail or Indian scouring rush, was not used in the Esselen fragments found. This contrasts with Ohlone twined basketry where Equisetum was regularly used for black designs.

Asphaltum was applied to the back face (the interior side, in this case) of three fragments. Asphaltum was used for sealing water bottles and to attach mortar hopper baskets to stone mortars. Fiber cordage, possibly of yucca, was used for sewing on patches for repairs (Dawson p.c.).

Types of Esselen Baskets

Cooking stones found in Isabella Meadows Cave indicate the use of basketry cooking pots. Since all the Esselen basket fragments found were twined (except for a single crude coiled patch), the Esselen almost certainly cooked in twined baskets. Fragments additionally show that a small mush serving bowl was present (Meighan 1955, 3, 25).

Fragment shapes indicate that close-twined conical burden baskets were made (Dawson and Shanks research; Moser 1987, 84). At least one fragment from near a basket's base has broken warp ends worn in a pattern comparable to burden baskets that were repeatedly rested on their pointed end. There is also extensive abrasion on the exterior of the fragment exposing the warp sticks, while there is less abrasion on the interior. This is common on burden baskets regularly carried through rough chaparral country. Interestingly, this conical basket has an oval start.

The Esselen made twined mortar hoppers. Asphaltum rings where basketry mortar hoppers were attached to stone mortars have been found elsewhere in Esselen country. A mortar hopper may also be represented among the Isabella Meadows Cave fragments, although this is not conclusive (Dawson p.c.; Breschini and Haversat 2004, 131). Diagonally twined mortar hoppers are reported from the neighboring Rumsen Ohlone. Since the basketry of these two groups was very similar, Esselen mortar hoppers may well have been diagonally twined, too.

The use of asphaltum coating on globular or cylindrically shaped basket fragments indicates the presence of twined water bottles. The asphaltum coating appears on the inside of these fragments. Chumash water bottles were similarly coated on the inside of the basket.

Some Esselen archeological fragments are virtually identical to the U-shaped twined walaheen winnowers found among the Ohlone (Dawson and Shanks research). This is true for weft fag end and weft moving ends, for most materials and for most design concepts. These fragments are permeated with seed oils and most heavily caked on the concave side. The walaheen fragments lack burned char marks, a common indicator of using hot coals on a basket to parch seeds. This absence of burn marks on walaheens suggests that yet another type of winnower probably existed for parching.

Esselen and Ohlone walaheen winnowers were not quite identical. First, there were slight differences in materials. There was the absence of equisetum root designs among the Esselen. Secondly, human hair was briefly used as a weft strand, a feature apparently absent among the Ohlone. Finally, there is a design technique that may be uniquely Esselen. This Esselen design technique involves wefts aligning in one slant contrasting with a background of wefts rows of alternating up-to-the-left/up-to-the-right slants (see illustration in this chapter).

Only a single surviving walaheen winnower has this aligned/non-aligned weft slant feature. It is in the Monterey County Historical Society collection in Salinas (cat. no. 60.1 MC2). This is the closest of all surviving walaheen winnowers to the archeological Esselen walaheen fragments. This basket may be from a weaver who was Esselen, of mixed Esselen-Ohlone heritage or Ohlone. It is at a minimum an Esselen-style basket (see the Ohlone chapter in this volume; also Shanks in Breschini and Haversat 2004, 136-137).

One other source of information on Esselen basketry exists. Esselen word lists preserved by linguists mention winnowing baskets, water tight baskets and a small woven jug, which was probably a water bottle.

PATCHES

Many Esselen fragments show patchwork repairs. This may be a time-honored custom, as among the Sierra Miwok. Or it may represent a desperate attempt at cultural survival during the Spanish mission period. If no skilled weavers remained among a band of former mission Indians, traditional food processing could only continue by repairing old baskets. The latter case seems possible since surviving baskets of the culturally closest group, the Ohlone, were seldom repaired. All Esselen repair patches are twined, except one that is coiled. This modest coiled patch is the only example of Esselen coiled work known (Meighan 1955, plate 2-A).

Comments

Esselen twined basketry was very closely related to that of the Ohlone. The closer an Ohlone group was to the Esselen, the more important twining became. For the Esselen and the Rumsen (the southwestern most Ohlone group), coiling was of little or no importance. Although Esselen twining was very close to that of the Ohlone, it was not quite identical.

The Esselen people were few in number, but the culture was an old and influential one. It is significant that the Esselen population was probably formerly widespread. Their twined basketry likely influenced the Ohlone, Bay Miwok, Southern San Joaquin Valley Yokuts and possibly the Coast Miwok. Esselen twined basketry was also related to even more distant Numic speaking people, such as the Paiute in the Great Basin desert. The Esselen population and territory may have been much reduced when non-Indians arrived in California, but the Esselen likely had a long and proud history of influencing other cultures.

Nearly every Pomo basket used for cooking, food processing, gathering, fishing or hunting was twined. This huge lattice twined storage basket, attributed to master weaver Jenny Miller, is a fine example of the way Pomo weavers combined art and function. Notice how the storage basket curves inward at the top rather than having vertical sides at the top as on cooking pots. Designs are in redbud on a sedge root background. D: 27", H: 14" (Collection of the Grace Hudson Museum, Ukiah, California)

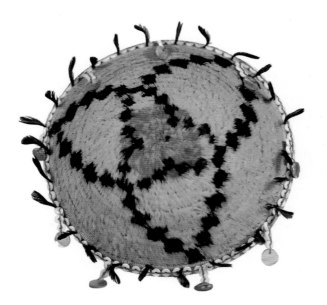

This Pomo feather basket has a burst of yellow meadowlark feathers accented with green mallard feathers and other plumage. The featherwork is encircled with clamshell disc beads, abalone pendants and quail topknot feathers. These coiled baskets were the result of many months of work to honor a beloved relative or friend. Feather baskets made prized wedding gifts. D: 9", H: 5" (Courtesy of Russell Kloer, Clear Sky, Sonoma)

The Pomo are notable for the complexity of their feather basket designs. This eleven inch wide coiled feather basket has yellow meadowlark, green mallard and brown robin feathers. Clamshell disc beads accent the basket and form chains tipped with round abalone shell pendants. Purchased by Samuel Barrett at Clear Lake, Lake County, in 1914. (Collection of the Milwaukee Public Museum, #15123/4250. Lisa Woo Shanks photo file)

POMO BASKETRY

The Land

Pomo country spreads across Lake, Mendocino and northern Sonoma counties. The northern edge of this land is near the present day communities of Fort Bragg and Willits. Pomo territory runs south through the Russian River watershed and Clear Lake. It includes Ukiah, Point Arena, Lakeport, Santa Rosa, Sebastopol and Jenner. Thus, Pomo lands range across the mountains and valleys of the Coast Range to the Pacific Coast. A detached group, the Salt Pomo, lived around Stonyford in northwestern Colusa County.[1]

This Pomo homeland had ample valleys filled with massive acorn bearing oak trees. Oak, manzanita, buckeye, bay, tarweed, miner's lettuce and other food plants abounded. Game was plentiful in the grasslands, chaparral and oak woodlands and salmon spawned in the coastal rivers and streams. Clear Lake was a rich source of waterfowl and fish. Along the Sonoma and Mendocino coast, Pomo people could find fish, clams, abalone, seaweed and other seafood.

This was a gentle land and numerous Pomo communities flourished in it. The Indian population here was perhaps the densest in California and was rivaled nationally only in a few other locales. The Pomoans spoke seven mutually unintelligible languages and comprised some seventy-five small sovereign nations (McLendon and Oswalt 1978, 274-288; Smith-Ferri 1998, 9). Yet, the people's lives and their basketry were sufficiently similar that we can speak of "Pomo basketry."

The History

The Pomo people have lived in west central California for a long time, probably for at least 4,000 to 6,000 years. Ancestral Pomoans probably first formed as a people around Clear Lake after moving into the area from the Sacramento Valley. From Clear Lake, the Pomo gradually spread west and south, eventually reaching the coast and valleys of northern Sonoma County (Moratto 1984, 543-552; Foster 1996, 87; Dawson, p.c.).

The Pomo expansion displaced an earlier people, most likely ancestral Yuki (Moratto 1984, 550). It also increased Pomo cultural influence throughout the region. Neighboring people such as the Wappo, Lake Miwok and Huchnom adopted major aspects of Pomo basketry techniques, forms and design styles.

Pomo Basketry and that of other Californian Indian Cultures

Alfred L. Kroeber wrote: "Pomo baskets have the name, among Americans, of being the finest…in the world. Such comparisons are perhaps best avoided. But it is clear that in a variety of ways Pomo basketry has undergone a special development quite unparalleled in California…" (Kroeber 1925, 244).

One of the striking features of Pomo twined basketry was that it offers exceptionally rich options for the weaver. Plain, diagonal or lattice twining could be selected for a variety of basket types. These techniques could be used separately or in combination with one another (or other types of twining) for almost every close-twined basket category. This was an almost unparalleled artistic choice in Native California.

A second outstanding feature of Pomo basketry was that weavers both twined and coiled with equally exceptional skill and artistic success. Some cultures rivaled the Pomo in the variety of twined basket types they made. Many other cultures made a greater variety of coiled basketry types than did the Pomo. But no one surpassed the Pomo for their skill and artistry in both techniques. The Pomo also made wickerwork baskets, a rarity in California, which added to the diversity of Pomo art.

The Wappo, Lake Miwok and Huchnom, whose basketry was much like that of the Pomo, were also exceptionally skilled weavers. But these cultures lacked the variety of basket types the Pomo made. They did not occupy nearly as

---

[1] All the groups of Pomoans formed a connected block of territory, except for one. These were the Salt (Northeastern) Pomo, so called because they owned a famed and exceptionally important salt deposit. The Salt Pomo became geographically separated from other Pomo by Patwin expanding into the region. Some archeologists and linguistics postulate an arrival date of between A.D. 1 to A.D. 500 for the Patwin in the Sacramento Valley and a slightly later spread of Patwin into the Coast Range Mountains. This would suggest the separation of the Salt Pomo from the main body of Pomo probably took place around 1,000 to 1,500 years ago (Kroeber 1925, 236; Moratto 1984, 652-563, 571; Foster 1996, 91). The Salt Pomo intermarried heavily with the Patwin and Yuki after European arrival. Therefore their basketry is poorly known and of mixed lineage. Salt Pomo basketry is discussed separately from that of the other Pomoan people at the end of the Yuki chapter.

large and varied territories as the Pomoans and had no need for so many different types of baskets.

Pomo Excellence in *Both* Coiled and Twined Basketry

Northwestern California tribes were great artists in twining and had no need for coiled baskets. All food processing could be managed handily using twined basketry alone. In contrast, all central and southern California tribes that coiled also had to twine. It was impractical to provide all the types of baskets required for food processing, storage and gathering without twining.

Yet people that both coiled and twined nearly always lavished their greatest artistic efforts on their coiled baskets. This was clearly the case for the Yokuts, Salinan, Chumash, Tubatulabal, Kawaiisu, Panamint, the Mission tribes and many others. The Ohlone, Coast Miwok, Maidu, and the Western Mono also excelled at both twining and coiling, but even in these cultures coiled basketry usually received the most artistic emphasis.

The Pomo were different. Kroeber saw the Pomo as "an island of semi-twining, cut off from the pure twining area" of Northwestern California by the presence of the Yuki. The Yuki were a coiling people, located between the Pomo and the Northwestern Californians (Kroeber 1925, 244). To the east of the Pomo were the Patwin and Valley Maidu, people heavily into coiling. Thus, geographical position alone cannot explain this exceptional Pomo skill at both twining and coiling.

Many Pomo feather baskets were decorated with a scattering of red woodpecker feathers. Along with the tufts of red woodpecker feathers, black quail topknot plumes and white clamshell disc beads, this coiled basket has black bulrush root designs on a background of sedge root. Made circa 1895. L: 12", W: 9", H: 4.5" (Turtle Bay Exploration Park, Redding, California, #1964.1.35)

Yuki Influence and the Development of Pomo Basketry

There are many differences between the basketry of the Pomo and that of Northwestern Californians such as the Hupa and Yurok. Both archeological and basketry studies have suggested that Yukian-speaking people once occupied the Redwood Coast from Sonoma County north to the Klamath River in Del Norte County. By the time of European arrival, the Yukian speakers had been reduced to a small fraction of this territory. Yet there remained some links between Pomo twining and that of Northwestern California which suggest a common Yukian inspired background. These include the use of pine root wefts (in some Pomo burden baskets, for instance), peeled shoot warps, some forms of twined baskets and the shared practice of making plain twined baskets with warps sticks trimmed at the rim. Mortar hoppers, plate-shaped baskets, some northern Pomo seed beaters and some openwork utility baskets evidence links in form and/or technique. Both the Pomo and the Northwestern Californians lack the scoop shaped baskets common in Central California. Both what was present and what was lacking serve as clues to once shared basketry traditions. Thus, there are basketry concepts that suggest possible ancestral connections between Pomo and Northwestern California basketry.

It may be that the Pomo and the Northwestern Californians independently adopted these ideas from ancestral Yuki. Twining predates coiling through out California. Lawrence Dawson's research led him to postulate that an early twining tradition in the North Coast Range would explain certain twining features shared by Pomoans and Northwestern Californians. He found that the oldest twined basketry designs seemed to be narrow, solid horizontal bands. Pomo basketry frequently used narrow horizontal bands in its twining, especially early Kashaya and Southern Pomo work. Dawson observed that the Yuki, the people most commonly suggested as living in the region when the Pomo arrived, frequently used narrow design bands on their coiled baskets and on at least two types of twined baskets (Dawson p.c.; see also Kelly 1930).

Dawson's basketry analysis is consistent with Michael Moratto's archeologically based hypotheses. Both scholars suggested that the territory historically occupied by the Pomo (and most Northwestern Californians) was once Yukian. Beginning about 6,000 years ago, most Yukians began being displaced by Pomo spreading into the Coast

Range from the Sacramento Valley by way of Clear Lake (Moratto 1984, 543-552; Dawson p.c.). Gradually, the Pomo displaced most Yukian people and by 1,000 to 2,000 years ago the Pomoans completed their settlement of most of Lake, Mendocino and northern Sonoma counties (Moratto 1984, 561).

The Kashaya and Southern Pomo portions of this territory, being the farthest away from Clear Lake, were the last areas settled by the Pomo people. This late displacement of Yukians in the southwestern part of Pomo territory would account for survival of narrow Yukian-type horizontal bands more commonly found on older Sonoma County Pomo baskets designs than are typically found among Pomo baskets from farther north and east (Dawson p.c.).

Still another link may be the presence of what the Pomo call the "dau." The dau was an interruption, or a break, in horizontal designs found on Pomo baskets. About 85% of Pomo twined baskets with horizontal band designs have dau marks, as do a few coiled Pomo baskets. One dau mark was usually placed in each design band. The Yuki also used a dau to interrupt horizontal designs on their coiled baskets.

It was not recorded why the Yuki used daus, but the Pomo did so for religious purposes. Many weavers believed they would be struck blind or suffer some other misfortune if they failed to include a dau (Barrett 1996, 171). Some daus were simple breaks in the design, but others were elaborately beautiful designs that provided a brief departure from the main design. The dau was found on close twined Pomo burden baskets, winnowers, mortar hoppers, storage baskets and cooking pots where horizontal band designs were used (Winther 1985, 52-53; Dawson p.c.).

Kroeber suggested that the mortar hopper might have been influenced by Northwestern Californians (Kroeber 1973, 60). But Pomo mortar hoppers rims were not braided in the Northwestern California style and instead had reinforcing rods the like those of the Yuki. The overall broad, open shape of Pomo, Yuki and Northwestern California mortar hoppers were similar enough in concept that they almost certainly shared a common ancient origin. But overall, Pomo mortar hoppers were closer in form and technique to those of the Yuki than to those of Northwestern California.

As their geographical position would suggest, the Yuki type mortar hopper was intermediate between those of the Northwestern Californians and the Pomo. For example, the Yuki used a reinforcing rod at the rim and another rod on the side near the base, along with three-strand twining for

Many Pomo close-twined burden baskets were plain twined with horizontal band designs. Note the "dau" or break in the pattern seen in each band. This pattern change is frequently found on Pomo plain and lattice twined baskets. Among some Pomo people it is believed that the dau allows Spider Woman to leave the completed basket and protects the weaver from blindness. This basket has redbud designs, plus a few clamshell disc beads added for decoration. The background is of sedge root. H: 18" (Private collection)

reinforcing. The Northwestern California people also used reinforcing rods on the side, but opted for rims that were braided. The Pomo used the reinforcing rod at the rim and lattice twined bands for reinforcing and located them similar to both groups.

If the Pomo did not invent mortar hoppers themselves, then they probably borrowed the concept of a mortar hopper from the Yuki and not from Northwestern California. The Pomo modified the mortar hopper both artistically and by using lattice twining for reinforcing.

Other Influences on Pomo Basketry

Pomo twining is so complex that it seems certain that a variety of cultures influenced its development. Kroeber wrote that "the usual rule in California is that a certain technique, or a certain variety of one technique, is invariable for an object serving a given purpose among one tribe… The Pomo break this natural inclination. Their carrying baskets are both plain twined and diagonally twined, their cooking baskets are made at will in plain, diagonal, or lattice twining; the [seed]beaters in [plain] twining or wicker." (Kroeber 1925, 245).

The Pomo made fine openwork burden baskets like this one for gathering acorns. Notice the beautifully spaced wefts and warps and the overall refined character of the basket. A nice Pomo touch is the broad, wave-like selvage that secures the warp ends at the rim. The basket is made of peeled willow. D: 20", H: 18" (California Academy of Sciences, #370-894)

Plain, diagonal and lattice twining were all widespread among Pomoan peoples. It might seem simple to account for the rich diversity of Pomo weaving by saying that the Pomoans were merely numerous distinctive people speaking seven different languages. But other equally large, diverse groups in California, such as the Yokuts and Chumash, lacked the unparalleled diversity of Pomo basketry techniques.

The Pomo region was a cultural focal point for basketry influences coming from several sources including the Yuki, Patwin and Valley Maidu.

Plain twining was a northern technique extending from Alaska south into California. The Pomo either had plain twining with them when they moved into the Coast Ranges or learned the technique from ancestral Yukians.

Lattice twining was more fully developed and used more extensively among Pomo than any other Native American culture. Both close-twined and openwork lattice twining were used in a wide variety of baskets. No one did lattice twining more extensively or better than the Pomo. Lattice twining is a technique that was long established in Pomo culture. It may have been invented by Pomo weavers.

Wickerwork has also probably been made by the Pomo for many centuries. Since archeological basketry suggests

that wickerwork declined in importance elsewhere in California and western Nevada, it may have once been more important among the Pomo as well. Wickerwork's only remaining important Pomo use was in seed beaters.

Diagonal twining was primarily a Central Californian and Great Basin basketry technique. This technique was almost unused north of the Pomo. In contrast, diagonal twining was extremely important to cultures east and south of the Pomo such as the Ohlone (Costanoan), Esselen, Western Mono, Paiute and others.

Diagonal twining probably first developed well south of the Pomo, perhaps among the Esselen (see the Esselen and Ohlone chapters in this volume). The particular style of diagonal twining made by the Pomo probably developed in the central Sacramento Valley. For example, very similar diagonally twined burden baskets were made by the Pomo, Patwin and Valley Maidu. The Pomo lived just west of the Sacramento Valley and they probably participated in the development of diagonal twining.

If diagonal twining came from the Sacramento Valley into Pomo country, the Clear Lake Pomo would have had diagonal twining prior to coastal Pomo. They would have had the most time to fully develop the art. In fact, diagonal twining is less common and early designs were less lavish among the Kashaya Pomo on the coast (Dawson p.c.). Broad, intricate patterns on diagonally twined baskets were especially common among inland Pomo people around Clear Lake and the upper Russian River. All this supports an interior origin for Pomo-style diagonal twining.

Some Pomo twined utility baskets combined both close-twining and openwork. This broad, lattice twined bowl is done in openwork for good air circulation and to allow liquid to flow through. The basket could be used for storage, drying, sifting, draining or gathering. Note that a reinforcing rod strengthens the rim. D: 15", H: 4" (Collection of the Milwaukee Public Museum, #60001, Lisa Woo Shanks photo file)

While Pomo coiled feather baskets were more famous, Pomo twined baskets were of equal artistic merit. Beautiful Pomo close twined burden baskets were creations used for seed gathering. These were typically bell-shaped baskets rather than conical. This is a diagonally twined burden basket using redbud designs on a sedge root background. Reinforcing rods on the rim were typically wrapped with wild grape or redbud. This basket may date back as far as the 1840s to 1860s. (Private collection)

Pomo diagonal twining had ties to the east, to Sacramento Valley Patwin and Valley Maidu basketry. Of the Pomo, Patwin and Valley Maidu, it was the Pomo who used diagonal twining most extensively and in the greatest variety of baskets. This suggests initial Pomo development of diagonal twining in the region. This development was not simultaneous among all Pomoans, but first occurred among the eastern Pomo, probably around Clear Lake. A Clear Lake area origin is suggested by the fact that diagonal twining was so extensively used around Clear Lake and Ukiah Valley. From there it likely spread west to other Pomo people and perhaps east to the Patwin and Valley Maidu.

To the south of the Pomo, the Ohlone (Costanoan) and Esselen made great use of diagonal twining. But Ohlone and Esselen diagonal twining was very distinctive and had major technical, stylistic and design layout differences from Pomo work. Any recent transmission of this technique from these southern people is highly unlikely. However, both Pomo-Patwin-Valley Maidu diagonal twining and Esselen-Ohlone probably have some ancient connection (See Esselen chapter this volume; also see Moratto 1984, 543-552).

Pomo Coiled Basketry Origins

The types of coiled baskets the Pomo made were very limited compared to the wide range of twined baskets they wove. True coiling people, such as the Maidu, Patwin, Yuki, Yokuts and others, made far more types of coiled baskets than did the Pomo. These cultures made coiled cooking pots, winnowers, storage baskets and other forms. In contrast, among the Pomo people all these types of baskets were twined.

Limited use of coiled baskets for every day purposes indicates a relatively recent adoption of coiling. The Pomo probably only began coiling after the Patwin arrival. Based on the Patwin's estimated date of arrival in the southern Sacramento Valley, if the Patwin were involved in the transmission of coiling to the Pomo then coiling would have reached the Pomo less than 1,300 to 1,500 years ago (Moratto 1984, 571; Foster 1996, 90).

It seems probable that coiling reached the Pomo from the Sacramento Valley. The only other likely source was the Yuki. But Pomo coiling was very different from that of the Yuki. Pomo coiling, in contrast, is very similar to Patwin and Valley Maidu coiled work. Since both the Valley Maidu and Patwin used coiled basketry far more extensively than the Pomo, this suggests that they had begun coiling earlier than the Pomo.

How the Pomo came to Excel in Both Twined and Coiled Basketry

How did the Pomo weavers come to excel at both twining and coiling? Simply borrowing ideas does not explain how the Pomo came to produce the most elaborate feathered coiled baskets in California, probably in the world. The beauty of Pomo baskets was elaborated and elevated to a high art by individual Pomo artists themselves. Kroeber believed that "the Pomo feel themselves freer than other groups to follow any type of design arrangement: horizontal or banded, diagonal, crossing, vertical or radiating, or isolated. The frequency is in about the order named. Elsewhere, one or two of these (design) schemes are followed to the practical exclusion of the others" (Kroeber 1925, 246). While neighboring cultures influenced the Pomo, this does not fully explain how the Pomo came to excel at both twining and coiling. Pomo cultural values must have also played a key part. What was great and special in this art is essentially Pomo, and this was the ultimate Pomo artistic achievement.

Pomo weavers are world famous for their coiled feather baskets. A variety of bird feathers, clamshell disc beads and abalone shell pendants were used to produce these artistic wonders. The feather basket shown here features white clamshell disc beads, abalone pendants and various species of bird feathers on a predominant background of green mallard feathers. (Private collection)

Basketry concepts were combined, elaborated and innovated in uniquely creative ways by Pomo people over the centuries. The diverse twining of the Pomo people was undoubtedly due to the ability to pull together in uniquely Pomoan ways twining traditions from different areas. The result was a distinctive form of twining all their own. Later, coiling was also elaborated into an unprecedented art form, particularly in feather work.

All cultures have both freedom and restriction in their art. There were important rules and cultural guidelines in Pomo weaving, as in every culture. But a general cultural openness to innovation probably played a part in the development of the diversity of Pomo basketry (Sherrie Smith-Ferri p.c.). This openness was not something that developed only after European contact, as occurred among some other tribes. It must have been a longstanding Pomo cultural value.

Pomo Coiled Basketry

Coiling is the most famous of Pomo basketry techniques. As with all basketry, Pomo coiled basketry had its cultural rules. Pomo coiling is done in a leftward **work direction**. Both three-rod and single-rod **foundation** coiled baskets were made (Dawson p.c.; Newman 1974, 3-24; Smith-Ferri 1998, 36). Pomo single-rod baskets have thin, pointed wefts. Because of the way they overlap the foundation rods, weft

stitches on single-rod baskets give designs a serrated look at their edges. Three-rod baskets have wefts that are broader in relation to their height than single-rod wefts. The wefts on three-rod baskets give an even look to the designs.

Seven different types of **starting knots** were used in Pomo coiled basketry (Bernstein 2003, 18). These were most

Sometimes feather-work was minimized or eliminated on fancy gift baskets and instead beads became the centerpiece. On this three-rod coiled Pomo basket, clamshell disc beads and magnesite pendants are strung on Native Indian hemp cordage. The golden tone of the sedge root wefts adds to the beauty. D: 11", H: 6" (Marion Steinbach Indian Basket Museum, Tahoe City, California, #724)

commonly overhand starting knots. Some coiled baskets began with a twining type start.

The outer surface of Pomo coiled baskets was quite smooth. **Weft fag ends** were hidden among the foundation rods. The **moving ends** of the weft were bound under stitches on the back face of the basket.

Pomo stitching was fine, even and firm. Sewing on three-rod foundation baskets has a free mixture of interlocking, non-interlocking and split stitches (on the back face only). Often all three types of stitches occurred together on the same basket (Dawson p.c.). Interlocking stitches seem to occur a bit more frequently than the other two types. But the use of pure interlocking stitches was only a minor usage among the Pomo (Elsasser 1978, 633). **Rims** were plain wrapped, never diagonally wrapped or overstitched. The **coil endings** were plain wrapped and tapered.

Decoration and Plant Materials

Pomo coiled basketry designs were almost always done in only one color, either red or black, on a light background. Redbud shoots (*Cercis occidentalis*) provided the red color. Black designs were made using black dyed bulrush root (*Scirpus*) or less commonly black dyed bracken fern root (*Pteridium aquilinum*). Both materials were dyed black by soaking in mud or ashes (Smith-Ferri 1998, 17). Walnut hulls or, in later years, rusty nails were also used to give weft materials a black color.

Bracken fern root, being more porous, darkens more quickly than bulrush root. The denser bulrush root was sometimes incompletely dyed black and it can be distinguished from bracken fern root by the presence of occasional pinkish streaks in it. Bracken fern root also has square edges while bulrush root edges taper.

Bracken fern root was especially common on coastal Pomo baskets, since redbud did not grow there and bulrushes were less common (Barrett 1908 (1996 reprint), 139; Gifford, 1967, 38; McLendon 1992, 59.). Bulrush roots (actually rhizomes) were also said to be of shorter length near the coast and this, too, contributed to the frequency of Kashaya Pomo use of bracken fern root for black designs (Mathewson 1998, 197).

The almost universal Pomo coiling background weft material was sedge root (*Carex*), which typically slowly changes from white to buff to deep golden to an almost black color with extreme age. Most existing Pomo coiled baskets were made for sale and are of an age giving them either a white or buff colored weft. Besides sedge root, split willow roots were occasionally used for wefts. The coiling foundation was most commonly willow shoots, or less commonly hazel (*Corylus cornuta var. californica*) or honeysuckle (*Lonicera interupta*) (Mathewson 1998, 155, 179). While ten or twelve materials were used in Pomo basketry, many only occurred in limited special uses (Kroeber 1909, 233-249). The most commonly used coiled basketry materials were sedge, redbud, bulrush root, bracken fern and willow.

The Pomo often put designs on the bottom of their coiled baskets. Bottom designs were a feature shared with Patwin, Yuki and Wappo coiled baskets, but the great majority of Maidu, Sierra Miwok and Washoe baskets did not use bottom designs (Dawson p.c.).

COILING VERSUS TWINING

There is an interesting paradox in Pomo coiling. Pomo coiled work is perhaps the most famous basketry in California. National books on Native American art frequently select Pomo feather baskets for illustration. But coiling was not as important as twining in Pomo daily life (Dawson p.c.). Many other tribes made more use of coiling than did the Pomo. Coiling did not serve the broad range of purposes among the Pomo that it did for many other Central California Indian groups.

Yet Pomo coiling was spectacular. Wefts were very narrow. Stitch work was so fine it often had over 60 weft stitches to the inch, an achievement rivaled by only a half dozen other tribes in North America. No culture exceeded the quality of Pomo feather baskets.

TYPES OF POMO COILED BASKETS

Pomo Feather and Beaded Baskets. Fully feathered baskets were made in three shapes. There were round globular forms, shallow plate forms and oval ("boat-shaped")

A little Pomo jewel decorated with lavish feathers, quail plumes and beads. D: 5", H: 1" (Gienger Enterprises)

baskets. Kroeber said that the Pomo "use the greatest variety of external ornament. Beads, shell ornaments, quail plumes, and feathering are employed to a far greater extent than elsewhere." (Kroeber 1905, 151). He was not quite correct. The neighboring Coast Miwok, Lake Miwok and Wappo may rival the Pomo. But no one exceeds the Pomo.

There were two broad types of feather decoration. Some baskets were decorated using spot feathering. In this style, small tufts of feathers, usually red woodpecker feathers, were scattered about the sides of the basket. The second type of feather decoration covered all or nearly all the surface of the basket with feathers. On both types of feathering, quail topknots might also be used around the rim and/or scattered on the sides.

Some anthropologists have suggested that originally only red acorn woodpecker (*Melanerpes formacivorus*) feathers and valley quail (*Callipepla californica*) plumes were used for feather decoration on Pomo baskets, but there is no

Some Pomo feather baskets had chains of clamshell disc beads attached, allowing the basket to be suspended and seen in all its glory. Meadowlark and mallard feathers with clamshell disc beads and abalone shell pendants were used on this feather basket. D: 5″ (Museum fur Weltkulturen, Frankfort, #NS 19055)

definitive documentation. Woodpecker feathers, widely used by interior Pomo, were not traditionally used on early coastal Kashaya Pomo baskets (Gifford 1967, 19).

The red feathers of the acorn woodpecker and the black plumes of the valley quail were certainly the most important

feathers. But mallard duck, oriole, bluebird, meadowlark and other types of bird feathers were also found on Pomo feather baskets. In later years, feathers from introduced, non-native birds were sometimes chosen by weavers as substitutes for native bird feathers (Mabel McKay p.c.). Traditional feather use was inhibited by laws protecting certain species of birds and by declining bird populations.

Although most surviving Pomo feather baskets were made for sale, feather baskets had an ancient and proud place in Pomo culture. Feather baskets were, and still are, used at weddings, as gifts and other important life events. Those intended for use in funerals were burned.

One other use of feathers should be mentioned, although the occurrence was in twined baskets. Flicker quills (the orange shaft portion of the flicker feather) were occasionally woven into the weft of Pomo twined baskets for a very short length. By observing this practice, the weaver was spiritually safe to continue to weave during her menstrual period. To break this rule might result in something bad happening to the weaver or a loved one. Many weavers simply avoided weaving during their monthly cycle. However, urgent events, such as a funeral that required a gift basket, could make a woman feel compelled to keep weaving during menstruation. To do so required special prayers and the addition of one or more flicker feather shafts to the basket (see: Smith-Ferri 1998, 32).

Besides feathers, Pomo people also used shell beads to decorate very fancy baskets. Beads were used extensively on coiled feather baskets. The use of beads on twined baskets was very limited. Occasionally a single bead or perhaps a few scattered beads were found on the sides of very fancy twined storage baskets and burden baskets likely made as wedding gifts. But beads were primarily used on coiled baskets.

Clamshell disc beads were sewn on rims and on the sides of coiled baskets. They were also made into chains used to hang feather baskets. Besides the round clamshell beads, triangular pendants of abalone shell were often used at the tip of short clamshell bead chains that hung from the side of very fine baskets. Less commonly, small magnesite pendants were also used at the ends of short clamshell chains (Smith-Ferri p.c.). Magnesite is a naturally white rock, but when properly treated by fire it turns pink. It was the fire-treated pink color that was used as pendants on baskets. It should be noted that magnesite can explode "like a hand grenade" when placed in a fire so this color treatment can be dangerous if precautions are not taken (David Peri p.c.).

Most often the Pomo and Wappo people attached clamshell disc beads to a basket using Native or commercial thread. This was different than the usual Ohlone (Costanoan) and Coast Miwok practice of using the basket's weft strands to attach the beads. The Ohlone and Coast Miwok primarily used olivella shell beads, which were much thinner than Pomo clamshell disc beads. All these tribes occasionally attached European glass trade beads to some baskets.

Pomo men usually made the clamshell disc beads and collected the feathers used for baskets. Originally, stone drills were used to perforate shell beads. The well-known wooden pump drill used to make holes in clamshell discs was not aboriginal. It was introduced to the Pomo about 1876 (Merriam 1967, 297).

Boat-Shaped Baskets

Boat-shaped baskets were oval baskets used for gifts, wedding presents, during feasts and in funerals. Indian doctors used the largest of these baskets to carry rattles, medicines and other doctoring gear. The largest baskets were said to have reached four or five feet in length. Boat-shaped baskets were often highly decorated. Clamshell disc beads were often sewn on the rim in groups of four, the culturally preferred number. At other times, clamshell beads might be sewn all the way around the rim. Quail plumes, red woodpecker feathers and/or clamshell beads and abalone pendants might be used to decorate the side. Both single-rod and three-rod foundations were used. In later years, large numbers of boat-shaped baskets were made for sale.

This oval "boat-shaped" Pomo basket's featherwork is a scattering of quail topknot feathers accented with clamshell disc beads. The basket's single-rod coiling foundation gives its black bulrush root designs a serrated effect on the sedge root background. Note the variations in the design layout. L: 12", W: 7.5", H: 3" (Private collection)

Ceremonial Child Washing Baskets and Other Flaring Bowls

Broad, flat-bottomed bowls that flared toward the rim were made. The largest were somewhat smaller than cooking pots, and varied in size. Either three-rod or single-rod

This Pomo Ceremonial Child Washing Basket serves as an indication of the love and respect given to infants. A newborn Pomo baby was carefully washed in soothing warm water each morning and each evening by the paternal grandmother. This coiled basket is decorated with glass European trade beads. Designs are bulrush root on a sedge root background woven over a three-rod foundation. (Private collection)

foundations were used. Often these baskets were ornamented with beads and sometimes with quail plumes as well. Food was served and eaten in these baskets, but they also had other important purposes.

Beautiful baskets of this type were used for a newborn baby's first wash. The basket was then saved as a family heirloom to give to the child later in life. Girls also used them at puberty to wash themselves while in seclusion during their first menstruation. Similar baskets were also made for sale (Barrett 1996, 286-287, plate 19, fig. 1; Smith-Ferri 1998, 225-26; McLendon 1992, 63; Bibby 2004, 19).

Globular Bowls

Small to medium sized coiled baskets usually with three-rod foundations were used for wedding gifts, storage, ceremonial purposes and miscellaneous other uses such as drinking cups and to store water. They were broad and low with the broadest point either at the bottom or midway up the side. Some of these bowls were decorated with beads or feathers (Smith-Ferri 1998, 26).

Feast Trays

Feast trays were used for serving food at special occasions. These flat-bottomed baskets had low, flaring sides and were typically made with a single-rod foundation. Some were beautifully decorated with elaborate designs. One use was during the Pomo Harvest Festival, to hold the first seeds gathered and processed by a weaver that season (Smith-Ferri p.c.).

Miniature Baskets (Both Coiled and Twined)

The Pomo have the distinction of making the smallest baskets in the world. Some coiled baskets are small enough

Fancy coiled feast trays such as this one were used for serving food at special occasions. Note the lavish designs. Jenny Jackson or a member of her family made this basket. Made at Pinoleville Rancheria near Ukiah in Mendocino County, prior to 1889. D: 18", H: 3" (Collection of Grace Hudson Museum and the Sun House, Ukiah, California)

to sit on the head of a pin! Some coiled baskets are so small that they are best viewed with a magnifying glass. Even the smallest willow rod might be too large to serve as the foundation on these tiny, coiled baskets, so finely twisted sedge had to be used as the foundation material.

Pomo weaver Mabel McKay made some of the smallest baskets. She explained to the author that the stitches were so small that she worked by feel rather than by sight because the

The world's smallest baskets were made by Pomo weavers. Some are so tiny they literally can sit on the head of a pin. Pomo weaver Mabel McKay explained to the author that she made these coiled baskets by feel since they were too tiny to see. The penny gives an indication of the remarkably small size of Mrs. McKay's miniature baskets. (California Department of Parks and Recreation, California State Indian Museum)

stitch work was too small to see (Mabel McKay, p.c.). Some of her smallest baskets have been on exhibit at the California State Indian Museum at Sutter's Fort in Sacramento. Other fine extremely small baskets are in the collections of the Grace Hudson Museum in Ukiah and at the Jesse Peter Museum at Santa Rosa Junior College.

Both coiled and twined miniature baskets were made by the Pomo as gifts to help teach girls the cultural roles they would play as adults. Miniature twined utility baskets such as burden baskets or mortar hoppers were for girls to learn adult roles through play. These baskets served as models for girls destined to become weavers. Sometimes miniature baskets were also hung from the hoop of girls' baby cradles, partially to entertain the child, but also as a prayer for the girl to grow up to be a fine weaver.

Later, non-Indian buyers spurred innovation in miniature basketry as they competed with one another to own "the smallest basket in the world." In response to this market, some Pomo artists wove incredibly tiny baskets the diameter of a pinhead or smaller. While this was a non-Native stimulated innovation, it was also an elaboration of virtuoso Pomo art (Smith-Ferri 1993, 61-67; Abel-Vidor Brovarney and Billy 1996, 63; Smith-Ferri 1998, 31, 148, 185 and p.c., 2003; Bernstein, 2003).

Pomo Twined Basketry

Although not as famous as Pomo coiled baskets, Pomo twined baskets were equally beautiful. This twined basketry was more varied, performed more functions and had been made by the Pomo for thousands of years longer than coiled basketry. Whereas coiled baskets were used primarily for special occasions, twined work was used for almost every activity of daily life. In so many ways, twined baskets were central to Pomo lives.

Pomo twining was complex, highly developed and had many variations. This twining may be distantly related to Northwestern California twining, but there were major differences. In Pomo twining, sharpened warps were added by wedging them, unlike Northwestern Californians where warp ends were chewed and then scraped (Dawson p.c.). Pomo twined weft fag ends were tightly secured under a twist of twining. The moving ends of the Pomo twined wefts were trimmed. In Northwestern California, by contrast, the moving ends of the weft were left hanging to be scraped off with a mussel shell when the basket was completed.

The elegant beauty of Pomo designs can be seen in this detail of a twined basket. Note the band of lattice twining between the two redbud designs amid the predominant plain twining. (Private collection)

DESIGNS AND MATERIALS ON POMO TWINED BASKETS

As with coiled baskets, Pomo twined baskets were nearly always done with either red or black designs on a white or buff colored background. Red designs were more often used on twined baskets. Black designs were more often found on coiled baskets. The red and black designs were rarely combined and probably were never used together traditionally.

On twined baskets, redbud furnished the red material while black was done in either bracken fern root or less commonly bulrush root (Barrett 1996, 137). The background material was either of sedge root (*Carex*) or split, baked pine root (*Pinus sabiniana*). A beautiful, subtle Pomo decorative technique was to include bands of lighter colored sedge root on a background of darker sedge root or pine root.

There were ten or more kinds of twined basketry starts used by the Pomo (Bernstein 2003, 18). Warps were either willow or hazel sticks. Willow was the primary warp material, but when a basket needed to be especially strong, hazel (*Corylus cornuta var. californica*) or creek dogwood (*Cornus*) were sometimes used for warps in twined baskets (Smith-Ferri 1989, 13; Mathewson 1998, 152-153). Sumac (*Rhus trilobata*) rods were used to make coarse baskets, such as fish baskets and rough burden baskets (Merriam 1967, 296). Wild grape (*Vitus californica*) was used to wrap rims where a reinforcing rod was used. In rough baskets, willow and sumac could have been used for weft material, too.

The digging of pine roots and gathering of pine nuts gave a favored tree (*Pinus sabiniana*) the common name of "Digger Pine." Sadly, Digger became a racist term for California Indians instead of the honored term it should be. Those women digging pine roots were great artists and should be remembered as such. Most contemporary botany books now use the term "Gray Pine," or less often "Bull Pine," for "Digger Pine." A better name would be "Basket Weavers' Pine."

TWINED BASKET DESIGNS

Pomo twined designs were most frequently horizontal or diagonal bands, although other design arrangements occurred. Where horizontal designs were used, a simple narrow band was usually placed near the base. Then the elaborate middle zone designs were added and finally a narrower and simpler uppermost band was usually woven near the top. This arrangement of a narrow band at the top and at the bottom was combined with the middle zone using either horizontal or diagonal patterns.

The bases of Pomo twined baskets may have no defining base line design or change in weave type (such as a row of three-strand twining) to visually set off the bottom from the side. The Pomo often had a defining base design on most large twined baskets, but it is seldom as pronounced as the base line among such Northwestern California people as the Yurok and Hupa. All the Northwestern Californian peoples routinely

A diagonally twined Pomo storage basket with redbud designs, sedge root background and willow warp sticks. Pomo weavers often used diagonal twining to produce particularly fine twined baskets. This was a cultural choice since diagonal twining can also be used to produce rugged utility baskets. D: 17", H: 11" (California Academy of Sciences, #154-58)

emphasize their bases by either weave type (three-strand twining was most commonly used) or design placement.

Unlike Northwestern California and Northeastern California baskets where designs are added by using an overlay material atop the weft, the Pomo did not use overlay for designs. Instead, the Pomo most commonly used weft substitution (changing from sedge to redbud, for example) to add designs. Weft substitution means one weft material (sedge or pine root) is replaced by another material (redbud or bracken fern root most commonly). Besides weft substitution, the Pomo also used the "turned weft strand" technique. This involved peeled redbud bark which has a red side and a white side. By twisting the peeled redbud weft strand over, it was possible to create alternating red and white designs. The turned weft strand technique was used on both plain twined and lattice twined baskets. Coastal Pomo people usually used the spiral lattice binding technique for their designs while inland Pomo more commonly used the turned weft method or weft substitution for creating designs (Dawson p.c.).

Major Types of Pomo Twining

Lattice Twining

It is likely that lattice twining was a Pomo invention. No one used it as extensively and with the diversity that Pomo weavers achieved. No other people made baskets virtually entirely done in lattice twining, except the neighboring Wappo, Lake Miwok and perhaps Huchnom. And even these three cultures are believed to have derived this style of basket from the Pomo people.

Pomo weavers made entire baskets using lattice twining. Both close twined and openwork lattice twining were used on many different types of baskets: burden baskets, cooking pots, winnowing trays, storage baskets and others. Pomo lattice twining was so strong that it could be used in place of reinforcing rods on the sides of baskets such as mortar hoppers and some winnowers and sifters. Pomo lattice twined baskets were marvels of art and engineering that offered strength and beauty.

Plain Twining

Plain twining was very common and was found on cooking pots, burden baskets, winnowers and bowls. Pomo twined baskets destined for hard use were either plain twined or lattice twined or a combination of both. Both lattice twining and three-strand twining (using three weft

Most North Central California people cooked in coiled baskets. The Pomo, however, cooked in twined baskets. This lattice twined cooking pot was purchased at Cloverdale, Sonoma County, in 1910. We only know that the weaver's first name was Susie. It is regrettable that so few baskets have had the weaver's name recorded. These women were great artists and deserve to be honored. This basket has redbud designs on a sedge root background. D: 16", H: 9.5" (Private collection)

strands) were used on baskets for reinforcing to strengthen the baskets.

Diagonal Twining

Diagonally twined Pomo baskets were less often used for culinary purposes, but were often made for lighter use such as ornate globular storage baskets, fancy burden baskets and as gift baskets. These closely woven, diagonally twined baskets seem more fragile than their counterparts that were made using plain twining and lattice twining. Most Pomo diagonally twined baskets seem more appropriate as gifts or for use on special occasions than as workbaskets. Perhaps they were rather like the way a woman's fine china dishes are used today. This delicateness was a cultural choice, since fragility is not inherent in diagonal twining. For example, the Western Mono, Tachi Yokuts, Paiute, Chemehuevi and others made very strong diagonally twined baskets.

Diagonal twining occupied a position similar to coiling in that it was often used for baskets made for special occasions such as presentations at weddings. It is true that diagonal twining was used on baskets made for storing, cooking or carrying harvested seeds. But for rough work, plain twining or lattice twining were preferred. With the possible exception of storage baskets, the Pomo made more daily use of baskets done in plain twining or lattice twining than in diagonal twining. This supports the view that diagonal twining had not been present among the Pomo for as long as plain twining and lattice twining.

Design layout is yet another indication that diagonal twining has a separate origin from other twining traditions. Horizontal designs predominated in plain twining and lattice twining, but diagonal designs were most common on diagonally twined baskets.

POMO CLOSE TWINED BASKETRY

Nearly all California **burden baskets** were either conical or flat-bottomed. However, the Pomo made bell-shaped burden baskets. This flowing artistic form was a unique Pomo invention. Bell-shaped burden baskets were made in not just one, but in two techniques.

The Pomo made two basic forms of seed gathering baskets: (1) plain twined burden baskets, and (2) diagonally twined burden baskets. It was very unusual to have two different types of close-twined burden baskets made by the same culture. Each type of Pomo burden basket had a separate origin. Virtuoso Pomo weavers raised both styles to high art.

Twined baskets such as this one have a woven look to them rather than the corrugated look of coiling. This plain twined Pomo burden basket has beautiful redbud designs on a background of rugged pine root. It was extensively used to gather tarweed seeds. The basket's beauty was always present even when used in the most ordinary of tasks. D: 23", H: 19" (Private collection)

Plain Twined Burden Baskets

On plain twined burden baskets, wefts were either of sedge root or split, baked pine root. Split, baked pine root wefts were especially useful on plain twined burden baskets that were destined for hard use, such as for gathering tarweed seeds. Designs were normally either horizontal bands or diagonals, although a few baskets departed from these layouts. Designs were typically in redbud. These baskets were almost entirely made in plain twining. Just below the rim, however, plain twining over two warps was used. Rims had a wrapped reinforcing rod of willow attached at the rim. The rim rods were usually wrapped using peeled bark from wild grape. The bottoms of these burden baskets were finished using three-strand twining.

Plain twined Pomo burden baskets have ties to the north and northeast. Plain twined conical burden baskets occurred among the Pomo's northern neighbors, such as the Yuki and the Southern Humboldt Athapaskans. People northeast of the Pomo such as the Nomlaki, Wintu, Achumawi and others also made conical plain twined burden baskets. But none were identical to the bell-shaped Pomo burden basket. The plain twined bell-shaped burden basket was probably the original and most ancient form of Pomo burden basket. It almost certainly pre-dates the introduction or development of diagonally twined burden baskets among the Pomoans.

Diagonally Twined Burden Baskets

Pomo diagonally twined burden baskets were made primarily using diagonal twining, but other types of twining were used as accents on these burden baskets. Plain twining wrapped over two warps was used just below the rim. Spiral lattice binding (not to be confused with lattice twining, which is different) was used to implement designs amid the background of diagonal twining. You can recognize spiral lattice binding by looking on the back face (normally the interior) of the basket where raised latticework can be seen contrasting with the smoother diagonal twining. This difference is not visible on the exterior work face of the basket. Spiral lattice binding was regularly found on Pomo diagonally twined baskets (Dawson p.c.).

Pomo diagonally twined burden baskets were most similar to those of the Colusa Patwin and Valley Maidu around Chico. These groups also used a down-to-the-right slant of weft twist, made designs woven in spiral lattice binding, and added warps by sharpening their lower ends. Just below the rim they used plain twining over two warps, which provided a lovely decorative touch. The most obvious departure from Pomo bell-shaped burden baskets was the conical shape of Patwin and Valley Maidu burden baskets

The Valley Maidu made diagonally twined burden baskets, but the Maidu of the Sierras made plain twined burden baskets. The Patwin made diagonally twined burden baskets, but their linguistic kinsmen and neighbors, the Nomlaki, made plain twined burden baskets. The Pomo are thought to have once occupied the Sacramento Valley. Lawrence Dawson noted that diagonally twined Pomo burden baskets were an interior Pomo trait. Pomo on the immediate coast did not as often make diagonally twined burden baskets. All this suggests diagonally twined burden baskets of the Pomo-Patwin-Valley Maidu type developed in the central Sacramento Valley. The Pomo, however, developed their own distinctive bell-shaped form of burden basket. The diagonally twined conical burden basket of the Patwin and Valley Maidu would remain in the Sacramento Valley.

Storage Baskets

One of the most spectacular of Pomo baskets was the large, globular storage basket. These baskets might be lattice twined, plain twined or diagonally twined. Designs were typically horizontal bands or diagonals. They were broader in relation to height than were cooking pots. Rims were simply trimmed. Incredibly beautiful huge storage baskets were often given as prized wedding gifts.

Cooking Pots

Very closely twined cooking baskets were used for boiling acorn mush, acorn soup and other foods. Cooking pots were very similar to storage baskets and were made in plain twining, lattice twining or diagonal twining. Plain twining was most commonly used for cooking pots. Lattice twining was especially good for cooking pots because it could be woven so tightly that it held water especially well (Gifford 1967, 38; Dawson p.c.).

Cooking pots did not reach the size of the largest storage baskets. They tended to have straight sides unlike storage baskets. Cooking pots were more open at the top than were storage baskets for ease in stirring and using cooking stones. Cooking pot designs, like those on storage baskets, were normally bands or diagonal designs. Rims were simply trimmed. There were no coiled Pomo culinary baskets.

Smaller Cooking Pot-Shaped Baskets

Shaped liked a cooking pot, but much smaller, this basket was most commonly used for pouring water and other liquids.

Winnowing trays had long been used to winnow, sift and parch seeds and acorn flour. Pomo winnowers, such as this one, were strengthened with bands of lattice twining, but lacked the reinforcing rod at the rim that mortar hoppers and close-twined burden baskets had. Both winnowers and mortar hoppers were typically made of sedge root wefts and decorated with redbud designs. Mortar hoppers were invented prior to the arrival of Europeans and were developed because they were more effective and lightweight than using a stone mortar alone. Pomo mortar hoppers were derived from winnowers. D: 16", H: 4.5" (Private collection)

Winnowing/Sifting/Parching Baskets

The Pomo made three main types of winnowers. The first type was a very large plate-like form. These were round, plain-twined slightly concave baskets usually with reinforcing bands of lattice twining. No reinforcing rod was used at the rim as the basket would lose its flexibility. The rim was simply trimmed, with warp sticks slightly protruding. Some were quite large, far bigger than plates.

A second, less common type of Pomo winnower was like the first type described above, except that it was made entirely of lattice twining.

A third type of Pomo winnower was also round and concave but had a short straight peg protruding from the apex of the broad cone. It lacked the lattice twining reinforcing bands. It was made by the Clear Lake Pomo (Dawson p.c.). It was possibly made elsewhere by other Pomoans, too. Occasionally a loop was substituted for the peg to aid in holding the winnower (Smith-Ferri p.c. 2003). The vast majority of surviving winnowers do not have either a peg or a loop.

The Pomo made close twined winnowers, while the Patwin, Maidu and Yuki made coiled winnowers. Round, close twined winnowers are a northern type of basket. The Northwestern Californians and the Southern Humboldt Athapaskans made round close twined winnowers, although they had differences from those of the Pomo. But clearly Pomo winnowers have Northern California, not Central California, affiliations.

Serving Plates

These nearly flat, round baskets were similar to the winnowers described above, but smaller and were used as plates for serving foods such as acorn mush, pinole (small, cooked seeds) or dried seaweed. Sometimes plate form baskets were used as covers for other baskets (Ilvina Brown p.c.; Smith-Ferri 1998, 23).

Mortar Hoppers

Mortar hoppers have a hole in the bottom to allow a long, narrow pestle to pass through to pound acorns into flour. Mortar hoppers were placed on a stone slab to pound acorns into meal. The mortar hopper kept the acorns in and dust and debris out. The Pomo replaced stone mortars with flat stone slabs centuries before non-Indians arrived. However, on rare occasions, some Potter Valley Pomo in Mendocino County did use wooden mortars (Barrett 1952, 181; Smith-Ferri p.c.).

Pomo mortar hoppers were either: (1) plain twined with horizontal bands of lattice twining for reinforcing strength, or (2) solid lattice twining (less common). A wrapped reinforcing rod was added to strengthen the rim. The rim wrapping was most commonly wild grape (*Vitus californica*). Designs were usually in redbud, but narrow black bands were found on some southern Pomo mortar hoppers. Mortar hoppers might have pine root wefts at certain places on the basket instead of sedge root wefts because pine root added strength.

Weft splices were on the interior with fag ends held in by one weft twist. Warp ends were sharpened when added and concealed in the weave. The weaving adjacent to the hole at the bottom of the mortar hopper was usually done in three-strand simple braiding or plain twining, but three strand twining or diagonal twining was also used (Barrett 1996, 139-140; Dawson p.c.).

Mortar Hopper-Start Baskets

When the mortar hopper was completed and the reinforcing rod added, the bottom was then trimmed off to form the hole. The disc-shaped bottom was said to be later reused to start new mortar hoppers with new warp sticks added (Elsie Allen, quoted in Abel-Vidor, Brovarney and Billy 1996, 41). However, analysis of the mortar hopper-start basket construction suggests that they more likely were used for other purposes, such as small trays, rather than as a start for a second mortar hopper (Smith-Ferri p.c.).

This closely woven disc-shaped bottom was actually a specialized type of Pomo basket—the Mortar Hopper-Start Basket. Being cut from the bottom of the mortar hopper, it was obviously the same diameter as the mortar hopper hole. This basket was close woven diagonal twining, but with plain twining (often over two warps near the out edge) in parts. They were carefully woven to provide a sturdy start and to be fairly easily removed.

Mortar hopper start baskets were undecorated. This distinguishes them from comparably sized centers of winnowers that were normally decorated. Some mortar hopper start baskets were a bit more conical than the bottom few inches of a winnower.

Mortar hopper start baskets occurred elsewhere in California in various forms. In contrast to the Pomo close twined mortar hopper-start basket, Northwestern Californians began their mortar hoppers with an openwork start. In northeastern California, a handle-like bundle of warp sticks was sometimes used to begin a mortar hopper.

The Origins and Spread of Mortar Hoppers

Pomo mortar hoppers and winnowing trays are virtually identical to one another in shape and in the kinds of weaves used. Pomo mortar hoppers differ from winnowers only in having a reinforcing rim rod added and in having their bottom cut out. Sherrie Smith-Ferri has pointed out that, prior to having their bottoms cut out and the rod added, Pomo mortar hoppers look like Pomo trays. This agrees

This is a mortar hopper start basket after being cut out of the bottom of the mortar hopper. Done in diagonal twining and undecorated, the six inch diameter basket corresponds in size to the hole in the bottom of a Pomo mortar hopper. These handy little baskets could be used for other purposes after being removed from the mortar hopper bottom. D: 6", H: 1.5" (Collection of the Milwaukee Public Museum, #15663/425. Lisa Woo Shanks photo file)

with Lawrence Dawson's research that suggests that mortar hoppers were first developed from winnowing trays.

Pomo mortar hoppers are essentially winnowers with their bottoms cut out. No other mortar hoppers are as close to their ancestral winnowers as Pomo mortar hoppers. The unbroken link between Pomo mortar hoppers and winnowing baskets indicates a long shared ancestry. Based on the closeness of these two types of baskets, Dawson believed that twined California mortar hoppers were first developed among the Pomo and/or the Yuki (Dawson p.c.).

The Northwestern and Northeastern Californians both made similar mortar hoppers. However, the mortar hoppers of these cultures have been more modified in their weaving and reinforcing methods and thus diverge more from their trays than do Pomo mortar hoppers from Pomo trays. The Southern Humboldt Athapaskan mortar hopper is intermediate between the Pomo and Northwestern California types and adapted from both.

No matter which area(s) first invented mortar hoppers, there was a remarkable spread of twined mortar hoppers. This diffusion was primarily along the coast. On the coast, mortar hoppers were found as far north as the Siuslaw around Florence, Oregon (Barnett 1937, 167) and as far south as the Kumeyaay (Diegueno) on the California-Mexico border. Mortar hoppers spread well inland less often, as among the Achumawi and Atsugewi in California and among the Upper Umpqua and Kalapuya in western Oregon. In the Sierras, the mortar hopper was absent among the Sierra Miwok, absent

Pomo twined mortar hoppers began much like winnowers, except that they had a plain undecorated center bottom. The bottom was cut out after the basket was completed. In this photo, we can see a Pomo mortar hopper prior to having its bottom removed. The portion to be cut out is inside the lattice twining below the bottommost design band. This removable section is called the mortar hopper start basket. On this basket, the mortar hopper's reinforcing rod at the rim has not yet been added. D: 23", H: 10" (Collection of the Grace Hudson Museum and the Sun House, Ukiah, California)

among most Maidu groups and used minimally by the Foothill Yokuts. The greater abundance of large, flat bedrock mortar sites in the Sierra Nevada Mountains probably made this coastal invention less appealing to Sierran peoples.

In Southern California coiled, not twined, mortar hoppers were used. Since twining came into California long before coiling, the southern California coiled mortar hopper must have developed well after the twined form. The Southern California coiled mortar hopper was probably derived from the twined Central California mortar hoppers.

Fine Tule Baskets, Some with Clamshell Disc Beads on the Rim

The Pomo made bowl-shaped, closely woven tule baskets. None of these baskets had designs, but they were nicely woven. The best were made with clamshell disc beads around the rim. This was the only decoration. Wefts were large compared to the finer Klamath or Modoc tule baskets. Yet, the Pomo tule baskets decorated with clamshell disc beads at the rim possessed their own special artistic beauty.

There were two sub-types of well-woven tule baskets: (1) the ones decorated with clamshell discs and intended as fancy baskets, and (2) the ones of the same shape, but without

Among the most interesting kinds of California Indian twined baskets were mortar hoppers. These bottomless baskets were placed over stone mortars or slabs to hold in the acorn flour when pounding acorns using a stone pestle. A woman rested both legs atop or along side the mortar hopper to hold it steady while crushing shelled acorns. These baskets endured hard use and mortar hoppers had to be among the most structurally strong of all baskets. This Pomo mortar hopper uses bands of lattice twining and a reinforced rim to maximize strength. D: 19", H: 5.5" (Private collection)

The Clear Lake Pomo, perhaps more than any other North Central California people, used tule baskets extensively for many utilitarian purposes. This tule bowl was purchased in Lake County in 1914. (Collection of the Milwaukee Public Museum, #15687. Lisa Woo Shanks photo file.)

clamshell discs and not quite as carefully woven. The second type was obviously a utility basket, but even these were more finely made than the usual tule workbasket used by the Pomo. These fine tule baskets were certainly made by the Clear Lake Pomo and perhaps elsewhere as well.

Sling and Clay Ball Baskets

This tule basket was shaped rather like a ping-pong paddle but with raised sides and a short handle. The sling and clay ball basket was used in tule canoes to hold a sling and clay balls. The sling was used to propel the clay balls at high velocity. Some clay balls were flattened so that they

Special pouch-like tule baskets were made to hold hardened "mud balls" that were hurled using slings when hunting waterfowl. Such baskets were often used by Pomo men while hunting on Clear Lake. (California Department of Parks and Recreation, California State Indian Museum)

skipped over the water and hit waterfowl when hunting (Barrett 1952, 226). Other clay balls were round or oval. Clay balls were sometimes called mud balls because they were formed from hardened mud.

Minor Tule Baskets

Many Californian tribes wove tule baskets. These were easily made and used for temporary storage of a variety of objects. Most were briefly used and discarded. The Clear Lake Pomo especially made tule baskets (Smith-Ferri 1998, 14).

POMO OPENWORK TWINED BASKETRY

Openwork twined baskets were often needed in order to: (1) allow for good air circulation to reduce spoilage or, (2) allow water or other liquids to flow through the basket. Openwork basketry required less time in weaving and allowed heavy-duty baskets to be lighter weight. Such baskets were used to collect or store acorns, buckeye seeds, fish and other items. Baskets were also woven using openwork to serve as fish traps or bird traps.

Both Pomo women and men made openwork baskets. Kroeber states that the "Pomo men performed the coarser labor of openwork twining in most instances." The men made all traps, basketry weirs, big, coarse burden baskets and some baby cradles. In general, Pomo men made the types of baskets they used in their daily work. Men tended to weave openwork baskets using unpeeled shoots while women more often wove using peeled shoots. (Kroeber 1925, 246; Smith-Ferri 1998, 30-31, Smith-Ferri p.c,. 2005).

Pomo close twined baskets, made by the women, generally had a down-to-the-right slant of twist. Pomo openwork twined baskets, made by the men, generally had an up-to-the-right slant of twist. It is believed that this was the result of different customs for the sexes, rather like the way buttons are sewn on one side of a shirt for women and on the opposite for men in contemporary American society.

Openwork Burden Baskets (Acorn Gathering Baskets)

Openwork burden baskets were used to gather acorns, firewood and other large objects. Perhaps because of their different functions, openwork burden baskets were not limited to a bell shape as were the vast majority of Pomo close twined burden baskets.

Unlike close twined Pomo burden baskets, openwork Pomo burden baskets came in a variety of shapes. Large openwork Pomo burden baskets come in any of four shapes: (1) bell shaped, like close twined burden baskets, (2) conically shaped, (3) truncated cones with nearly straight

Pomo men made very large, coarse openwork burden baskets of willow such as this one. These big, rugged baskets could be used to carry heavy loads of salmon, firewood and other heavy items. Pomo men often made the baskets that were needed in their work. D: 24", H: 24" (Collection of the Grace Hudson Museum and the Sun House, Ukiah, California)

flaring sides, or (4) rather barrel shaped. These different shapes reflected their different purposes. For example, the barrel shaped forms may have been storage baskets used as burden baskets for convenience. Men's burden baskets were larger than women's burden baskets and were used to carry large, heavy loads such as firewood or clamshells. They were made of unpeeled willow, were coarse and strong. The burden baskets made by the women were of peeled willow and usually beautifully made. The finest openwork burden baskets were designed to carry acorns (Gifford 1967, 38; Barrett 1996, 300-301, plate 26, figs. 1, 2; Smith-Ferri p.c.).

A distinctive feature of Pomo openwork burden baskets (and some openwork shallow bowls and trays, too) was the gathering of the warp stick ends in flowing, wave-like groups at the rim. Three or four clusters of warp sticks were typically braided giving a flowing, over and under, wave-like rim finish.

Openwork Sieves or Colanders

Openwork sieves, typically small enough to be held in the hand, were used to process berries, bulbs and other foods (David Peri p.c.).

Openwork Basin-Shaped Bowls and Trays

Various shapes of openwork bowls were used for purposes ranging from food processing to holding basketry. Most were low, broad baskets that varied from coarse to fine construction. These workbaskets could also be used to hold wet or messy food, such as shellfish, seaweed, roots, bulbs, fish and the like. They could also be used as serving bowls.

Baskets of this type might have a simple design, but many were undecorated. Some had selvages with the distinctive set of warp stick ends interwoven in a wavy pattern at the rim. If desired, a reinforcing rod might be added at the rim. Both techniques served to strengthen this utility basket. These baskets might be plain twined, lattice twined or even three strand twined (Barrett 1996, 298-299, plate 25, figs. 3, 5, 6).

Plain twined, openwork baskets using whole willow shoots were made in sizes ranging from small general purpose bowls to huge storage baskets several feet in diameter. Such baskets might be quite coarse, or finely made like this one. Note how the warps are braided to form a strong and artistic rim. Anthropologist Samuel Barrett purchased this basket at Clear Lake, California in 1914. D: 11.5", H: 5" (Collection of the Milwaukee Public Museum, #15697. (Lisa Woo Shanks photo file)

Openwork Storage Baskets

People who stored acorns, dried fish and other foods in their houses used openwork lattice twined or plain twined baskets for storage. There were two basic types of openwork storage baskets. The plain twined baskets were usually barrel-shaped and a bit roughly made (Barrett 1996, 301, plate 26, fig. 3).

The finely made lattice twined openwork baskets were usually globular in form and typically broader than tall. These were carefully made and most impressive with their entire lattice structure strikingly visible. The best of these baskets were both utilitarian and works of art.

A Clear Lake Pomo lattice twined storage basket from Elem Rancheria, Lake County. This openwork basket was used to store fishing nets. Its openwork construction allowed air to circulate freely, thus preventing mold. Purchased in 1906. D: 13.5", H: 10" (C. Hart Merriam Collection, University of California at Davis, #378)

Huge Openwork Storage Baskets

Giant openwork storage baskets up to seven feet in diameter were made of willow. These undecorated baskets were plain twined, but for strength two or three weft strands might be used at once. Some were set atop a table-like platform similar to the mesquite granaries of Southern California. The men made these baskets (Smith-Ferri p.c.).

Wickerwork Seedbeaters

The classic Pomo seedbeater was of wickerwork (Barrett 1996, 297, plate 24, figs. 1, 4). The handle of parallel warps was used as the "starting knot." These wickerwork seedbeaters vary in size. All the Pomoans living south of the present day Mendocino County community of Willits used them. Wickerwork seedbeater distribution also extended east from Coyote Valley and Ukiah Valley to the Clear Lake Pomo. The Patwin and some Valley Maidu made wickerwork seedbeaters, too.

Twined Seedbeaters

The only Pomoan people who made radiating warp, plain twined seedbeaters were the northern-most Pomo. These included the Little Lake Pomo, Sherwood Valley Pomo and Potter Valley Pomo people (Gifford and Kroeber 1937, 132; Dawson p.c.). This form of seedbeater had a roughly twined bowl form consisting of woven radiating warps to which a handle was added. The twined seedbeaters of the

northern-most Pomo had an attached handle similar to Yuki seedbeaters.

The Pomo used round shoot warps on their twined seedbeaters instead of the flat warps the Yuki used on their seedbeaters. The Pomo use of rounded shoots as opposed to the Yuki use of flat warps indicates that these twined Pomo seedbeaters were not trade pieces from the Yuki. They were a localized Pomo type. Yet both of these twined seedbeaters were closely related and likely shared a common ancestry. They were probably originally from the Yuki.

Fish Traps, Eel Traps, Quail Traps, Waterfowl Traps and Woodpecker Traps

Pomo traps varied greatly in size depending on purpose (Barrett 1996, 303, plate 27). Most were long and narrow with a wide mouth. They were made so that an animal or fish entering the trap could go far inward but could not turn around to escape. Traps could be quite large. As a result, some long traps were woven in segments that would telescope into themselves. This made for easier weaving and provided greater convenience when transporting them. The men made these traps to their own careful specifications. The size of the

Seedbeaters were important food gathering baskets. When harvesting small seeds, Pomo women skillfully knocked the seeds into close twined burden baskets using seedbeaters. Most Pomo people made their seedbeaters in wickerwork, the technique used in the seed beater shown here. L: 23", W: 13" (Collection of the Grace Hudson Museum and the Sun House, Ukiah, California)

basket's openings, form and shape all depended on the trap's purpose. The men usually worked using unpeeled willow while women usually peeled their willow shoots (Smith-Ferri p.c., 2003).

Fish traps were of several types. Most tended to be long and narrow, although there was a broad conical style, too. Most fish traps had a double mouth. There was a wide outer mouth that flared outward and an inner mouth that narrowed so that the fish could not get back out. Some fish traps were large enough to catch salmon and were used in conjunction with a weir. The fish trap was placed on the upstream side of the weir to trap migrating salmon on their return run. Once inside the trap, the salmon could not turn around to escape. (Barrett 1996, 303, figs. 2, 4, 6).

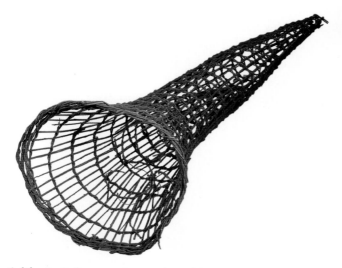

California Indians made a variety of ingenious animal and fish traps. This four-foot long, openwork Pomo basket was used to trap fish, especially salmon. It has an inner section that prevents fish from getting back out. This basket is made of unpeeled willow and was made in Lake County about 1915. (Collection of the Milwaukee Public Museum, #17207. Lisa Woo Shanks photo file)

Quail traps were long and narrow, up to eight or nine feet in length and made of young willow sprouts. A three-foot high brush fence was built amid quail habitat. At intervals, small openings were left in the fence where the quail traps were placed. Quail were driven slowly toward the six-inch diameter traps. They followed one another inside and were caught (Barrett 1952, 134-135; Merriam 1967, 289).

Waterfowl traps were about a foot in diameter. These traps were staked in marshes amid the tules so that they would float partially above the water allowing birds to easily

swim into them. Like the quail trap, once inside the birds could not back out (Barrett 1952, 141-142, fig. 4).

Woodpecker traps were typically about four inches in diameter and as much as two or three feet long. After dark they were tied to a hole in a tree to cover the entrance where woodpeckers were roosting. In the morning when the woodpeckers tried to leave the nest, they were caught in the trap. A single woodpecker trap might catch as many as six birds at once (Barrett 1952, 139; Barrett 1996, 166, 303, plate 27, fig. 1).

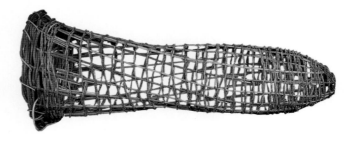

Woodpecker traps were placed on trees to catch woodpeckers as they left their holes. The Pomo needed red woodpecker feathers to decorate feather baskets. Elsie Allen made this trap. A major public high school in Santa Rosa, California, has been named in honor of this famed Pomo basket weaver. (Marion Steinbach Indian Basket Museum, Tahoe City, California)

Fish Catching Plunge Baskets were not really a trap but an open-mouthed, cone-shaped basket used to plunge down over fish in shallow, muddy water. It had a hole in the top so

A Pomo plunge trap used for catching fish. This basket, open at both ends, was used in muddy water with the large end down to plunge down over fish and trap them. Then the fisherman reached down into the trap and grasped the entrapped fish with his hand. This plunge trap was purchased in 1906 from the Lower Lake Pomo, Lake County. D: 23", H: 11.5" (C. Hart Merriam Collection, University of California at Davis, #381)

the fisherman could insert his hand to remove the fish trapped inside (Merriam 1967, 299). Grasping the narrow, upper end of the trap, the fisherman waded along in the stream, plunging the trap in likely places to catch a fish. When a fisherman felt a fish striking against the side of the basket, he reached in the small opening at the top and pulled up the fish (Kroeber 1996, 165; Barrett 1996, 203, plate 27, fig. 5).

Fish Scoop Baskets were made by the Pomo as a basket to scoop up fish from the water (Essene 1942, 6).

Bait Baskets were made by the Clear Lake Pomo for holding fishing bait (Smithsonian #203 267).

Surf Fish Baskets were baskets made of hazel twigs used to catch smelt and other surf fish during ebb tides. It had a funnel-shaped mouth and a handle across the top. It seems to have been used similarly to a dip net. A fisherman stood in the water with a pole attached to the basket. He dipped the basket into the sea as a wave came in, then lifted it up full of fish and carried the fish ashore to a hole in the sand. The women then gathered the fish and placed them in a burden basket (Gifford 1967, 20).

Hunting-Blind Baskets were huge, roughly woven bottomless baskets four to five feet in height that were carried to hunting sites. A mat of ferns or grass was placed in the bottom for the hunter to sit on. The hunter sat and waited for game to pass by close enough to be shot (Merriam 1967, 289). The concept was similar in concept to the duck blind used by contemporary duck hunters, but used on land.

Fisherman's Seat Baskets were U-shaped, made of tule and woven for use in tule canoes (Barrett 1952, 212).

Pomo Baskets Made in Other Types of Weaves

Cradles made with a Bound Weave

All California Indian baby cradle baskets were designed to be carried on the mother's back. These were U-shaped sitting cradles where the baby sat in the bottom of the cradle with the child's legs hanging down. A hoop was attached horizontally at the cradle's top. The hoop projected outward from the front of the cradle. It was handy to lift the cradle, protected the baby's head from a fall and could also support a screen or hood to protect the baby from insects and the sun. Miniature baskets, beads, shells and other interesting items might be hung from the hoop to inspire a girl to be a good weaver and gatherer. For boys, other role appropriate items related to running, hunting and other men's activities would be used (Barrett 1952, 171-171; Barrett 1996, 166).

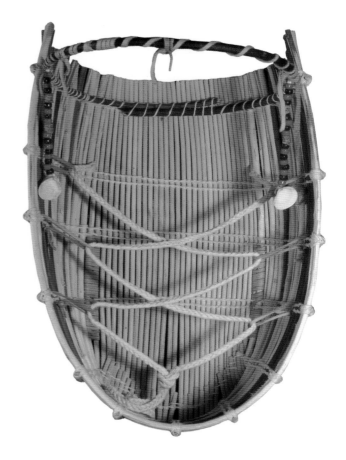

The Pomo cradle was designed for a baby to sit in, rather than lay on its back. These sturdy cradles were typically made with willow warps and were held together with a bound weave of either Native string or commercial cotton string. The hoop at the top was traditionally made of oak. Christine Hamilton made this cradle around 2004. Note the pendants of beads and seashells she has added to entertain the baby. Some Pomo mothers use such cradles today and infants love them. This cradle is woven in the Mendocino County-style where the back warp sticks come straight down to the U-shaped bottom. On Clear Lake Pomo baby cradles the warp sticks on the back loop down to the bottom and back up in a U-shaped pattern. L: 18", W: 12" (Private collection)

A tumpline was attached to the back of the cradle so the mother could carry it on her back.

Pomo baby cradles were technically not twined. They were made using a bound weave, a type of double half-hitch knot using string (Dawson p.c.; Smith-Ferri 1996, 36). While Pomo cradles on first impression look quite similar to one another, there were regional variations. Major regional cradle differences include whether the warps were bound inside the back of the cradle, secured outside the back of the basket or were carried around the back in a graceful U-shape.

Several regional types of early Pomo cradles can be identified. On early Upper Lake Pomo cradles the points of back-stitches were trimmed off on the inside and held down by a U-shaped stick (for example, UC Hearst cradle 1-480). Lakeport Pomo cradles had the warp sticks on the back arranged in a U-shape form (UC Hearst cradles 1-24253 and 1-24213). Kashaya Pomo cradles had straight, vertical warp sticks on the back. At the bottom of the cradle, these back warp sticks were either cut off or bent inside at the base (UC Hearst cradle 1-2362). Yet another type of cradle was found among the Southern Pomo and Wappo of Alexander Valley in Sonoma County. In this type of cradle the warp sticks were carried forward inside the back at a low angle to extend partially across the cradle's seat. The tips of these warp sticks were tapered to blend with the bottom. In at least some parts of Mendocino County, the warp sticks on the cradle's back were brought straight down. At the U-shaped bottom the warp sticks were bent upward for about an inch or inch and a half and secured tightly against the back. In later years, these cradle types seem to have spread among different Pomo groups so that early regional characteristics became blurred (Dawson p.c.; Smith-Ferri p.c., 2003; Bibby 2004, 35-36).

Around Clear Lake and elsewhere a temporary first cradle of soft tules was made for the child. It was used for about a month before the baby was moved to the regular cradle. Finely shredded soft, green tule was used as "swaddling clothes" for the baby's comfort (Barrett 1952, 172).

Tule fluff, the soft inner fibers of tule, and Spanish moss (long moss-like lichens that often hang from oaks) were used as diapers.

WICKERWORK

As discussed earlier, wickerwork seedbeaters were made.

Some Regional Variations in Pomo Basketry

Although Pomoan basketry is uniform enough in style and technique to be readily identifiable, there were regional differences. The regional styles were probably far greater than we realize today because no early studies documented local variations. After contact with Euro-Americans, there was increased movement and intermarriage among different Pomo groups. This almost certainly reduced local styles.

CLEAR LAKE POMO BASKETRY

The Clear Lake Pomo and other inland Pomo made lavish use of redbud designs, often in spectacular wide bands. Redbud was plentiful in the interior and Pomo artists took advantage of this opportunity. Clear Lake Pomo were lake people and they used tule for a wider range of baskets than any other Pomoans.

COASTAL POMO BASKETRY

From Lawrence Dawson's research on early twined baskets, he found that early Kashaya Pomo plain and lattice twined baskets often had warp ends bent over and bound down and outward at the rim, although the usual Pomo practice of trimming the warps was also done. This binding of warp sticks downward at the rim contrasts with the almost universal Pomoan practice of trimmed warp sticks cut off at or slightly above the rim.

Dawson's studies of Kashaya and coastal Pomo basketry also found some distinctive starting knots, less diversity of designs, narrower and more linear designs, and the use of pale bands of willow or sedge root wefts for contrast on some baskets that used pine root wefts. Diagonal twining was either lacking or uncommon, he believed. The basis for

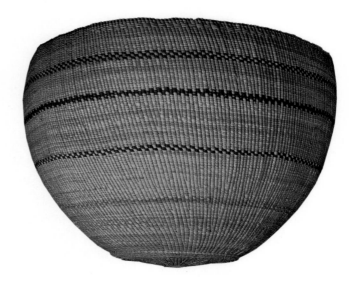

A Coastal Pomo cooking pot from the Manchester-Point Arena area, Mendocino County. Coastal Pomo weavers frequently used narrow, black designs. These designs were done in plain twining using bracken fern root on a sedge root background. Warps were of hazel. Peggy Burke Smith, whose home was the Manchester Rancheria, made this basket. D: 11", H: 8" (Marion Steinbach Indian Basket Museum, Tahoe City, California, #247)

The Pomo weavers of Lake, Mendocino and Sonoma counties excelled at feather-work as well as basketry. Pomo feather baskets combined three arts: basketry, feather-work and jewelry making. Jewel-like chains of clamshell disc beads were tipped with pendants of abalone shell or pink magnesite. This detail of a coiled feather basket shows Pomo artistry. (Private collection)

this conclusion was that he could find no diagonally twined baskets using bracken fern designs, which would suggest coastal Pomo origins (Dawson p.c.).

Old coastal Mendocino and Sonoma County Pomo baskets often have a slightly leftward lean in the warps, as opposed to the more vertical warps of the interior Pomo. Since redbud did not grow on the coast, black dyed bracken fern root designs were predominant among older baskets from the Kashaya, Point Arena and Fort Bragg Pomo (Barrett 1996, 139). Coastal Pomo basket banded designs were narrower in comparison to the broader bands of the Clear Lake Pomo and their neighbors. The Coastal Pomoans often used the spiral lattice binding technique when weaving designs on both plain twined and diagonal twined baskets (Dawson p.c.).

At least among the Fort Bragg Pomo, feathers were less often used on baskets than they were further inland (Smith-Ferri p.c., 2005).

SOUTHERN POMO BASKETRY

Southern Pomo weavers often used large, broad weft strands in lattice twining. They also bound down selvages on some twined baskets (Dawson p.c.).

THE DECLINE OF REGIONAL STYLES

With automobile transportation, intermarriage and the sharing of ideas among different Pomoan groups, later Pomo baskets showed fewer regional differences.

Comments

As Alfred L. Kroeber pointed out, the majority of the amazing Pomo basketry tradition was created by, or modified by, the Pomo weavers themselves (Kroeber 1925, 247). As in every culture, some ideas were borrowed from other groups. But ideas were reinterpreted by the Pomo artists to suit their own cultural and artistic tastes. New ideas were also added to basketry, creating an unexcelled art form. Pomo feather baskets, lattice twining and diagonal twining all were unsurpassed worldwide. The Wappo, Lake Miwok and the Huchnom were inspired by Pomoan weaving and largely adopted it. No people in California had richer, more varied basketry than did the Pomo. Great art flourished under the oaks amid the gentle, rolling hills of the Coast Range.

A magnificent Hill Patwin feather basket with red woodpecker feathers, blue feathers (possibly bluebird feathers) and dark green mallard feathers accented with clamshell disc beads and abalone pendants. Note that the top five coil rows are undecorated, except for the quail topknots at the rim. This coiled basket is from Rumsey on Cache Creek in Yolo County. D: 11", H: 3" (Turtle Bay Exploration Park, Redding, California, #1964.1.144).

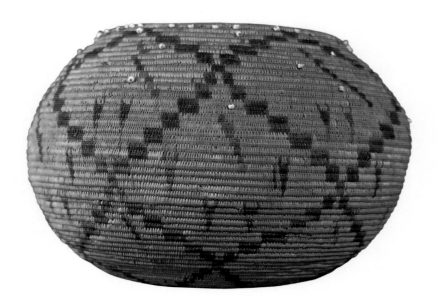

Great art has long flourished among the Patwin people in the southern Sacramento Valley and the inner Coast Range. This stunning Patwin coiled basket was created using black dyed bulrush root designs and is decorated with European trade beads on a sedge root background. Purchased in 1907 from the weaver in Long Valley at the Patwin village of Chenposel. This village was located on the North Fork of Cache Creek in eastern Lake County. D: 9", H: 6" (C. Hart Merriam collection, University of California at Davis, #785)

PATWIN BASKETRY

The great Wintun (Wintuan) language group comprised of the Patwin, Nomlaki and Wintu, extended from near Mount Shasta southward through the Sacramento Valley to the northeastern shore of San Francisco Bay. Wintuan speaking people came to live in the lands immediately north and west of the upper end of the Sacramento Valley, in most of the Sacramento Valley itself and along the eastern edge of the Coast Range Mountains and on south to the northeastern shore of San Francisco Bay (Kroeber 1925, 351-357).

Linguists and anthropologists using linguistic and cultural criteria saw that Wintuan speakers comprised three ethnic groups. The Wintu were the northern-most, the central group was the Nomlaki and the southern-most the Patwin.

The Wintuan people occupied such a large part of the state that cultural differences naturally developed among them. The northern groups, the Wintu, were twining people and their basketry resembled that of the Achumawi, Atsugewi and Yana to their north and east. The central group, the Nomlaki, was a coiling and a twining people. Their twining resembled some Pomo work and their coiling was closely related to the Patwin.

The southern-most people, the Patwin, were classic Central Californians in their coiled and twined basketry. Coiling had replaced twining to a large degree, indicating a deep commitment to Central Californian culture.

Wintuan speakers, including ancestral Patwin, are believed by some scholars to have entered the upper Sacramento Valley between 1,500 and 2,000 years ago. By about A.D. 700 the Patwin arrived at the lower Sacramento Valley and a bit later spread into the Coast Range Mountains (Moratto 1984, 562-563; Foster 1996, 90). As a result of this great expansion the Patwin came to occupy a large territory, including most of the lower Sacramento Valley.

Patwin territory stretched south from Colusa County, Yolo County and easternmost Lake County through the Sacramento and Capay Valleys. The present day cities of Colusa, Davis, Vacaville and Suisun City are all in Patwin country. The Patwin held all of Solano County and southern and eastern Napa County. In Napa County, Patwin land extended westward into Berryessa Valley, and along the Napa River estuary from the city of Napa to Vallejo. Patwin communities reached the north shore of the San Francisco

Bay estuary: at Suisun Bay, Carquinez Strait and northeastern San Pablo Bay.

Patwin people can be seen as coming from three areas. The River Patwin lived along the Sacramento River, from Colusa County south. The Hill Patwin lived along the eastern edge of the Coast Range Mountains. A third branch, the Southern Patwin, occupied what are today the southern portions of Solano and Napa counties (Whistler 1977, 160).

The Dramatic Effect of the Patwin Entry into the Sacramento Valley and North Bay Area

THE PATWIN AND THE MIWOK

When Patwin people entered the southern Sacramento Valley, dramatic changes in tribal territories occurred. When Europeans arrived in the region, they found the Miwok divided into Lake Miwok, Coast Miwok, Bay Miwok, Plains Miwok and Sierra Miwok groups. Some of these Miwok groups had even become isolated from one another.

It seems certain that the Miwok once occupied the lower Sacramento Valley that became Patwin territory. The people that occupy an area first name the native plants and animals. Patwin words for local native plants were borrowed from Miwok, including names for buckeye, manzanita, gray pine,

A flaring Patwin coiled bowl made by a member of the Tony Bill family, circa 1921. It has bulrush root designs on a sedge root background on a three-rod foundation. This basket has back-stitched over-stitching at the coil ending. When such over-stitching was found on Sacramento Valley baskets, it was nearly always only at the coil ending. D: 11.5", H: 6" (Courtesy of Russell Kloer, Clear Sky, Sonoma)

live oak, incense cedar and other plants (Whistler 1977; Foster 1996, 91). Both geographic location and linguistic data support a history of the Patwin displacing Miwok.

Some Miwok became separated from one another when the Patwin moved into the Sacramento Valley and adjacent Coast Range foothills. The Coast Miwok of Marin and southern Sonoma counties became isolated from all other Miwok groups. The Lake Miwok of the Middletown area in Lake County also became isolated from all other Miwok groups. The Bay Miwok were pushed south to the Mount Diablo region in Contra Costa County, although they still bordered the Plains Miwok at a narrow area around Rio Vista (Whistler 1977, 170-171).

The Coast Miwok separation resulted from two movements. First, there was the southwestern movement of Patwin to the northeast shore of San Francisco Bay. This Patwin expansion displaced the Miwok from below the city of Napa to the shore of San Pablo Bay. Almost simultaneously, the Wappo expanded south into the Napa Valley. Together, the Patwin and Wappo completed the geographic separation of the Coast Miwok from the Lake Miwok and Bay Miwok.

The Lake Miwok had long bordered the Pomo on their west and north. The Patwin and Wappo expansion cut the Lake Miwok off from other Miwok people to their southeast. Although occasional meetings still occurred at "Big Time" gatherings, in terms of daily life the Coast Miwok and Lake Miwok were now separated from other Miwok speakers.

The Bay Miwok nearly became separated from all other Miwok due to the Patwin expansion. Only a tenuous connection around Rio Vista in the Sacramento River Delta linked the Bay Miwok to the Plains Miwok. The Bay Miwok and Plains Miwok also were probably experiencing a gradual loss of their southern territory to the Valley Yokuts who were spreading into Miwok country from the San Joaquin Valley (Wallace 1978, 463).

Once the isolation of the western-most Miwok groups occurred, the influence of more populous surrounding groups increased. The Pomo heavily influenced the Lake Miwok and the Coast Miwok. Lake Miwok basketry became almost entirely Pomoan. The Coast Miwok adopted some features of Pomo basketry, and possibly Ohlone basketry techniques as well. Bay Miwok basketry is unknown, but it almost certainly was altered.

The great Patwin expansion had a major effect on all the Miwok peoples. But it was not that the Patwin moved in and influenced everyone else. Instead, the Patwin displaced other peoples, and this stimulated dynamic changes in basketry among many interacting groups. Tribes adopted new artistic and technical basketry ideas as a result of the Patwin expansion bringing about changes in territory. In some cases it was the Patwin themselves who were strongly influenced by other peoples. One such case involved the Sacramento Valley Maidu.

THE PATWIN AND THE VALLEY MAIDU

The coiled basketry of the Valley Maidu of the Sacramento Valley was very closely related to that of the Patwin. In fact, Valley Maidu coiling is more closely related to that of the Patwin than it is to the Sierra Maidu. For this to happen there must have been extensive interaction and/or intermarriage between the Valley Maidu and Patwin.

Because the Maidu had a long, pre-existing tradition of coiling present when the Patwin arrived in the Sacramento Valley, the Valley Maidu probably were the originators of this shared coiling tradition. The Patwin had come into California from Oregon and that was twining country. The Patwin would not have begun coiling until after they arrived in the lower Sacramento Valley where coiled was done. Here, both the Valley Maidu and Patwin eventually came to have shared basketry shapes, technical features and designs. Both groups used sedge root wefts, shared some designs, used similar weft fag ends and so on. But there were differences, too, and we will focus here on what made Patwin work distinctive.

Some Patwin versus Valley Maidu Basketry Features

Patwin coiled basketry was very similar to Valley Maidu coiled basketry, but it did differ. The Patwin placed designs on the bottoms of many of their baskets, unlike the Valley Maidu. Some Patwin designs were much narrower and had more open backgrounds than on Valley Maidu baskets. The Patwin sometimes used more than one design per basket, unlike the usual Maidu practice of using a single design on their baskets. If they included a second design, the Patwin used it either as a filler element between the main designs and/or placed it on the bottom of the basket.

In terms of design materials, the Maidu used redbud most often. The Patwin used redbud frequently, but not as often as the Maidu. The Patwin often used black designs done in bulrush root. The Maidu used black far less often and when they did, designs were done in bracken fern root or briar root (*Smilax*).

Again, we are emphasizing some differences here. Some Patwin and Valley Maidu baskets look very much alike and

This is a large Hill Patwin cooking pot made by the people around Rumsey in Capay Valley, Yolo County. It has a coiled, three-rod foundation and uses redbud designs on a sedge root background. Several variations of this design were used by both the Patwin and Valley Maidu. D: 17", H: 9" (C. Hart Merriam collection, University of California at Davis, #779)

it can be hard to tell them apart. The artistic concepts and forms of the two peoples' coiled work were very similar, although not identical.

In twining there were links between the Patwin and the Valley Maidu, although these ties were not as extensive as in coiling. The Patwin and Valley Maidu both made twined openwork scoop-shaped baskets, diagonally twined burden baskets and wickerwork seedbeaters, all of which show strong similarities. Patwin diagonally twined burden baskets were very close to Valley Maidu diagonally twined burden baskets in shape, weaving techniques, materials and design layout. Lawrence Dawson suggested that Patwin and Pomo burden baskets done in diagonal twining with wrapped-twined designs were almost certainly the invention of the Valley Maidu (Dawson, Bancroft notes).

The shared ideas of the Patwin and Valley Maidu were Sacramento Valley and the Coast Range Mountains practices. They were not the same as those of the Sierra Maidu. Weft material provides a good example. The Valley Maidu, Patwin and Pomo all used sedge root wefts, but significantly the Sierra Maidu used other materials. Sedge root wefts were not an old Maidu idea brought in from the east. Sedge root wefts probably came from the Pomo twining tradition. Thus, we come to yet another important influence in Patwin basketry, that of the Pomo.

THE PATWIN AND THE POMO

After the Valley Maidu, the Pomo had the second most influence on Patwin basketry. The Pomo influenced the Patwin primarily in twining, not coiling. This is not surprising since the Pomo had an incredibly strong and long-standing twining heritage.

The Pomo, unlike the Valley Maidu, were first and foremost a twining people and virtually all Pomo utility baskets were twined. Pomo winnowers, cooking pots, large storage baskets and many other types were twined. For example, we see shared ancestry in Pomo and Patwin mortar hoppers. Pomo and Patwin twined mortar hoppers are not identical, but they are close. Mortar hoppers spread from the Pomo to the Patwin, not from some northern source such as the Wintu or anyone else in far northern California.

Besides twined and coiled basketry, the Pomo also made wickerwork seedbeaters. Wickerwork seedbeaters were found among the Pomo, Patwin and a few Maidu. The Pomo made the largest and most elaborate wickerwork seedbeaters. It is probable that wickerwork seedbeaters were an idea that spread east from the Pomo to the Patwin and a few Maidu groups.

In terms of coiling, the Patwin probably adopted the decorative techniques of coiled feather baskets from the Pomo. No other culture equaled the elaborateness of Pomo feather baskets. Many tribes admired the beautiful Pomo feather baskets and were inspired to emulate them. Coiled Patwin feather baskets resemble those of the Pomo. But coiled Patwin utilitarian baskets such as cooking pots, trays

While most Patwin coiled baskets have three-rod foundations, this basket has a single-rod foundation. A fancy bowl like this might be used to hold valued possessions. Both redbud and bulrush root designs were used on a sedge root background. Purchased in 1903 from a Patwin elder at her home one mile north of Rumsey along Cache Creek in Yolo County. D: 8", H: 6" (C. Hart Merriam collection, University of California at Davis, #780)

and feast baskets are coiled much like those of the Valley Maidu. This is because Pomo coiling was largely limited to fancy baskets used as gifts or sometimes ceremonially. The Pomo did not have coiled food processing baskets. In contrast, the Valley Maidu had a full range of coiled food processing baskets to inspire Patwin weavers.

Did the Patwin have any influence on Pomo basketry? Patwin influence on Pomo twining seems nonexistent. When the Patwin arrived the Pomo already had a long established, fully developed twining tradition.

But coiling was another matter. Coiled basketry came to the Pomo long after twining. Compared to twining, coiling had a very limited, largely non-utilitarian place in Pomoan culture. Such limited use of coiled baskets suggests that the Pomo adopted coiling long after twining.

The Pomo adopted coiling from either the Patwin or the Valley Maidu. The Patwin were the Pomoan's eastern neighbors and if the Patwin arrived in the Sacramento Valley before the Pomo began coiling, then they most likely transmitted coiling to the Pomo. If the Pomo adopted coiling prior to the Patwin expansion, then the Valley Maidu probably would have been those who brought coiling to the Pomo. Once they began coiling, the Pomo elaborated it into an art that resulted in some of the finest feather baskets in the world. But Pomo coiling clearly has Sacramento Valley origins.

In conclusion, the Patwin adopted Pomo-style twining and Valley Maidu-style coiling. This supports that view that Patwin probably displaced some Pomo and some Valley Maidu upon entering the southern Sacramento Valley. It also indicates that the Maidu had coiling before either the Pomo or Patwin.

THE PATWIN AND THE NOMLAKI

Although only a tiny number of documented Nomlaki baskets exist in museum collections, Nomlaki coiled basketry appears to have been most similar to Patwin work. Coiled basketry was a Central California practice and the Nomlaki were on the northern fringe of coiling. The Patwin were the southern neighbors of the Nomlaki and likely introduced the Nomlaki to coiling after learning it from the Valley Maidu.

Nomlaki twining is even less known, but it seems to have some Pomo features. Nomlaki twining may ultimately be derived from Pomo twining and Nomlaki coiling from Valley Maidu coiled basketry. Both arts may have reached the Nomlaki via the Patwin.

The Patwin sometimes used two or even three different designs on their coiled baskets. This three-rod foundation cooking pot is from the River Patwin people, purchased from its weaver nine miles north of Colusa in 1903. It has black dyed bulrush root designs with a sedge root background. D: 13", H: 7.5" (C. Hart Merriam collection, University of California at Davis, #776)

THE PATWIN AND THE WAPPO

How much influence the Patwin had on the Wappo is uncertain, but it was never great. Wappo twined and coiled basketry was virtually identical to that of the Pomo, with one significant exception. The Pomo cooked only in twined cooking pots. While the Wappo also made twined cooking pots, they did something more. The Wappo also made coiled cooking pots (Driver 1936, 187). Interestingly, while Wappo twined cooking pots were like those of the Pomo, Wappo coiled cooking pots were very similar to those of the Patwin in form, technique and design concepts. The Wappo were in close contact with the Patwin in southern and eastern Napa County and probably adopted coiled cooking pots from the Patwin.

THE PATWIN AND THE OHLONE (COSTANOAN)

There were links between Patwin and Ohlone coiled basketry. The Patwin and Ohlone bordered each other along Carquinez Strait near Vallejo and Crockett. It is even possible that some of the people who lost territory during the Patwin expansion may have been Ohlone. But whatever happened, the two cultures clearly have shared coiled basketry characteristics.

In coiling, Patwin and Ohlone had many characteristics in common including: three-rod foundations, usually with bound down weft fag ends (some Patwin weft fag ends were concealed in the foundation); plain wrapped rims; designs sometimes placed on the bottoms of baskets; the use of bulrush root for designs; frequent favoring of narrow designs with ample background area; and feather and shell decoration. It is uncertain who influenced whom and in what ways, but the coiling traditions of these two peoples are clearly related.

SOME RESULTS OF THE GREAT PATWIN EXPANSION

In sum, the great Patwin expansion was one of the most significant events in the history of Central California coiled basketry. The Patwin migration into the Sacramento Valley, the Coast Range valleys and the northeast corner of the San Francisco Bay Area had an impact on many people. The Valley Maidu, Nomlaki, Ohlone, Coast Miwok, Lake Miwok, Wappo and Pomo were all affected. The Patwin were both the influencers and the influenced. In some cases, the Patwin may not have directly influenced a given culture, but by isolating that group from their linguistic kin they facilitated change throughout much of North Central California.

Patwin Coiled Basketry

Technical Features of Patwin Coiled Basketry

Patwin coiled basketry primarily used three-rod **foundations** of peeled willow. Single-rod foundations were were mostly used on winnowers and "boat-shaped" oval gift baskets. A very few Patwin baskets (and a few Pomo baskets, too) had foundations that began as a single-rod foundation and then changed to a three-rod foundation part way across the bottom (Dawson p.c.).

On many Patwin baskets overhand knots of shredded material served as starting knots. Patwin coiled **starting knots** were most commonly a tight spiral start made by wrapping a weft strand around a bundle of shredded material for about one inch, then kinking it around on itself to form a spiral. One Patwin coiled basket studied had a twined start knot, a feature sometimes found among the Pomo, Wappo and Yuki.

The Patwin coiling **work direction** was always to the leftward. The **work face** (the side of the basket facing the weaver as she sews) was the convex (outer) side of all Patwin baskets, except their nearly flat winnowing trays. In the case of winnowing trays, the concave side of the basket was held toward the weaver and the work face was on the inside.

The **weft stitches** in Patwin baskets using a three-rod Patwin foundation were un-standardized. On the same basket there could be a mixture of interlocking stitches, non-

The Patwin custom of leaving the top coil undecorated is clearly visible above the redbud designs on this Hill Patwin cooking pot. This basket was purchased in 1903 from the weaver at Cortina Creek, Colusa County. D: 14", H: 8". (C. Hart Merriam collection, University of California at Davis, #774)

interlocking stitches and split stitches. Split stitches were found only on the back face; that is, the interior on Patwin bowl-shaped baskets. Unlike three-rod baskets, single-rod Patwin work was regularly done with inter-locking stitches.

For splices, the **weft fag ends** were wound around a foundation warp and the end concealed under the successive stitches. In larger baskets, such as cooking pots and feast baskets, the moving ends appear as visible bumps on the interior of the basket. Moving weft ends were bound under successive stitches on the back face (interior) of the basket.

Rims were plain wrapped (self-rim) with no over-stitching. For strengthening purposes, rims are often a bit larger than the coils below them, a trait shared with the Valley Maidu as well. Patwin **coiling endings** usually tapered to an end and were plain wrapped. However, some Patwin coiled baskets had back-stitching for two or three stitches at the very end of the coil. Other Patwin baskets had a narrow back-stitched type of over-stitching atop the coil extending for an inch or so atop of the coil ending.

Rarely did the Patwin carry the design up to include the final coil. Thus, the basket's top coil normally had no designs on it. The Patwin did not use rim ticks (stripes) anywhere on their final coil.

Technologically, Patwin coiled basketry shared characteristics with the Valley Maidu and their work can be difficult to tell apart. It is in terms of design concepts that the Patwin often diverged from the Valley Maidu.

DESIGNS

Patwin coiled basketry is most easily confused with that of the Valley Maidu. Many designs were very similar. However, the Patwin often put designs on the bottom of their coiled baskets. This trait was shared with the Pomo and Ohlone, but was rare among the Valley Maidu, Sierra Miwok and Washoe (Dawson p.c.). Patwin bottom designs were often different from the designs used on the basket side, yet they blend tastefully. It is important to remember that some Patwin baskets lacked designs on their bottoms.

The Patwin often preferred narrower designs than did the Valley Maidu. There was also more open background space on Patwin baskets. The Patwin often used more than one design on a basket. The Valley Maidu usually used only a single design on a basket.

Kroeber noted that the Patwin used black designs more often than the red designs the Maidu so often favored (Kroeber 1932, 281). This was especially true for the River Patwin. But redbud designs were still common, especially among the Hill Patwin.

Historically only a single color was used on Patwin baskets. All older Patwin baskets have the designs in a single color, either black or red, but not both colors together. In late baskets, red and black were occasionally used on the same basket, but this was a post-European innovation.

Patwin baskets often, not always, have designs on the bottom as well as the sides. This large Patwin coiled storage basket also has a single small white glass trade bead sewn on with cordage, perhaps a maker's signature mark. On another very similar Patwin basket, a single black glass trade bead was used. D: 20.5", H: 8" (Private collection)

MATERIALS

Foundation rods for coiled baskets were of peeled willow (Kroeber 1932, 281; Johnson 1978, 356). Both three-rod and single-rod foundations were made.

Split sedge root (*Carex*) was the traditional weft background material for Patwin coiled baskets. The River Patwin used sedge root almost exclusively for background weft material. It was also the primary background material for Hill Patwin baskets. The River Patwin of Colusa and Grimes are said to have used a darker colored sedge similar to that of Valley Maidu. Split, peeled redbud or willow shoots were less commonly used for the weft and occurred primarily or exclusively on baskets made in later years for sale (see: Bates and Bernstein 1982, 195; Bernstein 1990, 218). Among documented older, finely made Patwin baskets sedge root was virtually the only background weft material.

For red designs, both the Hill Patwin and River Patwin used redbud. The Hill Patwin had redbud readily available and used it more often than the River Patwin. Interestingly, sometimes the redbud was darkened, giving a deep red, almost black tone (Bernstein 1990, 217). On most Patwin baskets redbud retained its natural strong red color.

For black designs, dyed bulrush root (*Carex*) was the standard material used. This material was regularly used by the Patwin, but rarely used by the Maidu. Unlike the Pomo who were very particular in dyeing their pinkish bulrush root completely black, the Patwin allowed for more variation and pinkish hues are fairly common in Patwin black dyed bulrush root wefts. Black designs were more common among the River Patwin than the Hill Patwin because bulrush root was so readily available, but both groups used it (Elsasser 1978, 629; Bates and Bernstein 1982, 197; Bernstein 1990, 217).

Two known Southern Patwin baskets, one from the Suisun Patwin in Solano County and the other from Napa, used black dyed bulrush root for designs. Another Southern Patwin basket from Napa used briar root (*Smilax californica*) for black designs. On rare occasions the River Patwin and Nomlaki also used briar root for black. Briar root was far more common on Valley Maidu baskets, especially those from Butte County (Bates 1982, 32-3; Bates and Bernstein 1982, 195).

Beads on Patwin Baskets

The Patwin decorated feather baskets with clamshell disc beads and abalone pendants. At an early date, European trade beads also began being used. Each bead was only of a single

A flaring Patwin coiled cooking pot with sedge root weft and black dyed bulrush root designs. Note the break in the design near the top center. All Patwin cooking pots were made with a three-rod foundation. This basket is a classic Central California beauty. D: 16", H: 7" (Private collection)

the beads were used very sparingly to tastefully accent black weft designs. The beads were generally placed on the buff colored sedge root background rather than on the black designs themselves.

Larger white trade beads were used only on two broad, globular baskets. One of these baskets using glass seed beads is documented from the Suisun Patwin of Solano County. The other was a Hill Patwin basket from Cache Creek. On a third early Patwin basket, larger glass trade beads were attached. White beads were scattered about the surface along with several red and green beads. This basket differs from the other two in that the beads are not confined to the upper half of the basket.

On two additional baskets, just a single glass seed bead was attached using a weft strand. On one of these baskets the single bead was white, and on the other lone basket the bead was black.

color. White beads were most commonly used. A few black, red and green beads also are found on some Patwin baskets.

Five rare early Patwin baskets, all decorated with small European glass seed beads were studied. On each basket,

Southern Patwin Coiled Archeological Basketry

Archeologically, three-rod foundation coiled basketry fragments were found at the Southern Patwin village at Glen Cove on Carquinez Strait, east of Vallejo in Solano County

A rare Suisun Patwin basket from Solano County. This Southern Patwin coiled basket has sedge root background wefts, black bulrush root designs and scattered white European trade beads. It is a good example of the ample background Patwin artists often liked on their baskets. Solano County is named after the Suisun Patwin leader Chief Solano. D: 17", H: 10" (Smithsonian Institution, #E313078)

(Sol-236). These archeological fragments are typically Patwin. They are very finely made, done with split stitches on the back face and with a leftward work direction. One fragment used a very pitted unidentified material that looks rather like conifer branches (Dawson, Bancroft notes).

Patwin Coiled Basket Types

Patwin Feather Baskets

The Patwin made finely coiled feather baskets. These baskets were sometimes decorated with abalone pendants and/or arranged clamshell disc beads. Red woodpecker feathers were the feathers of choice, although quail plumes, mallard feathers and bluebird feathers were used, too (Merriam 1967, 276). The background of Patwin feather baskets could be a solid field of red woodpecker feathers, scattered woodpecker feathers or a plain sedge root weft background. Feather baskets in the form of round bowls, open "soup bowl" shapes and oval "canoe-shaped" basket shapes were made (Johnson 1978, 356).

Barrett stated that originally the Patwin never completely covered baskets with feathers, as did the Pomo, but in later years they made fully feathered baskets (Barrett 1996, 83, 141). Barrett believed that originally the Patwin used feathers only to very limited extent. McKern, on the other hand, reported that some Patwin families traditionally specialized in making feather baskets (McKern 1922, 250). Such work specialization suggests a long-standing and well-established feather basket tradition. Feather baskets were used as wedding gifts, to honor someone, and in later years as sale items.

A Hill Patwin Feather Basket

A Patwin feather basket of special interest from the Hill Patwin at Rumsey in Yolo County was studied (Turtle Bay #1964.1.144). This basket had no feathers for the first several coil rows below the rim and then the remainder of the basket was fully feathered with a solid background of red woodpecker feathers. Designs were of blue bluebird feathers and green mallard feathers on a background of red feathers. Quail plumes and clamshell beads decorate the rim and shell pendants were placed on the top half of the side.

The basket had a three-rod foundation with a weft of sedge root. Having four or five undecorated coils below the rim is different from the usual Pomo feather basket layout. The Pomo typically either brought the feathers up to the rim or up to about two coils below the rim.

Southern Patwin Coiled Feather Baskets

Three Southern Patwin coiled feather baskets are known. They are of special interest because of their very early collection dates and the extreme rarity of Southern Patwin basketry. Two were in a private collection and were collected between 1840 and a devastating smallpox epidemic of uncertain date. They were from the village of Tulucay (also spelled Tulukai), just south of Napa. Both baskets were decorated with red woodpecker feathers.

In addition to the woodpecker feathers, one basket, five and three-eighths inches wide and four inches high, had small white glass trade beads attached with native twine. This basket had black bulrush root designs and the beads were placed on the designs. The red woodpecker feathers were placed between the designs. All red feathers and all beads were in the upper portion of the basket from the fifteenth coil from top upwards. This basket was curved at the base with rather vertical straight sides. The coil ending had three back stitches.

The second Southern Patwin basket from Tulucay was a flaring bowl eight and half inches wide and two and half inches high with clamshell beads and quail plumes at the rim. Its coil ending was missing. As with the other Tulucay basket, this one had a three-rod foundation and a simple plain wrapped rim. The background weft material is sedge root and the design was a reddish colored root. Dawson suggested this root might be briar root (*Smilax californica*), although briar root is generally blacker (Dawson, Bancroft notes).

A third surviving Southern Patwin feather basket was made by the Suisun Patwin in Solano County (Smithsonian

A much used old Patwin cooking pot from the Colusa Rancheria on the Sacramento River. This coiled basket was purchased from Mrs. Mitchell, an elder, in 1913. D: 15", H: 6.5" (Oakland Museum of California, #H16.1969)

#E313078). This Suisun Patwin basket is globular and broad (the diameter is seventeen inches and the height is ten inches). This basket is decorated with small white European trade seed beads and a scattering of feather remnants. These beads are all in the upper third of the basket, sewn on a background of sedge root. Sparse, thin designs using black dyed bulrush run down the side of the basket at a slightly diagonal angle. There is a bottom design. The basket is said to have been made as a Native wedding present. Like the two Tulucay pieces from nearby southern Napa County, this Southern Patwin basket also has a three-rod foundation and split stitches on the interior.

A very old Hill Patwin coiled bowl with redbud designs on a sedge root background. Purchased from the weaver at Cortina Creek, Colusa County, in 1903. H: 5.5", D: 8" (C. Hart Merriam collection, University of California at Davis, #760)

A large attributed Patwin feast basket with redbud designs on a sedge root background. Feast baskets were used at Big Times and other gatherings to feed large groups of guests. In an apparent misguided non-Indian restoration attempt at the rim, the designs have been brought up to include the top coil. Originally the top coil was left undecorated. D: 25", H: 11" (Private collection)

Coiled Cooking Pots

Patwin cooking pots were made in three shapes (Dawson p.c.). The first type of Patwin cooking pot flared sharply outward (Bernstein 1990, 217). These flared to a greater degree than on almost all Maidu baskets. The second type of Patwin cooking pot was more vertical with a slightly curving steep side; they are not straight-sided. These Patwin cooking pots are proportionately slightly smaller at the base than most Valley Maidu pieces. The third type of Patwin cooking pot was low and broad with curving sides.

Feast Baskets

Like the Maidu and Sierra Miwok, the Patwin made very large coiled feast baskets to serve acorn mush at major gatherings. Patwin feast baskets were proportionately broader and lower than Maidu or Miwok feast baskets, which tend to be tall and narrow in comparison. The Patwin feast baskets also tended to be wider at the mouth in relation to height than Valley Maidu feast baskets (Dawson p.c.).

Coiled winnowers were a Sierra Nevada type basket found among the Maidu and Sierra Miwok that spread to the Patwin. The Patwin made both single-rod and three-rod foundation coiled winnowing trays. This Hill Patwin winnower has a three-rod foundation. It was purchased in 1903 at Cortina Creek, Colusa County. The designs are in redbud with sedge root background wefts. D: 15.5", H: 2.5" (C. Hart Merriam collection, University of California at Davis, #767)

Acorn Mush Servers

These smaller baskets were used to dip acorn mush out of cooking pots for serving. They were typically low, broad, flaring bowls.

Globular Bowls

Small globular bowls were made as containers to hold small articles. There were two sizes made by the Patwin. One was about three and a half inches in diameter and the other about seven inches in diameter.

Winnowing and Parching Trays

The Patwin differentiated between two types of coiled trays. One was a flat type. These trays were large, typically seventeen inches or more in diameter. The second type was a somewhat concave meal tray, rather like a very shallow bowl. Both single-rod and three-rod foundations were used (Merriam 1967, 258; Dawson p.c.; see also Bernstein 2003, 58, fig. 25/4886).

Boat-Shaped Baskets

These finely woven oval shaped baskets were similar to those of the Pomo. They were used as gifts, burial offerings and probably by Indian doctors. Both three-rod and single-rod foundation types were probably made, as among the Pomo.

Patwin Twined Baskets

Patwin twined basketry was most often done in plain twining over a single warp, but in special, limited uses it was done over two warps. Diagonal twining was also practiced (Johnson 1978, 256). Lattice twining was used for reinforcing mortar hopper sides. Three-strand twining was apparently

A Patwin diagonally twined burden basket collected in 1903 near Princeton on the Sacramento River. This River Patwin burden basket is made with sedge root weft, redbud designs, willow warp sticks, and a reinforcing rod wrapped using wild grape. It was used when gathering small seeds. D: 19.5", H: 20" (The Field Museum of Natural History, Chicago, #79908)

This Patwin mortar hopper is woven in plain twining with three bands of lattice twining for added strength. At 22 inches in diameter and five inches in height, this is a broad, low mortar hopper. Purchased at Cortina Creek Rancheria, Colusa County, in 1903 from the Patwin woman who was using it (C. Hart Merriam collection, University of California at Davis, #761)

not done. Slant of weft twist was usually up-to-the-left (Elsasser 1978, 633). However, an up-to-the-right slant of weft twist was used on some twined openwork baskets made with whole shoots.

Twined weft fag ends were handled in two ways. Some were caught under a turn of twining on the basket's back face. At other times, fag ends were just pinched between warps and a trimmed stub was left showing inside the basket.

Warps were of willow. Warp rims were generally trimmed above the last row of twining. Twined weft strand materials were sedge root or conifer root. Redbud and possibly other materials were used for designs. Peeled redbud or wild grape bark was used to wrap rim reinforcing rods.

Charred archeological Southern Patwin twined basket fragments were found at Glen Cove on the north shore of Carquinez Strait, east of Vallejo (Sol-236). Analysis by Lawrence Dawson at the University of California at Berkeley found that these were plain twined basketry with both up-to-the-right and up-to-the-left slants of weft twist. The Patwin did both slants of weft, although an up-to-the-left slant was most common. Warps sticks were whole shoots. In one fragment up-to-the-right twining was used over pairs of warps instead of the usual single warp. The Patwin are known to have used paired warps for special purposes in their twined work.

According to Meighan and Baumhoff (1953, 10) the Southern Patwin also made soft cordage warp twining using tule. A fragment using this technique (called Catlow twining by some archeologists) was also found at the Glen Cove site on Carquinez Strait (Sol-236). It has a fine soft two strand warp described as being "of very fine grass." This "grass" is probably the basal leaves of tule or of cattail. The slant of weft twist was up-to-the-left, which was most typical of the Patwin. The fragment was decorated with very small rectangular olivella shell beads (Meighan and Baumhoff 1953, 10). Although this fragment could be a bag rather than a basket, the Southern Patwin made tule basketry and it is likely a basket (Kroeber 1932, 281).

PATWIN CLOSE TWINED BASKETS

Burden Baskets

The Patwin made two types of close twined burden baskets: plain twined and diagonally twined. These baskets were conical rather than bell shaped as among the Pomo. There was a flattening on the side that rested against the back of the woman carrying it. On at least some Patwin burden baskets, warp ends were bent over the reinforcing rod at the rim and lashed down when the rim rod was attached. Peeled redbud or wild grape was used to lash the reinforcing rod to the basket.

This winnowing basket is a good example of Patwin openwork twining. Note the twenty horizontal weft rows of redbud and tasteful handling of the warp sticks. Purchased in 1903 from a River Patwin woman at her rancheria on the west bank of the Sacramento River north of the town of Colusa. L: 15" (C. Hart Merriam collection, University of California at Davis, #775)

The River Patwin, and probably other Patwin, made diagonally twined burden baskets. The designs were woven with a spiral bound weave with latticework on the interior face (Dawson, Bancroft notes). A good example of a Patwin diagonally twined burden basket is in Chicago's Field Museum of Natural History (#79908). This basket's designs are in redbud on a background of sedge root. This Patwin burden basket has a horizontal primary band of chevrons below the rim. From this band diagonal patterns descend nearly to the bottom of the basket. The tip of the Patwin burden basket is heavily reinforced, unlike Pomo burden baskets. Valley Maidu burden baskets had similar heavily constructed tips, but these were less round than those of the Patwin piece. The Field Museum's Patwin burden basket designs contrast with Valley Maidu burden baskets, which favored horizontal bands. On this particular Patwin burden basket there are no small rectangles placed just below the rim, unlike typical Pomo diagonally twined burden baskets.

At the top of their diagonally twined burden baskets, the Patwin, Pomo and Valley Maidu all used plain twining over two or more warps below the reinforcing rod at the rim. Diagonally twined burden baskets of all three cultures have: (1) a down-to-the-right slant of twist, (2) warps that were added by being sharpened and inserted among the wefts, and (3) designs were woven with patterns done in a spiral lattice binding technique (Dawson p.c.). While the diagonally twined burden baskets of all three cultures are closely related, the Patwin diagonally twined burden basket was closer to the Valley Maidu than to the Pomo type.

The second type of Patwin burden basket was plain twined (Dawson p.c.). The Patwin, Pomo and Maidu all made close plain twined burden baskets. The presence of both diagonally twined and plain twined burden baskets among three adjacent cultures suggests these types spread from one group to the others.

Mortar Hoppers

Hill Patwin mortar hoppers are low and broad with simple linear bands for designs. A reinforcing rod bound with redbud strengthens the rim. Patwin mortar hoppers were primarily plain twined with three bands of lattice twining typically used on the side for strength. According to Gifford and Kroeber (1937, 138), the Hill Patwin made mortar hoppers, but the River Patwin did not. The Southern Patwin practice is unknown, although their Wappo neighbors are known to have made mortar hoppers.

The Hill Patwin mortar hoppers are similar to those of the Pomo and Wappo. However, there are some small differences. At least some Patwin mortar hoppers had only a single band design, whereas Pomo mortar hoppers typically have two to four bands of designs. The Patwin mortar hoppers studied

Small, conical baskets such as this was used by Patwin children to catch fish. It is a rare surviving example of a Patwin twined openwork basket. It was purchased from a Patwin woman at Cook Springs in Colusa County in 1903. D: 9", H: 6.5" (C. Hart Merriam collection, University of California at Davis, #777)

had designs comprised of simple rectangles of redbud on a sedge root background. The rectangles were each of similar size and all connected in a single band either two or three sets of rectangles wide. These simple designs contrast with Pomo designs, which are often more elaborate.

The documented Hill Patwin mortar hoppers in the Merriam collection (UC Davis #761) and the Field Museum of Natural History (Field #79885) are wider and shallower in relation to their height (respectively 22 inches and 21 inches in diameter and 4.5 inches and 5.25 inches in height) than most Pomo mortar hoppers. Their weft strands were also more coarsely woven. Patwin mortar hopper weft fag ends were mostly pinched between the warps and the weft stubs trimmed. In contrast, the Pomo secured their mortar hopper weft fag ends by catching them under a turn of the weft twist and trimming the weft stubs (Dawson p.c.).

Patwin mortar hoppers had wefts of pine root and possibly sedge root with designs of redbud. The reinforcing hoop was made of oak and wrapped with redbud or wild grape. The Field Museum Patwin mortar hopper has a distinctive feature: the redbud wrapping at several places along the rim extends well below the rod for two turns of the wrapping. The UC Davis Patwin mortar hopper lacks this feature.

OPENWORK TWINED BASKETS

Patwin openwork was done by weaving from the convex (outer) side of the basket typically in a rightward work direction.

Winnowers

The Hill Patwin wove circular twined winnowers. The River Patwin made a U-shaped twined winnower. As described earlier, both Patwin groups made coiled winnowers (Gifford and Kroeber 1933, 131-132).

Scoop Trays

The C. Hart Merriam collection at UC Davis includes an oval "scoop tray," which also seems to have been a winnower (Johnson 1978, 356, fig. C). On this basket, the vertical warp sticks were alternately drawn close and separated at each horizontal weft row presenting a pleasing appearance. This scoop tray is about 15 inches in length by 11 inches in width. It was collected from the River Patwin in Colusa County.

Cradles

Cradles were of the deep, sitting type like those of the Pomo and Nomlaki (Gifford and Kroeber 1937, 130). Patwin and Nomlaki men made cradles.

Openwork Burden Baskets

In addition to transporting acorns, the openwork burden basket was used to carry a variety of coarse materials. These burden baskets had warp ends interwoven and turned down at the rim, like some of the ancient baskets found in Lovelock Cave, Nevada. This conical openwork burden basket usually lacked designs; however, one basket was found with narrow horizontal band designs (Dawson p.c.).

Fish Traps

Salmon were caught using conical fish traps of willow (McKern 1922, 249).

Children's Fish Catching Basket

A rough, cone-shaped basket was used by youngsters to trap fish. It may have been like the plunge type fish trap described in the Pomo chapter.

Twined Tule Baskets

Modest baskets using split tules were made (Kroeber 1932, 281). These baskets were said to be shallow. According to Gifford and Kroeber, coiled tule baskets were also made by the Patwin (1937, 214). The presence of coiled tule baskets seems questionable, as tule baskets were twined, not coiled, throughout California and Oregon.

Seedbeaters: Twined and Wickerwork

There were two types of Patwin seedbeaters. There was a twined seedbeater and a wickerwork seed beater (Kroeber 1925, 244; Elsasser 1978, 629). Both wickerwork and twined seedbeaters were also found among the Pomo and Maidu. Wickerwork seedbeaters prevailed among the Pomo, and twined seedbeaters were dominant among the Maidu. It is unknown which type was most common among the Patwin.

Comments

The great Patwin expansion in Central California was one of the most significant events in Native history. This expansion had a significant impact on the basketry of most of the Patwin's neighbors. The results were among the most important changes in California Indian history. But while the Patwin influenced others, the other cultures also influenced the Patwin as well. It is clear that Patwin coiling is very closely related to that of the Valley Maidu and almost certainly derived from it. Pomo influence is also evident, particularly in some twined baskets and in coiled feather baskets. The results of the great Patwin expansion changed the basketry of many North Central California cultures, including that of the Patwin themselves.

The Coast Miwok are the First People of Marin and southern Sonoma Counties. From the moment Sir Francis Drake first gazed upon Coast Miwok basketry in 1579, people around the world have been awestruck by its beauty. This is an attributed Coast Miwok coiled basket with downward pointing patterns done using olivella shell disc beads. Abalone pendants accent the sides while some clamshell disc beads are on the rim. The basket has a three-rod foundation with sedge root wefts. (Museum of Anthropology and Ethnology, named after Peter the Great, St. Petersburg, Russia, #570-97. Courtesy of Chuner and Natalia Taksami)

Bottom view of the same Coast Miwok basket showing the overall design layout done in olivella shell disc beads. (Museum of Anthropology and Ethnology, named after Peter the Great, St. Petersburg, Russia, #570-97. Courtesy of Chuner and Natalia Taksami)

COAST MIWOK BASKETRY

The Coast Miwok are the Native people of Marin and southern Sonoma Counties. This is a land of wooded mountains and lovely valleys surrounded by grasslands rimmed by seacoast and bay estuaries. Coast Miwok territory extends from Sausalito at the Golden Gate north to Rohnert Park and Bodega Bay. To the west it reaches the Pacific Ocean at Point Reyes. To the east, Coast Miwok country runs along the low hills and wetlands at the north end of San Francisco Bay. Present day cities in Coast Miwok country include Mill Valley, San Rafael, Novato, Petaluma and Cotati.

To the north the Coast Miwok bordered the Pomo, to the northeast the Wappo and to the east the Patwin. Across San Francisco Bay were the Ohlone (Costanoan). Tule boats gave access across the Bay, and the Coast Miwok and Ohlone were the first bay mariners.

The Miwok probably began as people of the Sierras and the Delta of the Sacramento and San Joaquin Rivers. Gradually they began a great westward expansion. Over the centuries different branches of Miwok came to hold large areas. The Sierra Miwok held much of the central Sierra Nevada Mountains and foothills. The Plains and Bay Miwok extended Miwok territory across the Great Central Valley and the Delta. The Lake Miwok ranged up into northeastern Napa County and on into southern Lake County. The Coast Miwok settled the Marin Peninsula and southern Sonoma County after 1350 B.C. (Moratto 1984, 275, 554-556; Foster 1996, 89). The westward movement of the Coast Miwok into the North Bay seems to have been along the productive marshlands on the north and west shores of San Francisco Bay. Coastal southern Marin was probably the last area where the Coast Miwok replaced earlier peoples. At its height, the world of the Miwok ranged from the crest of the central Sierra Nevada Mountains to the Pacific Ocean (Moratto 1984, 557).[1]

For centuries, the Miwok people held a great land from the crest of the Sierras to the beaches of Point Reyes. But around A.D. 500 the Wappo moved into the Napa Valley and split the Lake Miwok and Coast Miwok apart. By A.D. 700 the Patwin had moved into the southern Sacramento Valley and settled in Colusa, Yolo, Solano and southern Napa counties. The Patwin assimilated some Miwok and pushed the ancestors of the Bay Miwok south to the vicinity of Mount Diablo. (Bennyhoff p.c.; Moratto 1984, 566; Foster 1996, 84)

We know that the Patwin borrowed words from Miwok for plant and animal species endemic to the Sacramento Valley (Foster 1996, 90). The earlier people in an area name the plants and animals they encounter. This use of Miwok names for local native plants and animals supports prior Miwok occupancy of the region and suggests the assimilation of some Miwok people into the Patwin.

The Patwin expansion had a great impact on the Miwok. It left the Coast Miwok and Lake Miwok isolated from the main body of eastern Miwok speakers: the Sierra Miwok, Plains Miwok and Bay Miwok (Moratto 1984, 562; Foster 1996, 90). Concurrently, the movement of the Wappo into the Napa Valley split the Coast Miwok off from the Lake Miwok. Non-Miwok speaking peoples now surrounded the Coast Miwok.

Make no mistake. The Coast Miwok have long been in their country. But after the Patwin and Wappo separated the Coast Miwok from their linguistic relatives, cultural influences on the Coast Miwok would come increasingly from their neighbors: the Pomo, Ohlone, Patwin, Wappo and perhaps even remnant Esselen (see the Esselen and Ohlone/Costanoan chapters). The development of Coast Miwok basketry would continue, but with rich, diverse influences.

The first recorded mention of Coast Miwok baskets was in 1579 when Sir Francis Drake and the crew of the ship *Golden Hinde* landed at Drake's Bay in Marin County. The Englishmen wrote that Coast Miwok "Baskets are made of Rushes like a deep boat, and so well wrought as to hold Water. They hang pieces of Pearl shell [abalone shell] and sometimes Links of these Chains [disc beads] on the Brims...they are wrought with matted down of red Feathers [red woodpecker feathers]" (Kroeber 1925, 276). The baskets described as "boat shaped" were probably a type of oval coiled feather basket made by the Coast Miwok and the Pomo.

[1] Preliminary mitochondrial DNA studies suggests a later arrival of Miwok speakers, perhaps as recently as 2,000 years ago. However, based on archeological, linguistic and basketry studies this date seems late (see: Eshleman 2002).

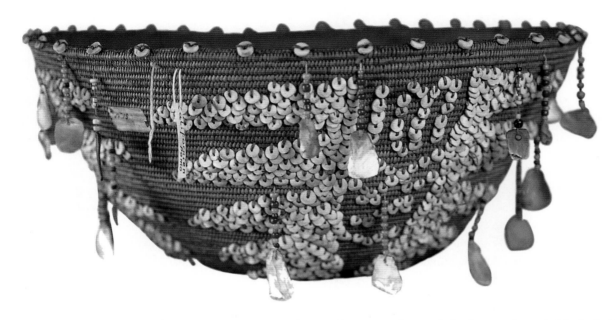

Exceptionally lavish use of olivella shell disc beads, abalone pendants and European glass trade beads cover this coiled basket's side while clamshell disc beads accent the rim. This is a classic San Francisco Bay Area coiled basket. An over-stitched rim, olivella shell disc beads arranged in downward pointing triangles, the use of pendants and the presence of clamshell disc beads along the rim indicate likely Coast Miwok origin. D: 12", H: 5.5" (Museum fur Weltkulturen, Frankfort #172. Photo by Jon and Betty Goerke)

Coast Miwok Archeological Basketry

A much richer source of information on early Coast Miwok basketry comes from archeological findings datable to late prehistoric and early historic times.

Two types of Coast Miwok basketry fragments have survived. The first are actual portions of burned baskets. These were found by archeologists at the Thomas site (MRN-115) in San Rafael. They are the remains of burned Coast Miwok twined baskets found nested one inside the other. The archeological report stated that one was a "coiled" basket fragment, but subsequent close study shows that it is actually a twined basket (Dawson p.c.). The Thomas site, a Coast Miwok village, appears to have been occupied from about A.D. 1200 until to about A.D. 1800 (Meighan & Baumhoff 1953, 1-12 and plates 2, A-D).

There is a second type of archeological basket preservation. These are basketry impressions on baked clay. A number of Coast Miwok village sites in Marin County from San Rafael to north of Novato have yielded baked clay basketry impressions. Among these sites is Olompali (MRN-193), now a state historic park between Novato and Petaluma.

Thus, we have both small basketry fragments and lumps of baked clay with basketry impressions. The baked clay impressions are deep and clear, the result of wet mud coming in contact with the baskets. Clay was pressed against a basket, probably accidentally, and the clay fired. The clay likely got on the baskets during the gathering of bay shellfish or the digging of bulbs in muddy soil. Later, the baskets were cleaned and the bits of mud knocked loose. Periodically, some fell into or close by the fire pit where a few pieces were accidentally fired when they were swept into household cooking fires. The impressions preserved were from plain twined and diagonally twined baskets with radial warps. They probably represent just two types of baskets.

Taken together, both archeological basketry fragments and baked clay basketry impressions provide exciting insights to the little known twining of the Coast Miwok.

The Distinctiveness and Variety of Coast Miwok Twining

One of the most important features of twined basketry is the slant of weft twist. The individual woven weft twists of twined baskets either slant up-to-the-right or slant up-to-the-left.

Isabel Kelly's ethnographic research reported that Coast Miwok twined basketry had an up-to-the-right slant of twist. Kelly's respected consultants, Coast Miwok elders

Tom Smith and Maria Copa, attested to this fact. The vast majority of Coast Miwok twined basket fragments and baked clay impressions found by archeologists confirmed their statements (Dawson p.c.; Meighan and Baumhoff 1953, 1-12; Collier and Thalman 1991, 156).

In contrast, the close-twined baskets of the neighboring Pomo, Wappo and Patwin have a down-to-the-right slant of weft twist. Some coarse openwork Pomo burden baskets, fish traps and flat sifting baskets made by the men have an up-to-the-right slant of twist (Barrett 1996, 147). But the overwhelming majority of Pomo, Wappo and Patwin twined baskets, including virtually all finely woven ones, have a down-to-the-right slant of weft twist. The Pomo, Wappo and Patwin slant of weft twist on close-twined baskets is the opposite of the Coast Miwok slant of weft twist.

Thus, the ethnographic information on Coast Miwok slant of twist data corresponds well to the majority of archeological fragments found in Coast Miwok territory. Down-to-the-left fragments do occur among the Coast Miwok but they are relatively few. The rare down-to-the-left pieces may be decorative touches, as were found on Ohlone twined baskets. Alternatively, they could be parts of a basket where the weft slant of twist had to be varied to produce a certain shape of the form. Finally, they could also be trade pieces from the Pomo, Patwin or Wappo.

The fact that the Coast Miwok and Pomo predominately used opposite slants of weft twists is significant. This is because other smaller tribes bordering the Pomo, such as the Wappo and Lake Miwok, virtually completely adopted Pomo-type twining. Even the populous Patwin, the eastern neighbors of the Coast Miwok and Pomo, used the same slant of twist as the Pomo (Elsasser 1978, 633). In contrast to all these ethnic groups, the Coast Miwok stand alone in the North Bay area in predominately using an up-to-the-right slant of twist in their twined baskets.

Why would this occur? Significantly, using an up-to-the-right slant of twist in twining is a Sierra Miwok trait. The Coast Miwok retained this tradition despite being cut off for about a thousand years from their eastern Miwok relatives by the Patwin and Wappo. Such long-term retention of a basketry practices is common throughout Native California.

Actually, the Coast Miwok may have had a tiny connection to eastern Miwok basketry ideas. There are some indications in archeological basketry remains that the southern-most Patwin around Vallejo preserved some Miwok concepts in their basketry. These southwestern-most Patwin probably absorbed Coast Miwok or other Miwok people when they settled in southern Solano and southern Napa Counties. Basketry may have become a mixture of Patwin and Coast Miwok concepts in these farthest west of Patwin communities. Having such a connection to Miwok twined basketry concepts would have helped Coast Miwok twined basketry to remain distinctive from the dominant Pomoan basketry of the North Bay area. (See the Patwin chapter for a discussion of Patwin twining along the north shore of Carquinez Strait near Vallejo.)

A Detailed Look at Coast Miwok Twining

The variety and high quality of Coast Miwok twining demonstrates that a strong twining tradition existed. It also indicates the importance of twining over coiling among the Coast Miwok. In California cultures where coiling was the dominant technique utility baskets such as winnowers, mortar hoppers and cooking pots were coiled, not twined. In these coiling cultures fewer kinds of close-twined baskets were made, although openwork twined baskets remained important. The Coast Miwok seem to have done a great deal of close-twining and this points toward a strong twining tradition.

Again, the most common twined basket fragments from San Rafael's Thomas site were of two types: plain twining and diagonal twining. One fragment also had designs done in spiral lattice binding, a technique used for designs. Shoot warps, cordage tule warps and splint warps were all used, an impressive variety from just five fragments. Shoot warps were most common. The baked clay basketry impressions show impressions of baskets that varied from medium coarseness to exceptionally fine weaving. Most were finely woven and show great variation in weaving techniques.

Throughout this discussion it should be remembered that the Coast Miwok also made finely coiled baskets. But, as among the Pomo, coiled baskets were less important in Coast Miwok daily life than was twined basketry.

The Unique Combination of Features in Coast Miwok Twining

Coast Miwok twining was distinctive in its diversity, slant of twist and the use of very fine tule cordage warps. Not only were there clear differences between Coast Miwok and Pomo twined basketry, there were also differences between Coast

This very old coiled basket is from the town of Sonoma in Coast Miwok territory. This early basket may be Coast Miwok, but Wappo or Southern Patwin origin is also possible. It is decorated with glass European trade beads. (State Museum Research Center, California State Department of Parks and Recreation, #155-5)

Miwok twined basketry and that of all other Miwok peoples. For example, Coast Miwok weaving of fine close-twined culinary baskets contrasts sharply with the basketry of the Plains Miwok and Sierra Miwok. These two Miwok peoples' basketry had strong coiling traditions and their twining was primarily utilitarian openwork basketry (Dawson p.c.).

Major dissimilarities between the basketry of the Coast Miwok and that of the Sierra Miwok indicate that differences occurred in their cultural history. These differences cannot be explained as being only the result of Pomo, Wappo or Patwin influences, since there are also important differences between Coast Miwok basketry and that of the Pomo, Wappo and Patwin.

Influences from Earlier Peoples?

Lawrence Dawson suggested that in part the Coast Miwok might have assimilated some ancient tradition of weaving from an earlier people in Marin County (Dawson p.c.). Those earlier people might have been from one of two groups. The ancestors of Yukian peoples are most commonly suggested as having occupied the Marin Peninsula prior to the arrival of the Coast Miwok (Moratto 1984, 281, 543-564; also see the Yuki chapter in this volume). Coiling foundations of tiny board-like splints, a highly distinctive Yuki trait, have been found in Coast Miwok territory and the Yuki were quite possibly pre-Miwok residents of the area.

The other people that could have preceded the Coast Miwok in Marin were the Esselen. The Esselen are thought to have occupied the East Bay and San Francisco prior to the arrival of the Ohlone. The Ohlone are believed to have

absorbed Esselen-speaking people as far north as the south side of Carquinez Strait in Contra Costa County. The Coast Miwok could have done the same thing in the North Bay, absorbing Esselen at some point in time. The possibility of ancestral Esselen occupation in Marin County prior to Coast Miwok arrival is plausible given the type and diversity of twined basketry found in Coast Miwok territory. The Esselen and Ohlone made complex plain and diagonally twined baskets and their presence as far north as Marin County would account for the diverse type of twining found there (see the chapters on the Esselen and Ohlone).

It is highly probable that ancestral Yukians or perhaps Esselen were living in southern Marin County when the Coast Miwok arrived. Or, least likely, there may have been an unknown group occupying the Marin peninsula that was completely absorbed by the Coast Miwok. In whichever case, Coast Miwok twining was so distinct from that of all other Miwok groups that it clearly had its own unique history and influences.

Types of Coast Miwok Twining

Plain Twined Basketry on Shoot Warps

Plain twined basketry using shoot warps and sedge root wefts was most commonly found in the archeological specimens. The most common type of twined basketry at San Rafael's Thomas site (MRN-115) was plain twined. The fine, close-twined weft materials on the baked clay impressions have been identified as being split sedge (*Carex*) root (Dawson p.c.). At least one piece may have pine root wefts. Warps were almost completely of whole shoots, probably willow, hazel or alder.

Diagonally Twined Basketry on Shoot Warps

Diagonally twined (twill twined) baskets were also found. This type of weaving was found both as a fragment at San Rafael's Thomas site (MRN-115) and in baked clay impressions in northern Marin County. The piece from the Thomas site consisted of a fragment of one basket that was diagonally twined with rather flat wefts (Meighan & Baumhoff 1953, plate, fig. C). Flat wefts were a Sierra Miwok trait that could have survived among the Coast Miwok.

Diagonally twined baked clay impressions were also found at Olompali State Park (MRN-193) between Novato and Petaluma. The impressions were very rounded, indicating probable split sedge root or split willow shoot wefts. These specimens consisted of diagonal twining with designs in spiral lattice binding and warp insertions like those of the Pomo.

But what was most striking about the Coast Miwok diagonal twining is that some of it ranks among the finest, closest woven diagonal twining in all North America (Dawson p.c.).

Another striking feature of Coast Miwok diagonal twining is the extreme slant of the weft twists, with a range of 23 degrees up to 48 degrees. The degree of slant at times is over twice as high as is found in some California ethnic groups (Dawson, Bancroft notes). In Coast Miwok diagonal twining, the weft slant is up-to-the-right and the warps are skewed to the left. The weft twists themselves have a short, rather broad appearance.

Besides the Coast Miwok, the neighboring Pomo, Wappo, Patwin and Ohlone all wove diagonal twined baskets and diagonal twining was common throughout the San Francisco Bay Area. But significantly Coast Miwok diagonal twining texture and slant of twist was unlike the diagonal twining of the Pomo or anyone else in California (Dawson p.c.). This underscores development of a strong Coast Miwok twining tradition that was in part created independently.

Spiral Lattice Bound Weave

A fragment using spiral lattice bound weave for decoration was found at the Thomas site (MRN-115) in San Rafael (Dawson p.c.). This piece has down-to-the-right slant of twist, a Pomo feature. This basket could be a variation in Coast Miwok weaving or a Pomo trade piece. The Pomo regularly used spiral lattice binding.

Splint Warp Basketry: Possible Yuki Influence?

The use of splints (thin, flat warps) was uncommon in Central California. The only major area where splints were used was among the Yuki and one or two of their neighbors in Mendocino County. These cultures used splint foundations in their coiled basketry. Interestingly, Yuki territory has repeatedly been suggested as anciently extending as far south as Marin County. If true, splint warps could be a remnant Yuki influence on Coast Miwok basketry. Archeological evidence in the Great Basin has shown that basketry traditions often remained unchanged for thousands of years.

The use of splints in twined Coast Miwok basketry was found at two archeological sites. A small baked clay twined impression using flat splints was found at MRN-374 on San Antonio Creek on the Marin-Sonoma County line. Additionally, at San Rafael's Thomas site, MRN-115, a fragment was found using flat splints for both wefts and for warps. Like nearly all other Coast Miwok twined baskets, it

has an up-to-the-right slant of weft twist. The dates of these archeological fragments are from the Coast Miwok period.

It should be remembered that round, peeled whole shoots or tule cordage warps were far more common in Coast Miwok territory than splints. Still, splints are an interesting occurrence that may be another clue to the history of Coast Miwok basketry.

An Interesting Variation in Slant of Twist

The variation in slant of weft twist found in the Thomas site fragments is interesting. Baumhoff suggested that this slant of twist variation might have been a decorative touch (Meighan & Baumhoff 1953, 10, plate 2, fig. A). Varying the slant of twist in twined baskets was a decorative touch commonly practiced by the Ohlone, the Coast Miwok's southern neighbors, and by the Esselen. It was a San Francisco Bay Area decorative twining technique that may have been used by the Coast Miwok, too.

Tule Cordage and Cattail and/or Tule Weft Basketry

One type of twined basketry found at San Rafael's Thomas site has cordage warps. Wefts are "of fine grass," usually less than one millimeter in diameter. Warps are composed of two strands of even finer "grass" twisted together in a clockwise direction. This is a flexible type of basketry archeologists sometimes call Catlow twining. It normally has tule cordage warps with wefts of tule or cattail, often using the plant's basal leaves, which would explain the look of "fine grass." Klamath and Modoc baskets from along the California-Oregon state line are good examples of type Catlow-type baskets. A number of Central California Indian cultures, including the Pomo, also wove tule baskets.

It is important to note that similar plain twined flexible cordage warp basketry fragments were found in the Sacramento-San Joaquin River Delta (Dawson, Bancroft notes). These would likely be Plains Miwok pieces. A Patwin fragment has also been found. Together, these tule cordage basket fragments suggest a cordage warp tradition extending from the Plains Miwok through the Patwin to the Coast Miwok. Thus, there possibly was a band of cordage warp basketry running from the Sacramento-San Joaquin River Delta to the Marin Peninsula.

The Patwin cordage warp fragment was found in southern Patwin territory, geographically adjacent to the Coast Miwok. The fragment was from Carquinez Strait's Glen Cove (Sol-236), just east of Vallejo. Like the Coast Miwok cordage warp piece from San Rafael, the Patwin fragment has two-strand warps and appears to be made of similar material (either tule or cattail or both) and is "apparently the same weaving technique" (Meighan & Baumhoff 1953, 10). The Glen Cove Patwin fragment has a slant of twist that is down-to-the-right, the opposite of the vast majority of Coast Miwok fragments. This difference is to be expected since the Patwin most often wove with a down-to-the-right slant of twist in their twined basketry (Elsasser 1978, 633).

This Patwin piece is decorated with rectangular olivella shell beads. In having rectangular olivella shell beads, the Glenn Cove fragment differs from Ohlone and probable Coast Miwok baskets, both of which used round olivella shell beads. Additionally, the Ohlone and Coast Miwok are only known to have used round olivella shell beads on coiled baskets. The Glen Cove Patwin piece was used on a twined fragment.

The Coast Miwok bordered the Patwin west of the Napa county line. The Patwin are believed to have displaced Miwok people in that area by about A.D. 700. Thus, it is probable that the Coast Miwok and southern Patwin use of tule cordage warps in twined baskets is linked. The presence of cordage warp basketry among Miwok in the Delta suggests that it was an old Miwok tradition, perhaps brought with them when they migrated into California from western Nevada thousands of years ago. Cordage warp basketry has been found in ancient Nevada archeological sites that also contain basketry similar to historic Sierra Miwok baskets (see the chapter on the Sierra Miwok).

Wickerwork

No definite wickerwork fragments were found, but a single basketry baked clay impression excavated at Olompali State Park (MRN-193) could be wickerwork. Wickerwork would suggest the presence of seedbeaters. The main wickerwork use in the North Bay was in Pomo and Patwin seedbeaters. Finding wickerwork seedbeaters among the Coast Miwok would be expected. However, the record is contradictory. Coast Miwok elder Maria Copa stated that their seedbeaters were twined, a response to anthropologist Isabel Kelly's self-stated presumption. Later, Kelly says they were "evidently twined." But then she refers to a Pomo wickerwork seedbeater (specifically, Kroeber 1925, plate 29, lower left) as "said to be similar" to Coast Miwok seedbeaters (Collier and Thalman 1991, 159). If so, this would indicate a wickerwork seedbeater of the Pomo type. Wickerwork can be easily confused with openwork twining. Between the archeological fragment and this statement by Maria Copa, Coast Miwok wickerwork seedbeaters seem likely.

Coast Miwok Twined Basket Types

The Coast Miwok made an extensive variety of twined baskets. These known types are discussed below (see also Collier & Thalman 1991, 86, 118, 145, 155-157).

Twined Feast Baskets and Cooking Pots

Large twined cooking baskets typically two feet in diameter were made. These were tightly woven with a rounded base. Due to their large size, they must have been used as feast baskets during special occasions such as "Big Time" gatherings. The Coast Miwok also made both coiled and twined smaller conventionally sized cooking pots.

Having both twined and coiled cooking pots was rare in California. However, both types occurred among the Wappo and Western Mono. These cultures were gradually changing their culinary baskets from twined to coiled and the same transition was probably happening among the Coast Miwok as well.

Large storage baskets for acorns were two to three feet in diameter. They were openwork twined baskets made of hazel or willow and were sometimes decorated with designs. These baskets were hung in the house and were stacked when empty. This storage basket was usually flat bottomed. It had a handle on each side so it could be lifted by two men. These handles probably were a post-European addition, as they were not normally found on other central California storage baskets.

Small storage baskets were made for holding berries. These baskets were probably made in openwork.

Conical close-twined burden baskets were used for seed gathering when using a seedbeater. These baskets were reportedly sometimes used as cooking vessels (Collier and Thalman 1991, 120, 145, 155). Using burden baskets as cooking pots was probably a late adaptation caused by a shortage of baskets due to the chaos of Euro-American disruption of Indian life.

Large twined burden baskets with a handle on each side were used to store dried acorns. These baskets were apparently openwork. Openwork burden baskets could be made by the women or men (Collier and Thalman 1991, 105, 157, 158).

Handles were not traditional on any other California burden baskets and would, if present, have been a modification begun after the arrival of the Spanish. Possibly the Coast Miwok elders were referring to a pair of loops used to attach a carrying strap to the burden basket. This was a common practice among some California peoples.

A coiled basket attributed to the Coast Miwok. Note the lavish display of Native California olivella shell beads and abalone pendants on the basket's side and the clamshell disc beads on the rim. D: 12" (Staatliches Museum fur Volkerkunde, Munich, #142. Photo by Jon and Betty Goerke)

Mortar hoppers. Coast Miwok mortar hoppers were used on top of a flat rock slab with a long pestle for pounding acorns. Coast Miwok mortar hoppers were probably twined as were all other north central California mortar hoppers. A watercolor done in 1818 by the Russian artist Mikhail T. Tikhanov of a Bodega Coast Miwok woman shows what is almost certainly a twined mortar hopper. However, Isabel Kelly's Coast Miwok consultants were in disagreement as to whether Coast Miwok mortar hoppers were twined or coiled. Significantly, two different names were given for mortar hoppers (Collier and Thalman 1991, 155). This suggests that two types of mortar hoppers existed, perhaps one coiled and one twined. It may be that the twined mortar hopper was the traditional one, but as life became difficult after the Euro-American arrival, increasingly coiled baskets began being used as mortar hoppers, too. An old worn out coiled cooking pot with its bottom cut out could serve as a mortar hopper.

Seedbeaters had the usual handle and were either twined or wickerwork or both. Using the seedbeater, the Coast Miwok raked seeds into a conical basket. The seed beater was also sometimes used to fan a cooking fire to help it burn well. As discussed earlier, a probable wickerwork archeological fragment and a statement by an elder suggests that Coast Miwok seedbeaters were like those of the Pomo and made of wickerwork (Collier and Thalman 1991, 106, 120, 155-156, 159).

Berry Baskets were used to collect huckleberries. They were also used as sifters. The neighboring Kashaya Pomo made a small, round openwork bowl for gathering and sifting berries. The Coast Miwok type may have been similar to these shallow baskets.

The **cradle** was flat on the bottom and made of flexible wood (probably willow shoots). A sunshade of twined tule was attached to the cradle to protect the baby.

Hunting Baskets were a type of small basket made of willow by men. They were used by the men for carrying hunting equipment, such as obsidian knives for butchering game (Collier and Thalman 1991, 156, 157, 205). Given this basket's purpose, it was probably an openwork twined basket.

Illustrations of Possible Coast Miwok Twined Baskets

In 1818, Mikhail T. Tikhanov, the artist on the Russian ship *"Kamchatka,"* visited Fort Ross and Bodega in Sonoma County. He did at least two watercolors of Bodega Coast Miwok women with baskets. One watercolor painting has a mortar hopper with a reinforcing rod at the rim, which would indicate a twined basket. A second painting shows a Bodega Miwok woman holding a large tub-shaped basket full of what appear to be surf fish. This basket also has a reinforcing rod attached to the rim and was probably twined as well. Unfortunately, the watercolors lack sufficient detail to draw further conclusions. The original paintings are at the Scientific Research Museum, Academy of Arts in Russia (Fort Ross Interpretative Association, p.c.).

Coast Miwok Coiled Baskets

All Coast Miwok archeological basketry fragments and baked clay impressions were of twined baskets. However, basketry awls have been found in Coast Miwok village sites and these were used to manufacture coiled baskets. Both historic accounts and the statements of Coast Miwok elders affirm that high quality coiled basketry was made.

We do not know for certain what Coast Miwok coiling was like. We do, however, have good examples of the coiled

Olivella shell disc beads form the diamond patterns that decorate the sides of this Coast Miwok basket. Note that the olivella shell disc beads are thinner, slightly convex and not quite as perfectly round compared to the flat, thicker clamshell disc beads on the rim. The clamshell disc beads and the beads with the abalone pendants are sewn on with Native twine while the thinner olivella shell disc beads are attached using the basket's sedge root wefts. (Staatliches Museum fur Volkerkunde, Munich, #142. Photo by Jon and Betty Goerke)

work of all their neighbors: the Pomo, Wappo, Patwin and Ohlone. A small group of baskets believed to have been collected by the Russian Ivan Gavrilovich Voznesensky during his 1840-1841 trip almost certainly includes some Coast Miwok coiled baskets. During his visit Voznesensky traveled extensively through Coast Miwok territory, including Bodega Bay, Petaluma, San Rafael and Sonoma (Bates 1983, 38, 40; Hudson 1984, 32).

Voznesensky was based at Fort Ross. The Russian port of entry for central California was Bodega Bay in Coast Miwok territory and the opportunities for acquiring Coast Miwok baskets were ample. When traveling to San Rafael he would have passed through Olompali. This was the largest Coast Miwok village and was located along the main route from Petaluma to San Rafael. In 1840-1841 the most important leader of the Coast Miwok at that time, Camilo Ynitia, resided in Olompali (Slaymaker 1972, 28).

Among the baskets Voznesensky collected were five coiled baskets that are different from Pomo, Wappo, Patwin, Ohlone and Plains Miwok baskets. These five baskets are intermediate in ornamentation and style between Pomo and Ohlone work, respectively the northern and southern neighbors of the Coast Miwok. They were, however, closer to Ohlone than Pomo baskets. Lawrence Dawson attributed these to the Coast Miwok and our subsequent research supports his conclusion. (The catalog numbers of the five baskets at the Museum of Anthropology and Ethnography, named after Peter the Great, in St. Petersburg, Russia are: 570-95, 570-96, 570-97, 570-99 and 570-100. Baskets #570-98 and 570-103 also should be added to this group.)

Although there are slight variations, the baskets can be described as follows. Their diameter ranges from about eight inches to about 19 inches. These finely coiled baskets have sedge root wefts and black designs of bulrush root. They are decorated with red woodpecker feathers and black quail plumes. The baskets have olivella disc shell bead decoration and some have abalone shell pendants.

The baskets are decorated with round olivella disc shell beads, not whole olivella shells which are oval and much larger. A small part of the olivella shell's side was worked into a round bead with a hole in the center. These beads are about the same diameter as Pomo clamshell beads, which are typically slightly over one-quarter inch in diameter. Coast Miwok olivella shell disc beads, however, are much thinner. They are also slightly concave rather than flat like Pomo clamshell disk beads.

The olivella disc beads are attached to the basket using weft strands rather than Native string. They are arranged in parallelograms or triangles pointing downward at one end, but are arranged vertically at the other end of the design. Besides using olivella shell disc beads, a few clamshell disc beads of about the same size occur. Olivella shell disc beads are placed on the rims, not below the rim where the Pomo often place their clamshell disc beads.

The five Coast Miwok baskets' foundations are all three-rod. Stitches on the baskets' back face (the interior side on these baskets) are normally split. The weft fag ends are concealed in the foundation and the moving ends of weft strands bound under on the back face. The work direction is leftward. The coil endings are tapered.

The fact that the baskets are all decorated with olivella shell disc beads places the baskets in the San Francisco Bay Area. All, or nearly all, olivella disc bead decorated baskets were collected around the San Francisco Bay Area.

We can eliminate all the San Francisco Bay Area groups except the Coast Miwok as being the likely weavers of these five baskets. The Pomo and Wappo used clamshell disc beads, not olivella shell disc beads to decorate their baskets. The Pomo and Wappo thus can be ruled out as the source of these baskets. No Patwin coiled baskets using olivella shell beads are known to exist.

P.M. Kojean, a Russian scholar, speculated that the five baskets under consideration were Plains Miwok (Kojean, 1979). His attributions were often widely off mark. For instance, a Chumash basket was called Huchnom and an Asian basket called Yokuts. In any event, while one or more of the baskets he studied may be Plains Miwok, they are not the five we are concerned with.

For the five attributed Coast Miwok baskets, the possibility of Plains Miwok origin in the Sacramento Valley

A San Francisco Bay Area basket attributed to either the Coast Miwok or the Ohlone (Costanoan). Note the olivella shell disc beads on the side of the basket. Using clamshell disc beads on the rim and olivella disc beads on the sides is more typical of the Coast Miwok. However, this basket lacks pendants and has crisscrossing Ohlone-style diagonal designs done with olivella shell disc beads on an open background of undecorated sedge root wefts. Thus, it could be from either of these two Bay Area Native American cultures. Note that the clamshell disc beads are generally larger than the olivella shell disc beads. D: 12", H: 5" (Staatliches Museum fur Volkerkunde, Munich #143. Photo by Jon and Betty Goerke)

can be ruled out on several counts. San Francisco Bay was the thriving center of olivella shell disc beaded baskets, not the Plains Miwok homeland in the Sacramento Valley. The Plains Miwok were not in an intermediate geographical position where baskets having exactly these characteristics would be likely to be found. Most importantly, Plains Miwok overstitched rims were done using a herringbone (V-shaped) overstitching around the rim. This was different from the diagonal overstitching of the Coast Miwok.

The five attributed Coast Miwok baskets are clearly geographically intermediate between Pomo and Ohlone work for the following reasons: (1) The Coast Miwok baskets use olivella shell beads, as do the Ohlone but not the Pomo. (2) The Coast Miwok baskets sometimes place shell beads on the black patterns, as do the Pomo but not the Ohlone. The Coast Miwok baskets use the disc beads to form the main pattern, as do the Ohlone but not the Pomo. (3) Most importantly, three and perhaps four of these five baskets have single strand over-stitched rims mainly over-stitched over one stitch, but periodically crossing over two stitches at a time on two of the baskets. The fifth basket, 570-95, has its rim checked with pairs of black and white stitches with strands floated on the backside giving the impression of over-stitching. Overstitching rims was a Miwok trait that was not done by the Ohlone or Pomo. The Coast Miwok overstitching is not the same as the distinctive type of herringbone overstitching so prominently visible on Plains Miwok baskets. The Coast Miwok overstitching is also different from the parallel weft type overstitching that the Wappo used on their cooking pots.

In short, these five baskets are not Pomo, Ohlone, Wappo, Patwin or Plains Miwok. The five baskets are certainly from the San Francisco Bay Area and the only people likely to have made them are the Coast Miwok. We began working with Lawrence Dawson on the origin of these baskets in the late 1960s. Our recent research strongly supports Lawrence Dawson's hypothesis that these baskets are Coast Miwok.

Other Possible Surviving Coast Miwok Coiled Baskets

There are other coiled baskets in the Museum of Anthropology and Ethnography (Peter the Great Museum) in St. Petersburg, Russia, some of which could be Coast Miwok. But their attribution is uncertain. These other baskets could be Ohlone, Patwin, Wappo or Pomo (see Blackburn and Hudson 1990, 150-151). Plains Miwok origin has been suggested for at least one basket in that collection (Bates p.c.).

A much stronger case can be made for a basket in the Museum fur Volkerkunde in Frankfurt, Germany (Catalog #E-172). This basket is probably Coast Miwok and is nearly identical to the Russian owned Coast Miwok baskets described earlier. It has olivella shell disc bead designs, an over-stitched rim, rim decorations of clamshell disc beads arranged with downward pointing (at one end) parallelograms and abalone pendants. The original feathering, unfortunately now destroyed, appears to have been red woodpecker feathers (see: Hudson 1984, 31). Another similar coiled basket at the Staatliches Museum fur Volkerkunde in Munich, Germany, basket #143, may be either Coast Miwok or Ohlone.

There is also a very old coiled basket collected around the town of Sonoma (State Museum Research Center, California State Department of Parks and Recreation, basket #155-5). This basket, decorated with glass trade beads, is from historic Coast Miwok territory. However, Wappo, Patwin and other Indian people were at Sonoma Mission along with the Coast Miwok. Thus, it is not possible to attribute this basket with any certainty. It may be Coast Miwok, but could also be Wappo or, less likely, one of the other groups.

Illustrations of Coast Miwok Coiled Baskets

The artist Louis Choris drew a number of baskets during his 1816 visit to San Francisco Bay. Most are fanciful and lack detail. However, one detailed illustration of two men and a woman in a tule boat on San Francisco Bay shows two baskets near the stern. These two baskets appear to have designs of the type found on the five attributed Coast Miwok baskets in Russia. Choris did portraits of Coast Miwok people, and the baskets are probably either Coast Miwok or Ohlone since they appear in a tule boat on San Francisco Bay.

C. Hart Merriam photographed the wife of Miwok Chief Huyumhayum holding a coiled basket (Hearst Museum negative #23214). This photo is illustrated in Theodora Kroeber's 1968 book "Almost Ancestors," page 105, photo 66, mislabeled as Coast Miwok. This photo has also been mislabeled in museum files. Merriam's notes refer to the people in the photo as Tuleyomi, his term for the Lake Miwok, not the Coast Miwok. The people shown are not Coast Miwok, according to Sylvia Thalman, genealogist for the Federated Indians of the Graton Rancheria, the Coast Miwok people (Thalman p.c., 2003; Goerke p.c., 2005). The basket illustrated is similar to Lake Miwok rather than Coast Miwok baskets.

Ethnographic Information on Coast Miwok Coiled Baskets

Historic accounts and statements by Coast Miwok elders provide important information about Coast Miwok coiled basketry. We know Coast Miwok coiling was done on three-rod foundations. Additionally, the Drake account of Coast Miwok basketry mentions baskets "like a deep boat" (Kroeber 1925, 276). This statement refers to the boat-shaped baskets made by the Coast Miwok and Pomo. This suggests that the Coast Miwok also used single-rod basketry foundations since most boat-shaped baskets had single-rod foundations. The Coast Miwok did in fact make boat-shaped baskets (Kelly 1978, 418).

The work direction of Coast Miwok coiling was to the left. Sedge root, willow and hazel are all mentioned as basket materials. Designs were usually in black, almost certainly dyed bulrush root and perhaps bracken fern root. Based on the five baskets in the Russian collection, rims on the early fancy coiled baskets were usually finished with a diagonal backstitch type over-stitching on the rim. Split stitches on the back face of baskets occurred in Coast Miwok coiling. Interlocking stitches were occasionally found, but this was a minor usage (Elsasser 1978, 633).

Feather Baskets

Traditionally the Coast Miwok made coiled feathered baskets decorated with a scattering of red woodpecker feathers. These feathers did not entirely cover the basket (Barrett 1996, 83-84; Collier and Thalman 1991, 159). Coast Miwok feather baskets had quail topknots around the top above the red woodpecker feathers. White duck feathers from under the wing might be used, too (Collier and Thalman 1991, 159).

Feathered baskets decorated with shell beads (the type of shell is not stated), abalone shell (pendants), red woodpecker feathers and quail topknots are specifically mentioned for Coast Miwok baskets from Nicasio in central Marin County (Collier and Thalman 1991, 159). The same materials were also reported from Point Reyes in the 1579 Drake account.

Both olivella shell and clamshell disc beads were made by the Coast Miwok. Olivella shell beads were worn as necklaces and earrings. Clamshell beads were used for money (Collier and Thalman 1991, 8, 156, 169-170).

Both types of beads were used on fancy baskets. Olivella shell disc beads were the predominant beads used on baskets. Clamshell disc beads were uncommon on baskets except on the rim.[2]

Other Types of Coast Miwok Coiled Baskets

Cooking Pots were so finely coiled that Coast Miwok elders remembered them as being watertight. These baskets were made of a white root material "something like willow" (Collier and Thalman 1991, 155, 157), which was almost certainly sedge (*Carex*) root. Coast Miwok coiled cooking pots were said to have a small, flat base. Small bases were also often found on Patwin and Wappo coiled cooking pots.

Cup/Server/Dipper Baskets were small, coiled baskets used to hold liquids (Kelly 1978, 421; Collier and Thalman 1991, 155, 157).

Winnower, Parching and Sifting Trays were large flat baskets. The parching tray was coiled and round, not fan shaped. It was large, up to two and a half feet in diameter. Basket sifters were coiled baskets. Anthropologist Isabel Kelly stated that "From descriptions, seems coiled, which is not understandable." (Collier and Thalman 1991, 106, 145-147, 155-158). Actually, coiled sifting trays were widespread in Central California. They were round, flat baskets. Coiled sifters separated flour particles by tapping the basket to separate particles by size; not by having the particles fall through a screen as with contemporary kitchen sifters. This difference in sifting technique may have been what confused Kelly. A later Kelly notation also mentions twined sifters. In fact, Kelly may have been dealing with two distinct types of sifters: (1) a coiled sifting tray for acorn flour, and (2) an openwork twined berry sifter. In some cases it is unclear from Isabel Kelly's research notes which trays were coiled and which were twined.

Shaman's Baskets were probably coiled (Collier and Thalman 1991, 157).

Mortar Hoppers were discussed in the twining section.

Comments

The Coast Miwok excelled at both twined and coiled basketry. Twined basketry was made in an unusually wide variety of techniques and was of exceptional quality. Besides making very finely woven twined baskets, Coast Miwok coiled basketry had become a vital and beautiful aspect of Coast Miwok life. This coiled basketry featured stunning olivella shell disc beads, abalone pendants and over-stitched rims ranked among the finest coiled basketry in California.

---

[2] **Later Coast Miwok Fancy Baskets**
    There were additional coiled fancy baskets made by weavers of Coast Miwok ancestry in the late 19th century and well into the 20th century. During these later years, Coast Miwok weavers covered entire baskets with feathers, although this was reportedly not done in aboriginal times (Barrett 1996, 141). One example of this later type Coast Miwok feather basketry was a small, low globular coiled basket from the aunt of David Peri, an anthropologist of Coast Miwok ancestry. Mr. Peri stated that "I guess you could call it Coast Miwok" (Peri p.c.). This basket was sewn in a leftward work direction and had a three-rod foundation. It was made with mainly interlocking stitches, but with some split stitches on the back face. The weft was sedge root with a simple plain tapered coil ending. The feather designs were diagonal bands of green mallard feathers outlined in blue feathers with a background of orange-yellow oriole feathers. A row of quail plumes was placed under the rim. A second late period basket belonging to a friend who is Coast Miwok and believed to be a Coast Miwok basket was also studied. It was of similar low globular shape but without feathers. Both baskets were small, finely woven baskets identical to Pomo baskets in quality and technique.
    The difficulty with such late baskets is that it is hard to know how much Pomo influence is present in the basket's construction. Coast Miwok people intermarried extensively with the Pomo and in historic times incorporated Pomo features in their basketry. These late Coast Miwok weavers were usually of part Pomo ancestry and the Pomo had a very active basketry tradition that remained strong. Thus, it is not surprising that late Coast Miwok baskets became virtually completely Pomo-like. But it is clear that earlier there were major differences in the coiled basketry traditions of the two cultures.

The Wappo are the First People of the Napa Valley and Sonoma's Alexander Valley. Shown here is a fine Wappo coiled cooking pot with a three-rod foundation, sedge root background wefts, black bulrush root designs and a plain wrapped rim. The Wappo made both coiled and twined cooking pots. This was an uncommon practice in California and indicates that a shift was occurring from twined to coiled cooking pots. Collected in Alexander Valley, Sonoma County about 1901. D: 12", H: 6" (Courtesy of Phoebe Apperson Hearst Museum of Anthropology and Regents of the University of California, #1-404)

A fine Wappo coiled cooking pot with a three-rod foundation of willow, sedge root background wefts and redbud designs extending onto the bottom. This Wappo coiled cooking pot has a distinctive type of over-stitched rim that ran completely around the uppermost coil. This basket was made by Mary Duggan of Alexander Valley, Sonoma County, and purchased from her in 1908. D: 14", H: 7" (Courtesy of Phoebe Apperson Hearst Museum of Anthropology and Regents of the University of California, #1-369)

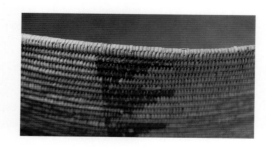

Detail of the unique style of over-stitched rim used on some Wappo coiled cooking pots. Unlike the over-stitched rims of other tribes, Wappo over-stitching was parallel to the wefts, not slanted diagonally or in a herringbone pattern. The Wappo over-stitching extended completely around the rim. (Courtesy of the Phoebe Apperson Hearst Museum of Anthropology and Regents of the University of California, #1-369)

WAPPO BASKETRY

The Wappo homeland comprises most of Napa County and a portion of Sonoma and Lake Counties. Napa Valley and Alexander Valley are the centers of Wappo country. The Wappo territory also spread out from Alexander Valley east over the mountain ridges to Middletown in Lake County. Wappo country even reached across the Mayacamas Mountain Range on the west side of the Napa Valley to include a portion of the upper Sonoma Valley. These valleys were once heavily wooded with valley oak, gray pine, manzanita and other plants vital to California Indian life. Fish were plentiful in the Napa River and Russian River. Major contemporary towns in Wappo country include St. Helena, Calistoga, Geyserville and Kenwood.

The Wappo language has long been linked to the north to the Yuki, Coast Yuki and Huchnom, but the connection was distant (Kroeber 1925, 217; Sawyer 1978, 256). The separation of the Wappo from the Yuki probably exceeds 3,000 years (Sawyer 1978, 256; Foster 1996, 83).

After moving away from the Yuki, the Wappo migrated south as far as the Napa Valley. Archeological research suggests that the Wappo moved into the Napa Valley around A.D. 500 (Bennyhoff p.c.; Moratto 1984, 566; Whistler 1977, 171).

The outcome of this movement had a profound effect on Wappo basketry. Perhaps due to such a long period of separation between the Yuki and Wappo, the basketry of the Wappo was not Yukian. Instead, Wappo culture became strongly influenced by the Pomo and to a lesser degree by the Patwin. Wappo basketry became almost entirely Pomoan, except for the Patwin influence on Wappo coiled cooking pots.

Wappo Coiled Baskets

Technical Features of Wappo Coiled Basketry

The Wappo made both three-rod and single-rod coiling with a work direction that was to the left. **Starting knots** used a wrapped segment of shredded foundation material. Twined starting knots were also occasionally used to begin coiled baskets. At least on three-rod foundation baskets, **weft stitches** were mixed interlocking, non-interlocking and split stitches. All three types of stitches were often used on the same basket. The split stitches were split only on the back face. Interlocking stitches were most often used on baskets with single-rod foundations (Elsasser 1978, 628, 633).

Wappo **weft fag ends** were concealed from view in the foundation by successive stitches. The **weft moving ends** were bound under successive stitches on the back face, thus concealing them. Rims were usually plain wrapped, except on coiled cooking pots (and possibly other types) where a unique over-stitching was sometimes used.

Wappo Coiled Basketry Materials

In coiling, the Wappo used willow as a foundation material. For black designs, mud dyed bulrush roots (most commonly *Scirpus fluviatus*, but also *S. maritimus* and *S. robustus*) were chosen. Red designs were done using redbud (*Cercis occidentalis*). Sedge root (*Carex barbarae*) provided the buff background color.

WAPPO AND POMO BASKETRY: A LARGELY SHARED, BUT NOT IDENTICAL, TRADITION

As Wappo/Southern Pomo weaver Laura Fish Somersall used to say of the Wappo and Pomo, "They all do the same weave." In terms of technical features, all Wappo twined weaving and most Wappo coiling was Pomo-style. Both people did plain, lattice and diagonal twining. Materials, shapes, weft splices, twining types, most designs and many kinds of baskets made were comparable for both the Wappo and Pomo (Heizer 1953, 245; Abel-Vidor, Brovarney and Billie 1991, 63).

However, there were some differences. The Wappo seem to have lacked some Pomo coiling and twining starting knots, some twining rim finishes (selvages), some twined and possibly some coiled basket types and reportedly wickerwork seedbeaters (Driver 1936, 187, 192; Elsasser 1978, 628). One kind of basket, however, was made by the Wappo and not by the Pomo. This was the coiled cooking pot.

WAPPO COILED COOKING POTS WERE DISTINCTIVE

Wappo basketry was overwhelmingly influenced by Pomo weaving, but with at least one major exception. The Wappo made both coiled and twined cooking pots. In contrast, the Pomo made only twined cooking pots and the Patwin made only coiled cooking pots.

The Wappo coiled cooking pot was distinctive. These coiled baskets were made on a three-rod foundation using wefts of sedge root (Driver 1936, 187, 191). Designs were in either bulrush root or redbud; the two design materials were never combined on the same basket. The basket's sides flared from the base, although not too sharply. One Wappo coiled cooking pot had a few scattered quail plumes attached, perhaps because it was intended as a wedding gift.

Surviving Wappo coiled cooking pots were twelve to thirteen inches in diameter and six to seven inches high. Known designs include crisscrossing diagonals or vertical designs with ample open space left in the background. Designs stopped one coil below the rim. On some Wappo cooking pots there was a highly distinctive type of over-stitching atop the final coil. This over-stitching was *parallel* to the top weft stitches onto which it was sewn. Unique in California, this special kind of over-stitched rim ran completely around the Wappo cooking pot's top coil. This over-stitching was not done just at the coil ending, as many other cultures did. Nor was it the diagonally backstitched rim or the herringbone over-stitched rim that completely ran around the rim on some Plains Miwok, Yokuts and Western Mono baskets; all these were different from those of the Wappo rim. Because Wappo cooking baskets are so rare we cannot say how widespread the over-stitched rims were.

How Wappo coiled cooking pots stand in relation to nearby cultures, however, seems clear. There were no connections to Pomo cooking pots since these were twined. The Patwin and Yuki, however, both made coiled cooking pots. Wappo coiled cooking pots were closely related to those of the Patwin, but not the Yuki.

Wappo coiled cooking pots were shaped much like those of the Patwin and Valley Maidu, but very differently from those of the Yuki. The Wappo, Patwin and Valley Maidu made three-rod foundation cooking pots, while only a minority of Yuki cooking pots used three-rod foundations. The Wappo, Patwin and Valley Maidu made deep, flaring cooking pots, while the Yuki made broad shallow ones. The Wappo, Patwin and Valley Maidu coiling work direction was invariably to the leftward, while the Yuki coiled in a rightward work direction about 85% of the time. The Wappo, Patwin and Valley Maidu normally left the final cooking pot coil undecorated, while the Yuki frequently placed designs on the rim. The bases of Wappo and Valley Maidu coiled cooking pots were undecorated and proportionately slightly broader than most Patwin ones. The Patwin made cooking pots both with and without designs on the bottom. Patwin cooking pot bases averaged slightly smaller in relation to their height than did Wappo and Valley Maidu ones. Thus, these and

other features point to a Valley Maidu or Patwin origin for Wappo coiled cooking pots rather than an ancient Yukian remnant tradition. Wappo cooking pots are most like those of the Valley Maidu, yet are very, very similar to Patwin ones. The Wappo were in close contact with the Patwin in Napa County, and the Wappo may have adopted coiled cooking pots only after the Patwin arrival in the Napa region after A.D. 700 (see: Moratto 1984, 652-563; Foster 1996, 90).

WAPPO COILED BOWLS AND GIFT BASKETS

The only Wappo coiled basket used for culinary purposes was the cooking pot. All other coiled Wappo baskets were fancy baskets made for special occasions or to hold treasured objects. These came in three forms: (1) low, broad flaring baskets, (2) globular-shaped baskets, and (3) oval "boat-shaped" baskets. Miniature baskets were also made.

Both bowl-shaped and oval (boat-shaped) coiled baskets were used for weddings and other important occasions. These baskets might be decorated with feathers or beads or both. Scattered red woodpecker feathers were traditionally preferred for decoration on feather baskets. According to Barrett, the Wappo originally never solidly covered their feather baskets with feathers, as the Pomo did. The Wappo originally only scattered feathers or partially covered the basket surface with feathers in certain areas. It was only after the arrival of Euro-Americans when making baskets for sale became widespread that some Wappo baskets became completely covered with feathers (Sawyer 1965, 7-8; Barrett 1996, 83-84).

The earliest coiled Wappo basket located (Oakland Museum H16.1376, circa 1840) was from Yountville in the Napa Valley, possibly from the village of Caymus. It had a band of clamshell disc beads sewn all around along the exterior of the final coil facing outward, not atop the rim as was so common among the Pomo. The clamshell beads were also sewn on singly, unlike most Pomo baskets where the thread ran from one bead to the next across the top of the beads.

On this basket, the rim was plainly wrapped without over-stitching. Sides were flaring. Wefts were of sedge root. The Yountville Wappo basket was once a feather basket decorated with red feathers, but the feathers have been eaten away. The basket is low (about three inches high) and broad (nearly nine inches in diameter) with flaring sides, a feather basket shape also found among the Patwin.

A very early Wappo coiled basket from the Napa Valley. The clamshell disc beads are sewn on individually using Native cordage and are placed on the side of the rim in a lower position than is typical of the Pomo. This basket was originally a feathered basket. It was made in the 1840s at Yountville, probably at the village of Caymus. D: 8.5″, H: 3″ (Oakland Museum of California, #H16.1376)

In later years the Wappo began making fancy baskets extensively decorated with tiny European-made glass seed beads. These trade baskets were a specialty of both the Alexander Valley Wappo and Southern Pomo living near Lytton and Healdsburg. These beaded baskets were made primarily for sale (Smith-Ferri 1996, 188; Turnbaugh and Turnbaugh 1997, 45, 184).

A herringbone rim finish like those of the Lake Miwok reportedly occurred on a very few Wappo coiled baskets;

however, our research did not support this claim. This type of coil ending was a Lake Miwok trait. While there could have been a sharing of this type of coil ending by the Wappo and Lake Miwok, the baskets in question are probably Lake Miwok trade pieces. Wappo, Lake Miwok and Pomo people mixed around Middletown in Lake County and it can often be difficult to determine which tribe made baskets from this area.

Wappo Twined Baskets

Wappo twined baskets were done in plain, lattice and diagonal twining. Both up-to-the-left and up-to-the-right slants of weft twist occurred. Crossed warp starts of the Pomo type were used. On close twined baskets, the rim selvages were trimmed slightly above the last weft row so that they protruded slightly above the top weft row. On some openwork baskets warps were bent downward and into the wefts to secure them (Elsasser 1978, 628). Warps were also bent and woven into a wave-like selvage on openwork burden baskets.

Wappo Twined Basketry Materials

Redbud, sedge root and pine root predominated in close twined work. Willow was used for warps in openwork twined baskets and split willow root for wefts. Besides willow, dogwood was used in rough baskets for both weft and warps (Sawyer 1965, 8; Moser 1987, 88; Mathewson 1988, 152-153, 179).

TYPES OF WAPPO CLOSE TWINED BASKETS

Twined Cooking Pots

The Wappo were unusual in that they made both coiled and twined cooking pots. Our knowledge of the twined Wappo cooking pots is limited due to so few surviving. But if the best-documented surviving example is representative, twined Wappo cooking pots had three-strand twining at the bottom, plain twining throughout the body of the basket and plain twining over two warps at the rim. The rim was trimmed with warp sticks protruding slightly above the top weft row. Background wefts were of sedge root. Designs were numerous narrow horizontal bands done in redbud. Some of these bands were plain, but others had designs within them. The Pomo-style dau (break in the design) was absent on some bands. A small floating design was present.

Mortar Hoppers

Mortar hoppers were said to be the same as those of the Pomo (Driver 1936, 186). Wappo mortar hoppers were plain twined. They used bands of lattice twining for reinforcement and had a wrapped reinforcing rod at the rim. One reputed

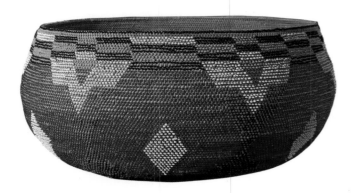

A Wappo beaded basket decorated with European glass trade beads. This basket was collected in 1904 at Alexander Valley, Sonoma County. The Wappo and Southern Pomo of Alexander Valley made this distinctive style of beaded basket. Baskets heavily covered with small European "seed beads" are uncommon in Central California, but are frequently found in the Great Basin. (The Field Museum of Natural History, Chicago, #103191)

This Wappo twined cooking pot is woven primarily in plain twining over one warp using sedge root wefts and redbud designs. This Wappo basket lacks the "dau," the break in the design usually found in horizontal designs on Pomo twined baskets. However, this Wappo basket has a small isolated rectangular design that may be a Wappo version of the dau mark. Collected in 1908 by Alfred L. Kroeber. D: 10", H: 7.5" (Courtesy of Phoebe Apperson Hearst Museum of Anthropology and Regents of the University of California, #1-14512)

Wappo mortar hopper examined was low and broad like the Patwin style. It had very narrow horizontal stripes for designs. This mortar hopper was constructed like Patwin and southern Pomo mortar hoppers rather than those of the Yuki.

Winnowers

Wappo winnowers were round, slightly conical plate forms like those of the Pomo. They had bands of lattice twining for reinforcing strength.

Burden Baskets

Wappo close twined burden baskets were said to be like those of the Pomo. If so, they would have been bell-shaped rather than truly conical. The Wappo used a carrying strap of either woven plant fiber or buckskin (Driver 1936, 192).

Storage Baskets

Wappo storage baskets were reported to be like those of the Pomo, which were quite large and beautifully decorated.

WAPPO OPENWORK TWINED BASKETS

Openwork Burden Baskets

Wappo openwork burden baskets were bell-shaped and undecorated. For strength, Wappo openwork burden baskets had three broad rows of warp sticks bent over to form a braided rim (Sawyer 1965, 7; Sawyer 1978, 262; Hearst Museum #114505). This type of selvage added strength and was similar to the Pomo type rim finish. These burden baskets were used to carry acorns, firewood and other items.

This Wappo openwork burden basket was made for gathering acorns. The wave-like braided rim was a beautiful Wappo and Pomo way of securing warps ends at the rim to strengthen openwork baskets. (Courtesy of the Phoebe Apperson Hearst Museum of Anthropology and the Regents of the University of California, #1-14505)

Globular Openwork Baskets

Fancy lattice twined bowls with broad bases and constricted mouths were made. These had redbud designs, an unusual feature for a Wappo openwork basket.

A Wappo twined storage basket woven with openwork lattice twining on the side and close-work diagonal twining near the top. Designs are in redbud, the background is sedge root and willow is the warp material. (The Field Museum of Natural History, Chicago, #103361)

Strainers and Sifters

Lattice twined, bowl-shaped openwork strainers with a band of close woven diagonal twining near the rim were made. The rim was reinforced with a wrapped rod. Sides were flaring. These baskets were used for sifting and for holding food (Driver 1936, 187; Sawyer 1978, 263; Fang and Binder 1990, 187, top right).

Cradles

A sitting cradle like those of the Pomo was made. Both women and old men made cradles (Driver 1936, 209).

A cradle made by Laura Fish Somersal, a Wappo and Southern Pomo weaver from Alexander Valley, Sonoma County. This cradle has the warp rods from the cradle's back brought forward on top of the U-shaped bottom. (Collection of the Grace Hudson Museum, Ukiah, California)

Woodpecker Traps

Various types of woodpeckers, including flickers, were caught using a long, narrow basket placed over holes in the trees where the birds were roosting (Driver 1936, 185). When the woodpeckers exited their hole they became stuck in the trap and could not back out.

Fish Traps

A brush fish dam or weir for salmon and other large fish was built in streams using stakes. Fish were driven toward the dam by noisily hitting rocks in the streambed with poles. Several openings were left in the weir. An openwork fish basket was placed at each opening to catch the fish. These fish traps were quite large, five to eight feet long and three to four feet at the mouth (Heizer 1953, 245; Sawyer 1965, 7). For luck, fishermen tied a string of clamshell beads to the mouth of the fish basket. Fish traps were woven by the men (Driver 1936, 184-186, 208).

Fish Scoops

Shallow scoop-shaped baskets were used to scoop up fish found in shallow water (Driver 1936, 184).

Seedbeaters

Driver stated that the Wappo made a twined seedbeater (Driver 1936, 187, 192). This is significantly different from the wickerwork seed beaters made by neighboring Pomo groups.

Wickerwork Baskets

A type of fish trap was made of wickerwork (Driver 1936, 184). This is the only type of wickerwork basket reported for the Wappo. Very widely spaced plain twining on rough openwork baskets, however, can easily be confused with wickerwork. It is possible that these baskets were actually plain twined, as among the Pomo.

Comments

The Wappo were major suppliers of obsidian used throughout much of Central California for projectile points. Glass Mountain on the Silverado Trail northeast of St. Helena was the source of this high quality black volcanic glass. Wappo baskets must have been regularly used to transport obsidian for trade. During trading sessions the Wappo would also have seen Pomo, Patwin and Coast Miwok baskets. This likely contributed to the Pomo and Patwin influence seen in Wappo weaving.

It should be emphasized that the Wappo excelled in the art of both coiled and twined basketry. As anthropologist Harold Driver wrote, Wappo basketry was "in every way comparable (in quality) to that of the neighboring Pomo, who have been judged to be among the finest basket makers in the world." (Driver 1936, 191). This is a high compliment and an accurate one.

The Yuki are generally believed to be one of the oldest cultures in Central California. The center of Yuki country is Round Valley in northern Mendocino County. Yuki coiled basketry deserves full recognition as one of the great arts in Native California. Yuki weavers made some of the most artistically interesting, unique and beautiful baskets in Native America. Note the fascinating designs on this large Yuki coiled basket. The designs are done entirely with unpeeled redbud while the light colored background is peeled redbud. All the Yuki baskets illustrated in this book were made at or near Round Valley in Mendocino County. D: 21.5", H: 6.5" (Private collection)

The Yuki used both peeled and unpeeled redbud as weft material. The dark design is unpeeled redbud from fresh shoots gathered in the spring. The light yellowish-brown background is peeled redbud. If you look carefully, you can see dark areas where the bark was not completely removed. Incomplete removal of redbud bark often occurs on Yuki coiled baskets. On some baskets this appears intentional and produces interesting background variations. D: 15", H: 6" (Maryhill Museum of Art, Goldendale, Washington, #0-10)

Yuki Basketry

The Yuki heartland is Round Valley in northern Mendocino County. This is still Central California with its oak woodlands in the valleys and pine and manzanita in the hills. Yet this is a land distinct from the more gentle country of the Pomo and Coast Miwok people to the south. For in Yuki country the mountains are steeper, higher and increasingly rugged. The rivers, especially the middle fork of the Eel River and its tributary creeks, run with startling force in winter. Within this challenging country are valleys and flats that offered a gentler home and the natural resources to live a Central California life.

The Yuki are said to be ancient Californians. Anthropologist Alfred L. Kroeber suggested that the Yuki may be the very first of all California Indian people (Kroeber 1925, 159). Archeologist Michael J. Moratto, in his "*California Archaeology*," proposed that ancestral Yuki might have once held all the land from the north shore of San Francisco Bay to the mouth of the Klamath River in Del Norte County (Moratto 1984, 545).

Gradually, over thousands of years, Yuki territory was reduced as Indian groups speaking other languages entered California. Yuki territory was probably still continuing to decrease when non-Indians began arriving. But the Yuki influence never disappeared. It remained in bits and pieces from the North Bay area to the Klamath River. There are Yukian influences in Kashaya and Northern Pomo basketry, in Wailaki and Cahto basketry and even among the basketry of Northwestern California cultures.

Yuki coiled basketry is unique in California. It was not as finely woven as the basketry of the Pomo nor as neatly done as that of the Maidu, but Yuki basketry possesses a charm and beauty all its own. Yuki basketry is best approached like an Impressionist painting, viewing the overall design layout, the texture and warmth of the piece. Judged by these criteria, this basketry stands out as a remarkable insight into a special kind of beauty. Yuki basketry has its own special character, charm and often an exotic quality that deserves appreciation by the art lover.

Yuki Coiled Basketry: A Unique and Fascinating Tradition

The Yuki made both coiled and twined basketry. Their coiled work especially stands out, as they were the only major group in Northern California to coil to the right.

Yuki rim decoration varied on coiled baskets. While some Yuki baskets had undecorated rims similar to those of the Patwin and Maidu, other Yuki coiled baskets had unpeeled redbud rims that provided a strong contrasting red border to the light colored peeled redbud background. This large storage basket was made prior to 1904. D: 21.5", H: 9" (Maryhill Museum of Art, Goldendale, Washington, #98-139)

True, a small percent of Yuki baskets are coiled to the left and the tiny number of surviving coiled Wailaki and Cahto baskets were coiled to the right.

But the significant fact is that at least 85% of Yuki coiled baskets have a rightward work direction. This is in stark contrast to the leftward work direction of all the rest of North Central Californians: the Pomo, Patwin, Maidu, Miwok, Wappo, Ohlone/Costanoan and others.

Why would we have an island of rightward coiling in a sea of leftward coiling? The answer could simply be local innovation, but when we carefully study California Native basketry we usually discover connections. California Indian people are dynamic people frequently interacting with each other. Isolated, unconnected developments were uncommon.

Whatever the reason, a rightward work direction in North Central California is a characteristic we are grateful for. It is one of several features that make it quite easy to distinguish Yuki baskets from those of other North Central California tribes. Kroeber said of Yuki basketry "a novice can tell it at a glance. It is of a character of its own" (Kroeber 1925, 270).

Yuki Coiling Foundations: The Use of Splints

Not only was the Yuki rightward work direction distinctive in North Central California, but so were the foundations of their coiled baskets. North Central Californians use either three rods or, less commonly, a single rod for the foundations of their coiled baskets. While about a third of

Coiled baskets require a foundation around and through which weft material is wrapped. There were several types of coiling foundations, including rods of peeled shoots (most often willow), splints (tiny thin board-like strips), grass bundles, and other materials. The Yuki used both rods and splints for their foundations, sometimes in combination with one another. Splints are shown here at the two points on the rim where wefts have broken away allowing them to be seen. (State Museum Resource Center, California Department of Parks and Recreation, #6002W)

Yuki coiled baskets do indeed use a three-rod foundation, approximately two thirds of them do not. Instead, most Yuki coiled baskets use what are called splints or welts, thin strips of wood, for the foundation. Splints look like thin, miniature boards, rather like the scale lumber model builders use. Most often these splints were combined with one or two rods to form the foundation of the coil. But in a few Yuki baskets splints alone comprised the foundation. Use of splints was a distinctively Yuki feature.

Perhaps the use of foundation splints accounts for the surprising fact that the Yuki lacked single rod coiling foundations, a feature common among the neighboring Pomo and Patwin (Kelly 1930, 424-425; Essene 1942, 60). Again, we wonder, why was Yuki basketry so distinctive?

Yuki Materials

Yuki coiling foundation splints and rods were most often of dogwood (*Cornus*) or western redbud (*Cercis occidentalis*). Sometimes, after a weaver had split her redbud weft materials, leftover redbud wefts were used as foundation splints. Willow (*Salix*), hazel shoots (*Corylus cornuta var. california*) or honeysuckle (*Lonicera interupta*) were also used as warp rods, but less often (Kelly 1930, 423; Foster 1944, 172; Dawson p.c.).

Yuki coiled baskets used peeled redbud for their wefts. Unpeeled red shoots were used for designs and peeled redbud shoots for the buff-colored background. All, or nearly all, Yuki baskets used redbud for their weft material (Kelly 1930, 423). Designs were overwhelmingly done in red only, using unpeeled redbud. Mud-dyed redbud was used on a few baskets for black designs (Winther 2000, 60). Sedge root was rarely, if ever, used.

Yuki Stitch Types Were Variable

Another unusual feature of Yuki coiling was stitch type. Most cultures produced a generally consistent type of stitching. For example, the Maidu regularly split their stitches on the interior face of their baskets, the Sierra Miwok primarily used interlocking stitches and the Yokuts coiled using non-interlocking stitches.

Among the Yuki, non-interlocking stitches were most common, but split stitches regularly occurred, too. The Yuki also left many stitches un-split. Lawrence Dawson observed that the Yuki "don't seem to be trying to produce a certain stitch type," as do practically every other California group. Once again, the uniqueness of the Yukian cultural approach to coiling is strikingly evident.

Yuki Weft Splices

Variations occurred among Yuki weft fag ends, too. Yuki weft fag ends were mainly bound under, but sometimes they were hidden in the coil foundation. Occasionally, some weft fag ends were trimmed. Moving ends were primarily bound under on the back face, usually the interior side (Dawson pc.).

Yuki Starting Knots of Splints

Some Yuki starting knots consisted of a ring of tightly wrapped layers using thin flat splints. In this type of knot, the tight spiral consisted of thin splints closely wound back-to-back like a clock spring. On worn baskets it can be seen that these layers of splints were used prior to stitching over the starting knot. Sometimes splints would continue along serving as the entire foundation. But more often the spiral of splints continued for only a short distance before rods were added to the foundation splints.

Other starting knots were used. Some Yuki coiled baskets actually began with a twined starting knot. There was, for example, a starting knot of layered crossed pairs of warps that looked similar to a Northwestern Californian's starting knot, but with different material. Another knot was a fist-like tightly knotted start.

Yuki Plain Wrapped Rims and Styles of Coil Endings

The Yuki made only plain wrapped (self-rims) rims, although coil endings varied. About half of Yuki baskets had a rather blunt coil ending, while other coil endings were tapered. In the final few centimeters of some coil endings, back-stitching and herringbone stitches were done. Using three different kinds of coil endings was not common in California.

Yuki Design Layout in Coiled Baskets

Yuki designs could be narrow or quite blocky. Only a few Yuki designs were outlined. One classic Yuki coiled basketry pattern consisted of narrow horizontal bands done in redbud. These bands were typically only one or two coils wide. Sometimes these parallel rows were not entirely on one level band, and for an inch or two each row dropped down a few coils and then returned to continue on at its original level. The dip would occur at the same spot along each band. The result was a series of very pleasing geometric dips in the design. These bands were typically three or four in number, but on a few Yuki baskets parallel bands with dips were much more numerous (see: Kelly 1939, plate 120).

These simple bands were probably derived from very ancient Yuki patterns. Simple narrow band patterns are often found on archeological baskets elsewhere. In the North

Coast region, simple narrow bands also occur among groups neighboring the Yuki. Cahto coiled baskets and Wailaki and Lassik twined baskets also used these narrow bands. Similar narrow bands also appear farther south among the Coastal and Southern Pomo on their twined baskets. This type of Pomo design may have Yukian origins. As Yukian groups were displaced and/or absorbed by neighboring people such as the Pomo, Yuki designs could have been transmitted. These narrow horizontal bands are a prime example.

Besides horizontal bands, other common Yuki designs include diagonal patterns, large vertical triangles (sometimes split vertically) and zigzags (see: Kelly 1930, plates 120-127). A particularly interesting Yuki design has vertically arranged horizontal lines outlined by very large, elongated triangles.

The Yuki frequently put designs on the bottom of their baskets. Yuki baskets often had a circle or partial circle design of redbud on the bottom. At times designs also extended out from this circle.

Yuki Rim Decoration

Some Yuki baskets brought the design on the side of the basket up to the rim rather than stopping it one coil below the rim. The entire final coil was sometimes finished in a narrow

Yuki coiled basketry is known for its "random rectangles." These are short sections of dark unpeeled redbud that irregularly appear on the background between the main designs. Such random rectangles seem to be an artistic choice by Yuki women since such highly skilled weavers could have easily eliminated them. This globular bowl has many dark red random rectangles visible on the light background. D: 9", H: 10" (Collection of the Milwaukee Public Museum, #31888, Lisa Woo Shanks photo file)

red band; at other times, the final coil was left undecorated. Rarely, rim ticks (red stripes) were used on the final coil.

Yuki Random Rectangles

Yuki basketry was quite distinctive in frequently having unpeeled redbud rectangular designs, usually one coil wide, that were randomly placed on the baskets. These rectangles varied in length from one to a dozen or more stitches. They appeared at unpredictable intervals in the overall pattern and showed no relationship to the overall pattern. With the exception of a small neighboring group or two, no one else used these isolated rectangles in their designs.

It has been suggested that Yuki randomly placed rectangles could be the result of simply careless, incomplete peeling of the redbud when preparing it for weft material. In a few cases this may have been true. But many Yuki weavers were highly skilled and obviously capable of properly preparing their materials.

Random rectangles were so widespread in Yuki basketry that they must have been purposely used. Given the high quality of some Yuki baskets, these "erratic splotches," as they have been called, could easily have been avoided by any careful weaver. There may have been a religious or esthetic reason for their use in the basket.

Sadly, early ethnographers did not inquire as to the reasons random rectangles were used, and we may never know their purpose. Some Pomo women inserted a flicker feather in their twined baskets when working during menstruation and the Yuki custom could be a related concept. Whatever the reason, these single coil-wide random rectangles are yet another distinctive feature of Yuki basketry.

The Importance of Coiling Over Twining in Yuki Basketry

The Yuki made coiled basketry quite extensively. Contrast Yuki basketry with that of the Pomo. In terms of key basket types, the Pomo made close twined cooking pots, storage baskets and winnowers. The Yuki made coiled cooking pots, storage baskets and winnowers. Coiling had displaced twining to a far greater degree among the Yuki than among the Pomo.

Twining long pre-dates coiling in California, and some tribes never adopted coiling. It takes time for a people to convert from twined to coiled basketry. The Yuki people's extensive use of coiling and reduced importance of twining suggests that the Yuki had coiled basketry for a long time. The Yuki almost certainly had coiled basketry prior to the Pomo.

MAJOR YUKI COILED BASKETRY FORMS

Yuki coiled baskets tend to fall into the categories: (1) medium size to very large broad, low bowls, (2) large storage baskets with upward curving sides, and (3) small to medium sized globular bowls.

The most common baskets were coiled **parching/winnowing/sifting baskets**. Using such baskets: (1) seeds were parched (roasted) using hot coals, (2) seeds were winnowed to separate husks, and (3) acorn meal was sifted.

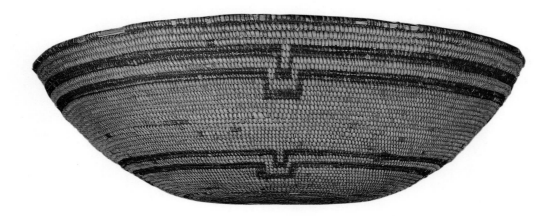

Yuki cooking pots were low and broad compared to those of all other California tribes. This very old Yuki cooking pot has been worn almost completely through the bottom by cooking stones being stirred to heat acorn mush and soup. Simple horizontal band designs such as these were very common among the Yuki. Note the interruption in the design bands, a feature found on some coiled Yuki baskets. This may be related to the "dau" mark that interrupts most horizontal designs in Pomo twined baskets. D: 17", H: 5" (Private collection)

A Yuki cooking pot for boiling acorn mush. It has the usual rightward work direction found on about 85% of all Yuki coiled baskets. D: 23", H: 7.5" (Mendocino County Museum, #84-2-7)

Very simple lines were used with strikingly beautiful results, as on this coiled Yuki basket. Simple horizontal bands are among the oldest of Native American designs. Horizontal band designs were found on woven bags, twined baskets and coiled baskets. Horizontal bands occurred first on woven bags. Bags and mats pre-date baskets, twined baskets predate coiled baskets and all three predate pottery along the West Coast. D: 17" (Mendocino County Museum, #84-2-9)

These multi-purpose baskets were also sometimes used as cooking baskets.

This form of Yuki basket was different from the coiled, flat parching trays of the Patwin and Maidu and the twined parching tray of the Pomo. The Yuki coiled winnower was about four to five inches deep and three times as wide. These parching baskets flared in a gently rounded manner from a flat bottom that was usually half the diameter of the basket or less.

Cooking Baskets. Yuki cooking pots and winnowers had similar shapes and some may have been used for both purposes. But there was a gradual transition in size from winnowers to the larger sized cooking pots. Yuki cooking pots ranged in size up to approximately two feet in diameter and up to about seven or so inches deep. Bases were small or medium size, which added a graceful flaring look to the basket's curving sides. Designs were quite attractive and were found on the bottom, the sides and sometimes on the rim (see: Kelly 1930, plate 122 c, d, e).

Using broad, fairly shallow baskets for cooking pots was unusual in California. However, evidence of cooking stone wear patterns and burns found in these baskets indicates that they served as cooking pots. Due to their greater width, the capacity of Yuki cooking pots rivaled that of the deeper cooking pots of other tribes.

Storage Baskets. Large, coiled storage baskets were a Yuki hallmark. Storage baskets were larger and deeper than cooking pots. These big, bowl-shaped baskets were used for storage, but they would also have made good feast baskets if desired. Storage baskets were typically about 16 to 20

inches in diameter and seven to ten inches deep. Isabel Kelly illustrates four examples with narrow designs, but blocky triangles were used, too (Kelly 1930, plate 120). It could take up to two years to weave one of these huge storage baskets (Mabel McKay, Pomo weaver, p.c.).

Fancy Baskets. Coiled, often globular, baskets were used to store small possessions (Kelly 1930, plate 124).

CONNECTIONS OF COILED YUKI BASKETRY TO OTHER CULTURES

Yuki-style coiled basketry was adopted to a limited degree by small neighboring groups such as the Wailaki, Cahto, Shelter Cove Sinkyone and Coast Yuki. This is discussed in a special section at the end of this chapter.

Yuki coiled basketry also shows superficial similarities to Maidu coiled basketry. At first glance coiled Yuki basketry looks much like Sierra Maidu basketry (but not the sedge root weft basketry of the Valley Maidu). The designs on some Yuki baskets were shared with the Maidu and the use of redbud was somewhat similar. In fact, Yuki baskets are frequently mislabeled as Maidu baskets in museum collections and art galleries (Winther 2000, 59-60).

However, closer inspection reveals major construction differences between Yuki and Maidu coiling. As viewed from the weaver's perspective, the Yuki predominantly coiled to the right; the Maidu coiled only to the left. The Yuki often had either a red band on the rim or brought designs up to include the final coil at the rim. In contrast, the Maidu left the top coil undecorated on nearly all their baskets, except for occasionally using a short section of rim ticks at the coil ending. The Yuki frequently used designs on the bottoms of their baskets or had a decorative band a single coil wide at the basket's base; the Maidu rarely did either. The Yuki most commonly coiled on a splint and rod foundation; the Maidu coiled primarily on a three-rod foundation. Thus, these and other features differentiate the coiled baskets of the two cultures.

Yuki Twined Basketry

Yuki twined basketry consisted of close twined and openwork. Both plain twining and three-strand twining was done. Starting knots were the crossed warp type. The slant of weft twist was up-to-the-right. Rim selvages were handled in two ways. On some twined baskets, the warp ends were bound down at the rim and woven in with the wefts. On other twined baskets warps were trimmed at the rim. Often these warp ends were allowed to protrude above the uppermost weft row (Kelly 1930, plate 126; Elsasser 1978, 628, 633).

Yuki twined basketry was very minimally decorated. When decoration was used at all, it consisted of simple bands. **Yuki close twined baskets** consisted of a plain twined **burden basket**, a plain twined **mortar hopper** and perhaps other types of baskets that have not been preserved. Three-strand twining was used for reinforcing. Reinforcing rods

The Yuki made large coiled storage baskets. These storage baskets typically ranged from about sixteen to twenty inches in diameter. Most large Native California storage baskets were twined, but the Yuki once again show their unique and fascinating approach to basketry with their big coiled storage baskets. (Center basket from a private collection. All others from Kelly 1930, courtesy of the Phoebe Apperson Hearst Museum of Anthropology and Regents of the University of California, #1-11962, #1-11963, 1-12002, #1-11982)

Seedbeaters were baskets used to collect small seeds in conjunction with a gathering basket. By gently hitting plants such as tarweed or sage with a seedbeater, tiny seeds could be efficiently gathered in close twined burden baskets. Note how this twined seedbeater's handle is attached to the radiating warp spokes of the bowl. Maggie Pike made this plain twined seedbeater. L: 18.5", D: 7" (Phoebe Apperson Hearst Museum of Anthropology and Regents of the University of California, #1-12016)

were attached to mortar hoppers and close twined burden baskets.

Openwork baskets include **seedbeaters, burden baskets, trays, cradles** and **coarse bowls** and **sifters** (Kelly 1930, 438 and plates 125-127). A variety of **plate-shaped openwork baskets** were made for various culinary uses. Miller illustrates a Yuki woman using a mortar hopper and a deep openwork tray, probably for holding shelled acorns (Miller 1979, fig. 7). Yuki **openwork burden baskets** had rounded bottoms, as did bowls (Dawson p.c.). The openwork tray was coarsely made and had a slightly raised edge (Kelly 1930, plates 126h and 127c). Yuki cradles were sitting **cradles** like those of the Ukiah Pomo (Kroeber 1932, 371). Yuki openwork twined baskets often have either trimmed or bound-down warp selvages. Kelly describes Yuki twined basketry rim finishes in detail (Kelly 1930, 442).

Twining materials for warps included willow, hazel, dogwood and redbud. For wefts, the materials used were willow, hazel, pine root, dogwood and redbud. Wild grape was used to wrap reinforcing rods on the rims on mortar hoppers and possibly on burden basket rims as well. Some of these materials were restricted to either openwork or close-twined baskets. For example, willow and hazel were primarily openwork weft materials.

Designs were minimal or absent on most Yuki twined baskets. It was generally nonexistent or limited to narrow horizontal bands. Kelly found some Yuki twined basket decorations that consisted of one or two rows of brown weft on the basket's side or near the bottom (Kelly 1930, 438-442). Evidence of an unpeeled redbud design was reported on one mortar hopper (Winther 2000, 69). Openwork twined baskets were occasionally made entirely of redbud.

Yuki Burden Baskets

There has been some question whether surviving burden baskets purported to be Yuki are actually Yuki made or trade pieces (Dawson pc.). Kelly (1930, plate 125h) illustrated a highly decorated, close-twined burden basket. This basket's designs were numerous narrow bands, similar to the concentric bands sometimes favored by the Wailaki and Lassik. A second photo shows a group of baskets labeled Yuki (Miller 1979, fig. 6). Unfortunately, some of the baskets in this photo are clearly not Yuki. One of the baskets in this illustration, which may actually be Yuki, is a close twined conical burden basket. This burden basket has six bands of broader zigzag designs. While we cannot rule out the possibility that these burden baskets are Wailaki or Lassik, one or both may be Yuki. Both baskets are consistent with the Yuki use of narrow band designs.

Baskets Used in Ferrying People and Supplies

During winter in Yuki country, heavy rains cause creeks to run high. The Yuki utilized baskets to cross these treacherous streams. Children and any women who were poor swimmers were ferried across the streams by the men using large carrying baskets (Kroeber 1925, 174). The huge coiled baskets were probably also used for storage, as they would seem ideal for this purpose.

Sometimes baskets were partially filled with ashes so that wood coals could be safely placed inside them. In this way, fires could be transported across streams to warm everyone after the ordeal of a cold winter crossing (Kroeber 1925, 174).

Yuki mortar hoppers were plain twined, functional baskets made of conifer root wefts. They were strong, well-engineered baskets that saw hard use. The oak reinforcing rod is visible at the top where the rim wrapping of wild grape has broken away. A second reinforcing rod is near the bottom where Native repair work can be seen. Mortar hoppers were either a Yuki or Pomo invention, that spread over most of California and in to western Oregon. A Yuki man made this basket. All mortar hoppers were bottomless to allow a pestle to pass through to the stone mortar. D: 20", H: 8" (Phoebe Apperson Hearst Museum of Anthropology and Regents of the University of California, #1-11968)

Yuki Mortar Hoppers

Five Yuki mortar hoppers have survived with enough documentation to allow detailed study. Lawrence Dawson analyzed four mortar hoppers that were clearly Yuki and not trade pieces. They were Hearst Museum basket numbers: 1-11892, 1-11968, 1-11886 and 1-11896. He also included a fifth mortar hopper (Hearst 1-732) that was collected from the Hull's Valley Wailaki, but which was completely unlike all other Wailaki mortar hoppers. Instead, this basket was like Yuki mortar hoppers and was almost certainly a Yuki made basket traded to the Wailaki. Hull's Valley is located just north of Round Valley, the heart of Yuki country.

Yuki mortar hoppers are predominantly plain twined with an up-to-the-right slant of twist. Wefts are of conifer root and warps are of dogwood. Warp ends are trimmed flush. Yuki mortar hoppers are broad and flaring with a reinforcing rod of willow attached to the rim. Another reinforcing rod was attached lower on the basket's side using lattice twining. It was located on the exterior about two inches above the hole in the basket's bottom. Two rows of three-strand twining were typically used just above this lower rod.

Yuki mortar hoppers had three-strand twining in four positions on each basket: (1) directly adjacent to the bottom, (2) above the lower hoop, (3) in the middle height of the side,

and (4) at or near the top edge. Weft fag ends were caught under one twist of twining; warp ends projected into the interior. A row of coiling was used at the bottom of at least one mortar hopper to repair and strengthen it. Dawson and Shanks found no designs on these mortar hoppers, but evidence of an unpeeled redbud design was reported on one mortar hopper (Winther 2000, 69).

Yuki mortar hoppers were technically intermediate between Pomo and Wailaki mortar hoppers, a fact consistent with Yuki territory being located between these two cultures. Pomo-type features included the mortar hopper's shape, the type of weft splices, the general neatness and the rim sewing. The use of some diagonal twining also occurs on at least one basket (Hearst 1-732), the Hull's Valley mortar hopper.

Shared Yuki, Pomo and Wailaki mortar hopper traits included a reinforcing rod at the rim, warp ends trimmed fairly flush at the rim and three-strand twining used adjacent to the basket's bottom.

Wailaki characteristics found on the Yuki mortar hoppers included a lower hoop with lattice twining about two inches above the bottom hole, two courses of three-strand twining above this lower hoop, an up-to-the-right slant of weft twist, warp butts projecting on the interior face and the positioning of the various three-strand twining courses.

Thus, Yuki mortar hoppers are very closely related to those of the Wailaki and Pomo, although in different ways. In fact, mortar hoppers of the Yuki, the Pomo, the Wailaki and other Southern Humboldt Athapaskans, the Northwestern Californians, the Patwin and the Wappo all probably share a common ancestry. Each culture's mortar hoppers evolved into culturally distinctive types over the centuries, but their shared low, broad form and overall structural concepts remained quite similar. The shared features probably resulted from a common origin. That origin was likely either Yuki or Pomo.

Yuki Seedbeaters

Yuki seedbeaters were round with an attached handle of sturdy warp sticks. Both warps and wefts were typically made of willow. These seedbeaters were roughly made, but strong (Kelly 1930, plate 126, d, f). Similar seedbeaters were used from northern Mendocino County to just above the Oregon state line.

The Yuki probably invented this type of seedbeater. The Yuki were probably the first inhabitants of the Redwood Coast, and their style of seedbeater came to be used by people speaking several different languages. Immediately to the north of the Yuki, the Wailaki, Lassik and Nongatl made Yuki-style seedbeaters. The very northern-most Pomo wove Yuki-style seedbeaters, although the rest of the Pomo made wickerwork seedbeaters. The seedbeaters of Northwestern Californian peoples, such as the Yurok, Hupa and others, were also closely related to the Yuki. The Northwestern California seedbeater was more finely made than were those of the Yuki, but the structural concepts were much the same.

It is not surprising to find Yuki connections to the seedbeaters of all the Redwood Coast tribes. Yukians were almost certainly displaced over the centuries by these very peoples (Moratto 1984, 550-568). It is probable that the Northwestern California seedbeater, a classic Central Californian type basket, was originally developed by the Yuki. It was adopted by later arriving tribes who realized its value in seed collecting. The seedbeater did not come from the north, for it is almost completely absent in Oregon.

Leaching Baskets

The Yuki made openwork baskets for leaching poisonous and bitter aesculin, an alkaloid, from buckeye seeds (*Aesculus californica*). Buckeye seeds are highly toxic and require mashing and a long leaching process involving repeatedly gently pouring hot water through them before they are safe to eat (Heizer and Elsasser 1980, 100).

Yuki Cradles

Yuki cradles were said to have resembled Pomo cradles (Kroeber 1937, 371; Foster 1944, 171). This may indicate yet another significant Yuki-Pomo connection in the development of Mendocino County basketry.

Comments

The Yuki are an ancient and influential North Coast Range people. This coiled basketry was different in many aspects from that of other North Central California cultures. Yuki coiled basketry probably did not come from the Maidu-Patwin-Pomo coiling predominant in the region. Yuki coiling may be distantly related to Yokuts-Southwestern California coiled basketry, or it could be a local innovation.

Yuki coiling was at least in part a distinctively Yuki invention. No one made coiled basketry like the Yuki, except the Wailaki and Cahto and both these people are thought to be of Yukian ancestry (see sidebar at the end of this chapter). The Coast Yuki and Shelter Cove Sinkyone also made a few coiled baskets that seem derived from Yuki coiling.

On the other hand, Yuki twined basketry, while largely simple and plain, could have been the prototypes for seedbeaters, mortar hoppers and perhaps other major types of baskets adopted by peoples over a wide range of territory. Yuki art reached its highest development in coiled basketry, but Yuki influence probably spread farthest in twined basketry.

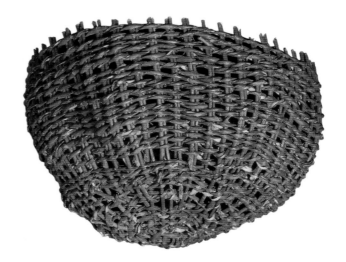

Most Yuki twined basketry was utilitarian and usually undecorated. This rough, plain twined openwork bowl, however, uses unpeeled shoots to give it a festive color. Note that the warp sticks protrude above the rim in a manner similar to the Pomo technique. (Phoebe Apperson Hearst Museum of Anthropology and Regents of the University of California, #1-11901)

Yuki Coiled Basketry's Influence on Their Neighbors

Yuki-type coiled basketry was made by several neighboring cultures. Although none were exactly like that of the Yuki, they were in some cases closely related. Each had an interesting history and had some distinctive characteristics. Only their relationship to Yuki basketry is discussed here. Most of these neighboring cultures' basketry will be discussed in detail in Volume III on northern California and western Oregon basketry.

CAHTO AND WAILAKI COILED BASKETRY

Yuki coiling definitely influenced Wailaki coiled basketry and may have influenced Cahto coiled basketry. Unfortunately, surviving examples of Wailaki and Cahto coiled baskets are extremely rare and documentation often poor, especially for the Cahto.

Wailaki Coiled Basketry

The few documented coiled Wailaki baskets show definite Yuki influence, such as rightward work direction. Wailaki coiling was only done sporadically and was apparently limited to smaller, but very high quality, fancy baskets. Wailaki coiling was said to average better quality than most Yuki baskets. If the tiny surviving sample is any indication, Wailaki designs were finer and more intricate than those of the Yuki. Yet the Wailaki were primarily a twining people and coiling was both uncommon and limited. All or nearly all Wailaki baskets used in daily life were twined (Kroeber 1925, 153, 169).

Cahto Coiled Basketry

Some Cahto baskets also are Yuki-like, but it must be noted that these baskets may actually be trade pieces from the Yuki (Dawson pc.). Baskets said to be Cahto and having Yuki traits are more roughly made and usually smaller than most Yuki coiled baskets.

There are also three baskets said to be Cahto that are not Yuki-like at all. These baskets are in the Southwest Museum of the American Indian collection and are labeled variously "Kato," "Cahto Pomo," and "Pomo Cahto." The terms "Kato" and "Cahto Pomo" are both early synonyms for the Cahto. The baskets all have three-rod foundations, sedge root wefts, redbud designs and leftward work direction. These are all Pomo coiling characteristics, but all three baskets vary from typical Pomo work in shape, roughness of workmanship and in some designs. They could be Cahto baskets. If so, they indicate Pomo rather than Yuki traits in Cahto coiled basketry.

Wailaki and Cahto Linguistic Heritage

Interestingly, both linguists and archeologists have suggested that the Cahto and Wailaki were originally Yukian speakers who adopted the Athapaskan language after Athapaskan speaking people entered Yukian territory in relatively recent times, perhaps even as late as 700 years ago. When the Athapaskan language arrived in Yuki country, it apparently became a prestigious and dominant language among ancestral Wailaki and Cahto. As a result, many scholars believe that these two groups gradually changed from Yukian to Athapaskan speakers (Foster 1996, 84 Moratto 1984, 495, 541).

Although they were Athapaskan in language, the Cahto and Wailaki were clearly Yukian in physical type (Gifford 1926a). The Yuki were said to be the shortest Indian group in the United States, averaging barely five feet in height and Yuki skeletal type is readily identifiable (Heizer and Elsasser 1980, 7). Skeletal remains show that the Cahto and Wailaki were physically Yuki. Even after the language switch occurred, some of their material culture retained Yuki features. Coiled basketry was one of these surviving features, at least among the Wailaki.

The Extent of Yuki Coiled Basketry Influence

Among the small tribes surrounding the Yuki, it is only certain the Wailaki made baskets resembling those of the Yuki. The Cahto may have also done so. On key technical features, such as work direction or foundation type, the coiled baskets of other small neighboring groups such as the Coast Yuki, Shelter Cove Sinkyone and Salt Pomo differed from the Yuki. Nomlaki basketry, with exception of a questionable basket or two that were likely trade items, was very different from Yuki basketry and more like that of the Patwin.

This leaves only the Wailaki and possibly the Cahto as doing coiling similar to Yuki coiled basketry. Virtually all Yuki-type baskets in museum collections were made by Yuki weavers and in most cases can be differentiated from Wailaki and Cahto baskets. The few surviving Wailaki baskets are smaller and more finely made than is typical of Yuki baskets. The few possible Cahto baskets that are Yuki-like in their technique are smaller and rougher than typical Yuki baskets. Other possible Cahto baskets are actually like Huchnom and Pomo baskets and are very different from Yuki work.

In short, the Yuki clearly influenced the Wailaki and may have influenced the Cahto. The possible existence of both Yuki-style and Pomo-style coiled basketry among the Cahto would suggest a culture in transition. In any case, both Wailaki and Cahto coiling were of limited importance and all, or nearly all, utilitarian baskets were twined.

COAST YUKI AND SHELTER COVE SINKYONE COILED BASKETRY

The Coast Yuki were a separate tribe closely related to the main body of Yuki. Their territory centered around Westport on the Mendocino Coast. Kroeber stated that no Coast Yuki baskets have survived (Kroeber 1925, 214), and we have been unable to locate any in our research. Some Coast Yuki elders' recollections, however, were recorded. Driver (1939, 333-335) lists the Coast Yuki as having the following types of baskets: a coiled mush boiler, a coiled storage basket which was covered with a basket bowl or tray to keep rodents out, a seed parching basket, a mortar hopper, a seedbeater, a small coiled globular basket, a fish scoop, a cradle with pendants hung from the top and a child's toy basket with a stone inside. As with the Yuki proper, both coiled and twined work was made. Yuki influence was clear in coiled cooking pots and storage baskets.

Importantly, however, the Coast Yuki denied using splint and rod foundations in their coiled work, which was the most common Yuki foundation type for coiled work. Instead, the Coast Yuki reported using a single rod foundation.

The Shelter Cove (Usal) Sinkyone stated that, like the Coast Yuki, they too only coiled using a single-rod foundation (Driver 1939, 333; also see Kroeber 1925, 214). Both the Sinkyone and Coast Yuki were on the very fringe of where coiled basketry was made. The use of only single-rod foundations points toward a recent and limited adoption of coiling by both the Coast Yuki and Sinkyone.

SALT POMO COILED BASKETRY

The Salt Pomo (Northeastern Pomo) were a small group separated from all other Pomoan people. The Salt Pomo lived around Stonyford in northwestern Colusa County and were surrounded by the Yuki, Patwin and Nomlaki. After European arrival, the Salt Pomo suffered a tragic population decline. By the time anthropologists began attempting to collect Salt Pomo baskets, sadly few Salt Pomo remained alive.

Yuki people from a place called Gravelly and perhaps Round Valley were known to have settled among the Salt Pomo after the arrival of Euro-Americans, perhaps as early as the 1870s (Kroeber 1932, 364). Surviving Salt Pomo had also intermarried with the Patwin and Nomlaki who lived around Stonyford in northwestern

Colusa County (Bean and Theodoratus 1978, 304; Bibby 2005 p.c.). What Salt Pomo basketry was originally like remains uncertain, but some things are known.

There are both Yuki-style and Patwin-style coiled baskets collected from the Salt Pomo circa 1900 in the C. Hart Merriam collection at the University of California at Davis. At least one of these baskets collected among the Salt Pomo was documented as Yuki (Winther 2000, 59). This and other Yuki-style baskets collected from the Salt Pomo at Stonyford were almost certainly of Yuki, not Salt Pomo, origin (Dawson pc.). Barrett concurred, noting that Yuki-style baskets among the Salt Pomo were undoubtedly due to the late association of the Salt Pomo with the Yuki (Barrett 1996, 158).

Although collected among the few surviving Salt Pomo, these baskets show every indication of being made by Yuki weavers. Yuki type baskets came in when Yuki people began arriving among the Salt Pomo in the 1870s. Salt Pomo, Patwin and Nomlaki baskets were woven in a leftward work direction, not rightward as the Yuki usually wove (Dawson pc.).

The other coiled baskets C. Hart Merriam collected from the Salt Pomo were probably made by the Nomlaki or Patwin. These baskets, done in a leftward work direction, were collected from people Merriam called the "Nomenkla." Nomenkla (from "Nomen," plus the suffix "kla" or "tla," meaning community) was a Paskenta Nomlaki term for the people of Grindstone Rancheria in southern Nomlaki territory (Brian Bibby p.c., 2005). A study of Merriam's field notes indicates that he also may have used the term Nomenkla to refer to Salt Pomo around Stonyford (Lisa Deitz p.c., 2004). These field notes do indicate that Merriam went to Grindstone Rancheria and Stonyford and that there were surviving Salt Pomo people at both locations. Merriam, however, lists the Nomenkla as being a part of the Wintun language group, which would make them Nomlaki or Patwin. While Merriam purchased coiled baskets from Salt Pomo people, there is the likelihood that they were made by weavers from other tribes. By 1900, Salt Pomo culture was so shattered that obtaining baskets from other cultures could have been a necessity.

The Salt Pomo were known to have made a parching tray, wickerwork seedbeater and a mortar hopper with lattice twined reinforcing rods (Dawson pc.). These tiny bits of information suggest Pomo, not Yuki affinities. Salt Pomo coiled basketry is poorly known, but it was almost certainly not Yuki-style.

This is the earliest known Huchnom basket. This coiled basket was collected in 1871-72 by the author Stephen Powers in the heart of Huchnom country on the South Fork of the Eel River in Mendocino County. Few Huchnom baskets survive today. D: 7", H: 4" (Smithsonian Institution, #E021371)

A fine old Huchnom coiled bowl made of redbud and sedge root. Note how the sedge has darkened with age. Sedge is one of the few materials that provides some indication of its age by its darkened color. (Southwest Museum of the American Indian, Autry National Center, #811-G-1412)

Huchnom Basketry

The Huchnom lived in a mountainous section of interior Mendocino County centering along the South Fork of the Eel River. The territory of this small group Yukian speaking people was northeast of Willits, along the Eel River upstream from Outlet Creek almost to Dos Rios. Huchnom culture was a mixture of Yuki and Pomo traits (Kroeber 1925, 203; Miller 1978, 255). In early anthropological literature the Huchnom were sometimes called the "Huchnom Yuki."

Tragically, the Huchnom people suffered horribly during the period of European-American settlement. As a result, only a tiny number of surviving documented Huchnom baskets exist. They show fine artistic taste, but give us only a glimpse into the art of a brutally destroyed culture.

Huchnom Coiled Baskets: Few Known Survivors

Our firsthand knowledge of Huchnom coiling comes from a tiny number of documented baskets. At least two baskets were collected directly from the Huchnom. These are Smithsonian Institution basket (#21371) and Phoebe Hearst Museum of Anthropology baskets (#1-12057). Two other coiled Huchnom baskets were acquired from respected Pasadena, California, basketry dealer Grace Nicholson in the early part of the last century. How she obtained them is unknown, but she regularly visited Indian communities. One of these baskets is in the Field Museum in Chicago (#103174) and the other at Harvard's Peabody Museum in Cambridge, Massachusetts (#05-7-10/64494). Finally, the Southwest Museum/Autry National Center in Los Angeles has two Huchnom baskets (#811-G-1410 and #811-G-1411). Who collected them is uncertain, but the Southwest Museum is just a few miles from where Grace Nicholson had her home and gallery.

Our knowledge of Huchnom basketry is not limited to these few baskets. As will be discussed, we also have valuable basketry information provided by a Huchnom elder.

A coiled Huchnom cooking pot from the Eel River, Mendocino County.
D: 13.5", H: 5" (The Field Museum, #103174—Photo by Brian Bibby)

Huchnom Coiled Basketry:
Materials and Designs

The work direction of Huchnom coiling was to the leftward. The rims were plainly wrapped (self rims) with no over-stitching. Sedge root, redbud and black dyed bulrush root were used in coiled basketry for weft materials. Warp materials were probably willow and perhaps redbud.

The Huchnom basket at the Smithsonian has black designs covering much of its sides and is decorated with small white beads and remnants of feathers. The coiling foundation consists of one or two rods combined with a thin splint (Mason 1902, 459-460). Stitches are split on the interior (back face) of the basket. The final coil at the rim appeared to be finished with a three-rod foundation (Felicia Pickering p.c.). The journalist Stephen Powers collected this basket in the 1870s from Huchnom people on the South Fork of the Eel River. The Smithsonian Institution acquired it in 1876. This is the earliest known Huchnom coiled basket.

The coiled Huchnom basket at the Phoebe Hearst Museum lacks beads, but has ample designs done in redbud on the sides and bottom. It has a three-rod foundation. Anthropologist Samuel Barrett collected it at Round Valley in 1907. The other Huchnom coiled baskets also have three-rod foundations.

The Smithsonian basket has sedge root wefts for the background weft with black designs done using bulrush root wefts. The Hearst Museum basket has sedge root for the background and redbud designs. Designs on both baskets are carried up to include the rim coil. Both baskets have designs of split parallelograms arranged diagonally. The designs cover most of the baskets' sides. These two baskets are fairly small bowls. The Huchnom basket at Harvard's Peabody Museum has blocky diamond-shaped designs (Fang and Binder 1990, 187, bottom left illustration). The Field Museum basket has fancy upward pointing black triangles with a sedge root background. Both baskets are flaring bowls.

Both Huchnom baskets at the Southwest Museum are woven on three-rod foundations with redbud designs on a sedge root background. One is a seventeen-inch diameter cooking pot with flaring sides and the other a bowl.

The Huchnom baskets at the Field Museum and Southwest Museum leave the top coil undecorated. The designs on the other baskets include the top coil. The Huchnom favored designs of triangles, diamonds and split parallelograms arranged diagonally or in V-patterns on their coiled baskets.

A small Huchnom coiled bowl with a three-rod foundation, redbud designs, sedge root background and leftward work direction. The weft fag ends are clipped. Made by Louise Hudson, circa 1907, in Mendocino County. (Phoebe Apperson Hearst Museum of Anthropology and Regents of the University of California, #1-12057)

"HUCHNOM YUKI" BASKETRY: AN ELDER SPEAKS

There is an additional source of information on Huchnom basketry. Anthropologist Frank Essene interviewed Eben Tillotson, then age 72. Mr. Tillotson had a white father and a Huchnom mother. Both Mr. Tillotson and his mother were born on Salt Creek about three miles south of Dos Rios on the South Fork of the Eel River. This was in the northern part of Huchnom country.

Essene calls the Tillotsons "Huchnom Yuki." This was a term sometimes used for the Huchnom by early anthropologists because the Huchnom spoke a Yukian language. Although listing Eben Tillotson's information as Yuki, Essene makes it clear that Tillotson was in fact Huchnom (Essene 1942, 2).

Mr. Tillotson's basketry information clearly refers to his Huchnom family heritage, rather than to the Yuki. Essene lists this information as Yuki because he considered the Huchnom a linguistic branch of the Yuki rather than a separate tribe. Culturally, however, the Huchnom were a distinct people and had much in common with the Pomo. It is clear from Mr. Tillotson's basketry descriptions that he is referring to Huchnom rather than Yuki basketry.

Types of Huchnom Coiled Baskets

Huchnom coiled baskets included cooking pots, winnowing trays, globular or flaring bowls and storage baskets (Essene 1942, 21). The surviving coiled Huchnom baskets are all bowls or cooking pots. One is low and globular, another with gently curving sides and the others flaring. Southwest Museum cooking pot (#811-G-1411) is the largest.

Eben Tillotson reported that Huchnom coiling was done in a leftward work direction (Essene 1942, 51). This is consistent with all six surviving documented Huchnom coiled baskets. A leftward work direction was the same as the Pomo work direction. It was the opposite of the usual Yuki work direction. About 85% of all Yuki coiled baskets had a rightward work direction. The Huchnom definitely coiled in a leftward work direction. But as will be discussed later, they may also have coiled in a rightward work direction as well.

While work direction and materials were Pomoan, making coiled cooking baskets, storage baskets and winnowing trays were Yuki concepts. The Pomo used twining for their cooking baskets, storage baskets and winnowing trays. The Huchnom had adopted Pomo materials, some technical features and work direction, but they still retained important Yuki type coiled basket types.

Mr. Tillotson reported that the Huchnom used single-rod and three-rod foundations. The Pomo also regularly made both single-rod and three-rod foundations. An extensive study by Isabel Kelly reported no Yuki single-rod baskets (Kelly 1930, 424).

The Huchnom also used rods in combination with splints for their coiling foundations, and this is a Yuki trait. Thus,

some Yuki coiling influence remained among Huchnom weavers. Huchnom wefts on the Hearst Museum basket are wider than those typical of the Pomo. Wide wefts are another Yuki trait. The Huchnom used both wide and narrow wefts. Huchnom coiled baskets are neither purely Pomo nor purely Yuki, but were a blend of traits from both cultures.

A POSSIBLE HUCHNOM COILED BASKET

An unusual coiled basket in the Oakland Museum of California (#H.16.1934; illustrated in Winther 2000, 61, fig. 6) is from Round Valley where some surviving Huchnom lived. While it has been attributed to the Yuki, it may be Huchnom. This basket uses sedge root wefts and white trade beads, both of which are known Huchnom characteristics. The Yuki used peeled redbud wefts rather than sedge root wefts. Yuki baskets decorated with beads are almost nonexistent (Winther 2000, 61). We have seen only one, and it had fairly late commercial beads attached with thick commercial yarn. It did not look at all like the Oakland Museum basket. The unique combination of materials, style and work direction of the Oakland Museum basket does not indicate either Yuki or Pomo coiling.

The characteristics of the Oakland Museum basket, however, suggest possible Huchnom origin. But the work direction on the Oakland Museum basket is rightward. Both

Many a meal of acorn mush was prepared in this very old Huchnom cooking pot. This coiled flaring bowl has a three-rod foundation with redbud designs on a background of sedge root. Note the white bloom that naturally and harmlessly sometimes forms on old redbud. D: 17", H: 7" (Southwest Museum of the American Indian, Autry National Center, #811-G-1411)

A Huchnom mortar hopper woven with redbud designs on a background of sedge root. This predominantly lattice twined basket is similar, but not identical, to Pomo mortar hoppers. Made by Louise Hudson and purchased in 1907 in Mendocino County. D: 18", H: 5" (Phoebe Apperson Hearst Museum of Anthropology and the Regents of the University of California, #1-12056)

documented baskets and the tribal elder's statement indicate a leftward Huchnom work direction.

Could the Huchnom, like the Yuki, have coiled in both directions? Essene lists only a single Huchnom work direction, but then he footnotes this in a manner that indicates two work directions were used (Essene 1942, 20, 60, fn. 807). Two Huchnom coiling directions would not be surprising. Most cultures coiled in only one direction, but the Yuki coiled in both rightward and leftward work directions. The Huchnom were a people whose basketry was in transition from Yuki-like coiling to Pomo-like coiling. It would not be surprising if the Oakland Museum basket were Huchnom.

Huchnom Twined Baskets

A number of kinds of twined Huchnom baskets are reported. Twined Huchnom baskets included carrying baskets, conical close twined burden baskets, conical openwork gathering baskets, mortar hoppers, seedbeaters, cradles, fish scoops and fish carriers made of hazel wood. Men made some twined openwork baskets, including some cradles. Openwork storage baskets were probably made, too. Basketry caps were not made (Essene 1942, 6-14, 22-21, 50-51).

Anthropologist Essene doubted Mr. Tillotson's statement that no twined storage baskets were made and questioned

him about it. Mr. Tillotson said he could be mistaken and that twined storage baskets may also have been made (Essene 1942, 60). The confusion may have resulted from Essene thinking of openwork storage baskets while his consultant was thinking of close twined ones. Instead of close twined storage baskets, the Huchnom made coiled storage baskets and Mr. Tillotson may have been remembering these baskets, hence a negative reply about twined storage baskets.

Mr. Tillotson's descriptions of twined basketry contain too many differences from Yuki twining for him to have been describing that culture's twined work. It was his family's Huchnom twining heritage that he was discussing. It is clear that, as with coiling, Huchnom twined basketry was a mixture of Pomoan and Yuki type basketry ideas.

Two Rare Twined Huchnom Baskets

Two rare documented twined Huchnom baskets were found at the Phoebe Hearst Museum of Anthropology. One basket (#1-12056) is a mortar hopper. It is very much like a Pomo mortar hopper in shape, technique, design layout and materials. It even has the Pomo "dau," a break in the design. This Huchnom mortar hopper uses a sedge root weft and featured horizontal redbud designs.

The Huchnom mortar hopper was plain twined with rows of lattice twining reinforcing on the basket's side. The slant of weft twist was up-to-the-left. This is opposite the slant of twist on Yuki mortars, but the same as on Pomo mortar hoppers. This Huchnom mortar hopper was much more like Pomo mortar hoppers than those of the Yuki. Lattice twined reinforcing on mortar hopper sides was a Pomo, not a Yuki, practice. The use of bands of redbud designs is also Pomoan. Yuki mortar hoppers were usually undecorated.

The reinforcing rod at the rim was, however, attached to the Huchnom mortar hopper in a different manner than was typical of the Pomo. Beyond wrapping the reinforcing rod as the Pomo usually did, this Huchnom basket deviated by having groups of about four large, long stitches at several places around the rim. These long weft stitches run side by side from the rim rod down a number of weft rows on the side. They neatly strengthen the rim's attachment of the reinforcing rod.

The second twined Huchnom basket in the Hearst Museum (#1-12058) was a small, conical, openwork gathering basket. Its warps were sometimes bunched in twos or even threes. They are bent over at the top of the basket to form a reinforcing rim. The basket is plain twined and undecorated. It had up-to-the-right slant of weft twist. This means that, like a few other tribes, the Huchnom used both leftward and rightward weft slants. This was also probably because their basketry was in a transition period from Yukian to Pomoan style.

Comments

While Huchnom culture in general was becoming more Pomoan than Yukian, it was still a mixture of the two traditions (Kroeber 1925, 203). Huchnom coiled basketry reflected this mingling of Yuki and Pomo traditions. Some old Yukian forms and coiling traditions were being retained, while other Pomo coiling techniques and materials had begun being adopted. A similar process of becoming more Pomo-like also was occurring in Huchnom twined basketry.

This transition was not surprising since the basketry of two other cultures neighboring the Pomo, the Lake Miwok and Wappo, had already become almost totally Pomoan. The Huchnom were not as far along with their Pomo acculturation, but the process had begun.

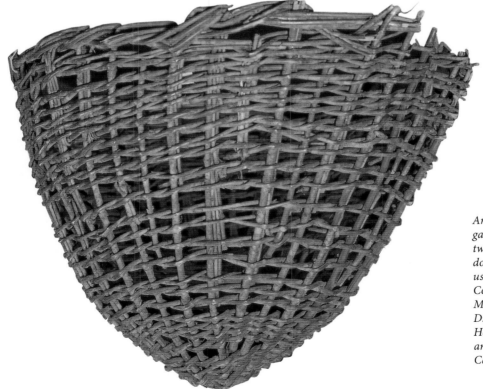

An openwork Huchnom twined gathering basket woven in plain twining. Note that sometimes double and triple warps were used, probably for added strength. Collected at Round Valley, Mendocino County, in 1907. D: 11", H: 9" (Phoebe Apperson Hearst Museum of Anthropology and Regents of the University of California, #1-12058)

Amid the rugged hills of eastern Lake and Napa Counties, the Lake Miwok weavers added their lovely baskets to the scenery. This is a Lake Miwok feathered basket with scattered red woodpecker feathers, black valley quail topknot feathers and a few blue feathers, perhaps bluebird. The weft designs are in bulrush root, with a sedge root background on a three-rod coiled foundation. This basket was a gift in 1906 to C. Hart Merriam from a Lake Miwok weaver living in Coyote Valley, northeast of Middletown, Lake County. D: 6.5", H: 2.5" (C. Hart Merriam collection, University of California at Davis, #253-254)

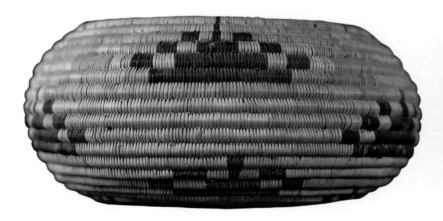

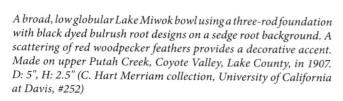

A broad, low globular Lake Miwok bowl using a three-rod foundation with black dyed bulrush root designs on a sedge root background. A scattering of red woodpecker feathers provides a decorative accent. Made on upper Putah Creek, Coyote Valley, Lake County, in 1907. D: 5", H: 2.5" (C. Hart Merriam collection, University of California at Davis, #252)

A distinctive Lake Miwok coiled basketry feature was to use a herringbone back-stitch at the coil ending. Note the contrast between the herringbone stitching and the plain wrapped rim of the rest of the coil. (C. Hart Merriam Collection, University of California at Davis, #252)

LAKE MIWOK BASKETRY

The Lake Miwok are isolated from other Miwok speakers by their Pomo, Patwin and Wappo neighbors. Their territory is in southern Lake County and northeastern Napa County. It extends from near the present day Lake County towns of Lower Lake and Middletown to Snell Valley and Pope Valley in Napa County. This rolling country is beautiful with small creeks and valleys enclosed by steep hills. Lake Miwok land is rich in oak, manzanita, pine and other native food plants.

Sometime in the past, ancestral Miwok populations began spreading out from the Sacramento-San Joaquin River Delta region. The Lake Miwok had apparently entered southern Lake and northeastern Napa Counties, displacing Pomo and Wappo inhabitants. Prior to this period, the Coast Miwok had spread west into Marin and southern Sonoma Counties. Miwok borrowing of certain local plant and shellfish names implies prior occupancy of the region by the Pomo and Wappo (Moratto 1984, 555; Foster 1996, 89).

The Lake Miwok and Coast Miwok languages were closely related and they almost certainly shared a common ancestry (Callaghan 1984, 264). But the Patwin expansion in the Sacramento Valley separated both the Lake Miwok and Coast Miwok from Sierra Miwok and Plains Miwok (Whistler 1977, 163; Foster 1996, 90). To the west, the Wappo entered the Napa Valley and almost simultaneously separated the Lake Miwok and Coast Miwok from each other (Bennyhoff p.c.; Whistler 1977, 171). As a result of these population movements, the Lake Miwok and Coast Miwok emerged as two distinct cultures.

Over the following centuries, the Lake Miwok, numbering perhaps 500 people, became strongly influenced by the Pomo (Kroeber 1925, 272-275). Only a few documented Lake Miwok baskets remain and our knowledge of their basketry is limited. But what has survived points more to Pomo than Sierra Miwok influence. Perhaps as the Lake Miwok people spread into Pomo Country, intermarriage with Pomo women slowly revolutionized Lake Miwok basketry until it was largely Pomoan. At the very least, Lake Miwok women must have admired Pomo basketry and made it their own.

Lake Miwok Coiled Basketry

The sample of Lake Miwok basketry is small, but informative. Like the Pomo, the Lake Miwok seemed to have made most of their coiled work as fancy gift baskets.

The surviving Lake Miwok coiled gift baskets are not large baskets. All are under a foot in diameter and most less than eight and a half inches wide. Larger coiled utilitarian baskets may have been made too.

Known Lake Miwok coiled basketry forms were either flaring or globular. Designs on all the coiled Lake Miwok baskets examined were in bulrush root (*Scirpus*) dyed black by being buried in mud. These black designs included split parallelograms or triangles, some with modified quail plume designs. These designs were arranged as diagonals or zigzags. Sometimes small filler designs were used to complete the overall pattern on the baskets. Isolated floating designs were also occasionally used. Designs were used on the rims and bottoms of some baskets. The rim was undecorated on some coiled baskets.

On feathered baskets, scattered red woodpecker feathers and quail plumes were most frequently used. Clamshell disc beads and/or abalone shell pendants were sometimes added for decoration (Gifford and Kroeber 1937, 132; Callaghan 1978, 267, fig. 4). While scattered placement of red woodpecker feathers and quail plumes were seen on the majority of Lake Miwok feather baskets, fully feathered baskets were made at least in later years. Feather baskets were stored with dried bay leaves (*Umbellularia californica*) to protect them from insects (Callaghan 1978, 266).

Foundation warps were predominantly of peeled willow shoots. Background weft material was sedge root on fine baskets. On all the coiled Lake Miwok baskets we studied only black bulrush root was used for designs. But the Lake Miwok reportedly used redbud for designs, too (Callaghan 1978, 266; Dawson p.c.). On any single basket, only a single color, either black or red, was used on a light buff colored background. The two design colors were never traditionally used together.

Lake Miwok Herringbone Coil Endings

Despite having only a tiny sample of Lake Miwok coiled baskets, we did find one significant distinctive feature. All of the coiled Lake Miwok baskets studied had a fine symmetrical herringbone finish at the coil ending. The Pomo, Wappo, Coast Miwok, Patwin and Valley Maidu did not use the herringbone coil ending. The herringbone coil ending was the major distinguishing characteristic of Lake Miwok coiled baskets.

Lake Miwok Coiled Basketry Technical Features

The work direction of Lake Miwok coiled baskets was to the leftward. Starting knots included the small overhand knot type used with shredded material. Lake Miwok coiled basketry stitches were a mixture of interlocking stitches with some split stitches. On single-rod baskets interlocking stitches were predominant. Split stitches were found only on the basket's back face (in this case the basket's interior). On at least one Lake Miwok basket the weft fag ends appeared as short stitches on the interior of the basket. Directly under these fag ends were the preceding strands' moving weft ends, bound under by successive stitches on the basket's back face. Generally, all Lake Miwok baskets were technically similar to Pomo baskets (Elsasser 1978, 628, 633).

A More Extensive Use of Coiled Basketry by the Lake Miwok

Both three-rod foundations and single-rod foundation were used. Lake Miwok single-rod baskets were used for meals and three-rod baskets held liquids such as acorn mush (Gifford and Kroeber 1937, 214). This statement is significant because it indicates that the Lake Miwok used coiled baskets more extensively for utilitarian purposes than the range of surviving documented baskets show us. If so, this would be an important difference between Lake Miwok and Pomo basketry since the Pomo only used twined baskets for culinary purposes.

Based on Gifford and Kroeber's statement, the Lake Miwok could have used coiled baskets for more purposes than we presently know. The mention of single-rod "baskets for meal," for example, would indicate the presence of single-rod coiled winnowing trays. For now, however, we only have definite information that the Lake Miwok used twined culinary baskets.

A Rare Lake Miwok Photograph

In October 1905, ethnologist C. Hart Merriam photographed "the wife of Chief Huyumhayumm" along Putah Creek near Middletown in Lake County. In Merriam's photo she holds a beautiful coiled basket. This picture has been previously labeled as a Coast Miwok photo. Actually, Merriam said this is a Tuleyomi picture, his term for the Lake Miwok. Consultation with scholars of Coast Miwok culture and history has confirmed that this is not a Coast Miwok photo (Sylvia Thalman p.c., 2005; Betty Goerke p.c., 2005). This is apparently a rare image of a Lake Miwok basket weaver holding her finely coiled basket. Merriam returned to Lake Miwok country the following two years and acquired

The wife of Lake Miwok Chief Huyumhayumm proudly holds her lovely coiled basket. The photo was taken along upper Putah Creek in Lake County, in October 1905. (Phoebe Apperson Hearst Museum of Anthropology and Regents of the University of California, #15-23214)

two different Lake Miwok baskets. Perhaps this very weaver made one of these baskets.

Lake Miwok Twined Basketry

The Lake Miwok were also a twining people and some twined baskets were quite beautiful. All or most utilitarian baskets were reportedly twined. The Lake Miwok wove in diagonal twining, lattice twining and probably plain twining. On fine baskets, sedge root wefts were used with warps probably of willow. For rougher twined baskets, the Lake Miwok used willow or dogwood (*Cornus*) for warps and willow for wefts.

Cooking Pots

Although both twined and coiled cooking pots may have been made, only twined cooking pots are known for certain. A basket illustrated in Callaghan (1978, 266, fig. 2) may be a cooking pot.

This Lake Miwok storage basket is woven mainly in lattice twining with plain twining near the rim. Redbud designs appear on a sedge root background. Made by Lucy Knight. D: 15", H: 8" (Phoebe Apperson Hearst Museum of Anthropology and Regents of the University of California, #1-230649)

Storage Baskets

Lattice twined globular storage baskets were made. Known designs on some storage baskets were simple bands.

Winnowers

Round, twined winnowers were woven. These were probably like those of the Pomo. No coiled winnowers were made (Gifford and Kroeber 1937, 131-132).

Burden Baskets and Gathering Baskets

Large burden baskets were made. These were almost certainly either bell-shaped or conical. Linguist Catherine Callaghan also mentioned that a certain bowl-like basket's name probably came from the Patwin word for a small burden basket. This probably indicates that small gathering baskets were made by the Lake Miwok (Callaghan 1965, 202). It is likely that two sizes of conical baskets were made; a larger size carried on the back and a smaller hand-held type.

Mortar Hoppers

Twined mortar hoppers were made. Mortar hoppers were used on flat rock slabs with mortar holes worn into them (Gifford and Kroeber 1937, 138). A good example of a Lake Miwok rock mortar slab used with a mortar hopper was found in Butts Creek, Snell Valley, in northeastern Napa County. It was a triangular-shaped, reddish flat rock 17 by 20 inches across. The center of the flat surface of the rock has a two and half inch deep mortar hole that is seven inches in diameter.

Cradles

Sitting cradles of the standard Pomo types were made. As with Pomo cradles, a horizontal rod was attached at the top for strength and ease of handling. The cradle was made

using willow warps woven with a bound-weave (Callaghan 1978, 266, fig. 3).

Seedbeaters

Seedbeaters were believed to be of wickerwork, as were most Pomo seedbeaters (Gifford and Kroeber 1937, 132).

Tule Baskets

The Lake Miwok reportedly did not make tule baskets (Gifford and Kroeber 1937, 131). If true, this is surprising since the neighboring Clear Lake Pomo probably made more tule baskets than any other North Central California tribe.

Other Lake Miwok Baskets

In Catherine A. Callaghan's *"Lake Miwok Dictionary"* she adds to our knowledge by listing such baskets as plate forms, parching trays, bowl-like baskets, fish gathering baskets and "a basket to cover doorway." It is not certain which of these baskets were twined and which coiled (Callaghan 1965, 202; Callaghan p.c., 2005).

Conclusions

In summary, Lake Miwok basketry was much like that of the Pomo. However, at least some Lake Miwok coiled basketry had a distinctive herringbone coil ending. Based on limited evidence, there is also the possibility that coiling may have been used more extensively among the Lake Miwok than among the Pomo. But in general, Lake Miwok coiled and twined basketry had become very Pomoan. The Lake Miwok did twining more extensively than coiling, but very finely coiled gift baskets decorated with feathers were made.

A Lake Miwok coiled basket done in a three-rod willow foundation with black dyed bulrush root designs, sedge root background and having remnants of quail topknot feathers. The basket has the distinctive Lake Miwok herringbone coil ending. This basket is missing and anyone knowing its whereabouts should contact the Vacaville Heritage Council through the Vacaville City Manager's Office. D: 8.5", H: 4" (Vacaville Heritage Council)

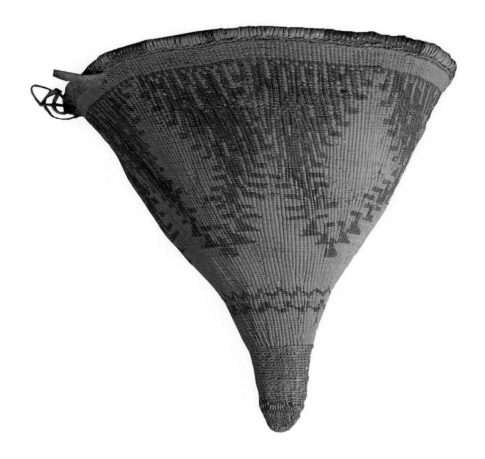

The central Sacramento Valley and adjoining interior Coast Range is the home of the Nomlaki people. This Nomlaki close twined burden basket has redbud designs on a sedge root background. While distantly related to Pomo burden baskets, this burden basket is uniquely Nomlaki in form and design. Purchased at Thomas Creek, near Paskenta, Tehama County in 1903, this basket is done primarily in plain twining with three-strand twining at the tip. H: 18", D: 18.5" (The Field Museum, #79839)

A coiled Nomlaki cooking pot with redbud designs on sedge root background and a three-rod foundation. Note the distinctive designs. Purchased on the west side of the Sacramento Valley in 1902. D: 12.5", H: 7" (C. Hart Merriam Collection, University of California at Davis, #752)

Nomlaki coiled basketry was similar to that of the Patwin. This fancy coiled Nomlaki basket is from Paskenta in Tehama County. It has black bulrush root designs on a sedge root background with attached quail topknot feathers. The three-rod foundation is of willow. D: 11", H: 5.5" (The Field Museum, #79836)

NOMLAKI BASKETRY

The Nomlaki are the people of the central Sacramento Valley and the adjoining Coast Range Mountains. Their territory includes Tehama County and northwestern Glenn County. The towns of Red Bluff, Corning and Paskenta and the Grindstone Indian Rancheria north of Elk Creek are in historic Nomlaki land. Culturally there were two main groups of Nomlaki, the River Nomlaki and the Hill Nomlaki. River Nomlaki life centered along the Sacramento River. The Hill Nomlaki occupied the upper reaches of the Sacramento River's tributary creeks and the western Coast Range Mountains from the foothills to the summit (Goldschmidt 1978, 141).

Ancestral Wintuan speaking people (the Wintu, Nomlaki and Patwin) entered the Sacramento Valley probably from Oregon. They spread south through the Sacramento Valley to northeastern San Francisco Bay.

The Nomlaki occupied the middle section of this vast Wintuan land. The Sacramento River portion of Nomlaki territory seems to have been occupied first. Then the Nomlaki spread from the Sacramento Valley west into the Coast Range hills.

Due to the Nomlaki's central position in the Sacramento Valley, they became participants in a trade network that extended from Mount Shasta south to San Francisco Bay (Goldschmidt 1984, 344-354). The Nomlaki must have observed a variety of basketry traditions during their extensive trading activities. Their immediate southern neighbors, the Patwin, had the most influence on Nomlaki basketry.

The Nomlaki language is a branch of the Wintuan language group comprised of the Nomlaki, Patwin and Wintu. The Wintu live immediately to the north of the Nomlaki. The Nomlaki language is more closely related to Wintu than to Patwin (Whistler 1977, 161). But the Wintu were never a coiling people and their basketry is Northeastern Californian.

Adjoining the Nomlaki to the south are the Patwin who are also close linguistic relatives. Nomlaki culture was more Central Californian and consequently most directly related to the Patwin. The fact that both Nomlaki coiled and twined basketry was more closely related to that of the Patwin than to the Wintu is a clear indication that Central California basketry was expanding north up the Sacramento Valley.

Today, two main Nomlaki communities, Paskenta and Grindstone, remain. Both are in Hill Nomlaki territory. Grindstone is a mixed Nomlaki and Patwin community, although other ancestries are found there as well (Bibby p.c., 2005). Baskets from Grindstone could be either Patwin or Nomlaki, and it can be difficult to distinguish them. This obviously makes the study of Nomlaki basketry more difficult. There are, however, a few surviving baskets from the Paskenta area that are clearly Nomlaki.

Nomlaki Basketry

The basketry of the Nomlaki is one of the least known in California. The documented sample is tiny. Too often, surviving baskets have confused documentation. Nomlaki basketry also does not seem to have the exceptional distinguishing characteristics of, say, Pomo or Yuki baskets which make them comparatively easy to identify. In part, this results from the Nomlaki having had long-time relations with the Patwin, Salt Pomo and the Yuki.

The Nomlaki were at the northern edge of Central California coiling and probably got it fairly late. There may not have been time enough to develop a highly distinctively Nomlaki coiling style prior to the arrival of non-Indians.

When anthropologist Walter Goldschmidt conducted his extensive research among the Nomlaki in 1936, Nomlaki baskets were no longer being made. Our statements about Nomlaki basketry are based on the statements of early tribal elders and the study of surviving documented Nomlaki baskets.

NOMLAKI BASKETRY MATERIALS

Basketry weft materials included sedge root, pine root and redbud (Goldschmidt 1951, 427). Redbud was used in both coiled and twined basketry (Gifford & Kroeber 1937, 132). Hazel and willow were used as warps. Use of pine root was confined to twined baskets. Wild rose stems were also reportedly used. Black briar root (*Smilax californica*) was rarely used by the Nomlaki (Bates and Bernstein 1982, 196).

The Nomlaki also decorated some fancy baskets with feathers. Feathers were probably only used on coiled baskets. Red woodpecker feathers were used as well as lark, flicker, and quail feathers (Gifford & Kroeber 1937, 132; Goldschmidt 1951, 427). One particularly attractive coiled

Nomlaki basket has a few scattered quail plumes tastefully attached to the basket's sides.

Nomlaki Coiled Basketry

Coiled basketry was made from the northern edge of Nomlaki territory at Cottonwood on the Tehama-Shasta County line, and southward (Kroeber 1932, 362; La Pena 1984, 335). The Nomlaki made three-rod coiled basketry, in common with the Patwin, Pomo, and Maidu. While non-interlocking stitches appear, the Nomlaki primarily used split stitches and interlocking stitches on the back face of their baskets (Dawson p.c.).

The work direction of documented Nomlaki baskets was predominantly to the left (Elsasser 1978, 633). Possibly, rightward work direction was done, too, but some or all of these rightward coiled baskets may be trade pieces.

Almost all tribes had only a single coiling work direction. Having two work directions would be unusual, although the Yuki did. In any event, it is clear the Nomlaki coiled in the leftward work direction. Whether or not the Nomlaki also coiled in a rightward work direction is uncertain.

Cooking Pots

Coiled, three-rod mush boiling baskets were made. These usually resembled Patwin cooking pots.

Small Bowls

Small bowls with flaring sides, straight sides or curving sides were made for a variety of purposes. The various forms of these baskets probably served as food bowls, as dipping baskets for scooping acorn mush from cooking pots and for storing objects such as basketry awls and beads.

A Nomlaki coiled bowl done with a three-rod foundation with redbud designs on a sedge background. Purchased in 1914 by Grace Nicholson, a prominent early Indian basket dealer. D: 13″, H: 7″ (Marion Steinbach Indian Basket Museum, Tahoe City, #869)

Winnowing and Sifting Trays

A round, flat winnower was made. These coiled baskets were probably similar to those made by the Patwin. They were made for sifting acorn meal and other seeds. Making coiled sifters is a trait the Nomlaki shared with the Patwin and Maidu, but not the Pomo.

Feather Baskets

As described earlier, the Nomlaki made fancy feather baskets. The feathers probably did not cover the entire basket, according to Barrett (Barrett 1996, 83, 141).

Nomlaki Twined Baskets

Close Twined Burden Baskets

Nomlaki carrying baskets were distinctive in that they had a gently curving funnel shape. An exceptionally long and narrow tip expanded to a broad flaring upper portion. Warp ends were trimmed flush with the last twining row at the rim. A reinforcing rod was sewn onto the back face of the basket rim.

The main portion of the basket was done in plain-twining. Three-strand twining was used around the base of these burden baskets. One burden basket also had a narrow band of three-strand twining by the rim.

One well-documented Nomlaki burden basket from near Paskenta had plain-twining done in an up-to-the-right slant of twist. Its base was done in three-strand twining with a down-to-the-right slant of twist. A second Nomlaki burden basket was the opposite. It had plain twining with an up-to-the-left slant of twist and three-strand twining done with an up-to-the-right slant of twist. This was unusual since most tribes used the same slants of twist on any specific type of basket.

On Nomlaki close twined burden baskets either sedge root or pine root or both were used as the background weft material. The designs were done in redbud in a wrapped twine technique. Designs are either horizontal bands or blocky designs using triangles and quail plume designs. Rims had a reinforcing rod wrapped with wild grape or redbud. The warp sticks were of willow or hazel. Ceanothus was sometimes used, probably for warp sticks (Kroeber & Gifford 1937; Goldschmidt 1951, 427-8; Dawson p.c.).

Inside one burden basket there were two thin reinforcing rods. One interior rod was midway down the side and the second interior rod was near the narrow tip. Both interior reinforcing rods were quite thin. While these Nomlaki bur-

This Nomlaki coiled bowl was collected in 1903 on Thomas Creek, near Paskenta, Tehama County. The designs are primarily redbud on a sedge root background. Three willow rods comprise the coil foundation. D: 9", H: 5.5" (The Field Museum, Chicago, #79838)

den baskets show Pomo influence in color tones and texture, the shape and design layout were uniquely Nomlaki.

Openwork Burden Baskets

An openwork burden basket was also made, probably of willow. It was larger than the close twined burden basket. It was undoubtedly used for carrying acorns, firewood and the like.

Parching and Winnowing Trays

A circular shallow basin-shaped twined winnowing and parching basket was made, at least at Grindstone Rancheria, a mixed Patwin and Nomlaki community. This basket shares with the Nomlaki burden baskets the use of three-strand twining around the start and again near the rim. Three groups of reinforcing rods were held on the back face of the winnower using occasional twists of twining. The three-strand twining was done up-to-the-right and the plain twining slant of twist was up-to-the-left. The weft appears to be split pine root, apparently over willow shoot warps. All these features are shared with one of the Nomlaki burden baskets described above.

Mortar Hoppers

Close-twined mortar hoppers were made.

Sifters

An openwork sifter was woven (Goldschmidt 1951, 427).

Cradles

The Nomlaki made sitting type cradles. Inner fibers of cottonwood bark padded the bottom of the cradle to provide a comfortable padded seat for the baby. For diapers, willow or maple bark was rolled into soft, absorbent balls. The child stayed in the cradle until he or she was old enough to crawl; sometimes the child would actually crawl with the basket still on (Margolin 1981, 11-12).

Men made cradles. This cradle was of the same general sitting type as used by the Patwin, Pomo and Wintu (Gifford & Kroeber 1937, 131 and Goldschmidt 1951, 428).

Wickerwork

Seedbeaters

Seedbeaters were of wickerwork, as were those of the Pomo and Patwin (Gifford & Kroeber 1937, 132).

Small Nomlaki coiled baskets, such as this one, were used to store valued possessions. The basket has redbud designs on sedge root over a three-rod foundation. Collected at Round Valley Indian Reservation, Mendocino County. D: 5", H: 3" (The Field Museum, Chicago, #103355)

Comments

Nomlaki coiled and twined basketry was clearly Central Californian. Its ties were to the Patwin, Valley Maidu, Pomo and perhaps even the Yuki. Nomlaki basketry seems most closely related to that of the Patwin. Few documented Nomlaki baskets survive, but those that are known are beautiful and well made.

The Plains Miwok people brought a special kind of beauty to the Delta region of the Sacramento and San Joaquin Valley. Shown is Plains Miwok Chief Wallentine's (also spelled Wallentien) personal basket from the village of Mokelmo (Mokelumne). This village was located east of Lodi between Lockeford and Clements in San Joaquin County. All the Plains Miwok baskets shown in this chapter have herringbone over-stitching atop the uppermost coil running completely around the rim. D: 7", H: 6" (Phoebe Apperson Hearst Museum of Anthropology and Regents of the University of California, #1-211527)

Plains Miwok coiled baskets were sometimes lavishly decorated with abalone pendants, feathers and glass trade beads. This basket was made in San Joaquin County by the daughter of Chief Wallentine. D: 7.5", H: 5" (University of Pennsylvania Museum of Archaeology and Anthropology, #NA 8010)

A Plains Miwok coiled feather basket with mallard, meadowlark and an uncertain species of red feathers arranged in triangular patterns. The daughter of Chief Wallentine made this basket. It was collected at Mokelmo village, San Joaquin County, circa 1900. D: 7", H: 5" (University of Pennsylvania Museum of Archaeology and Anthropology, #NA 8011)

PLAINS MIWOK BASKETRY

The Plains Miwok are the people of the Delta of the Sacramento and San Joaquin Rivers from Rio Vista north almost to Sacramento. They also held the lower Mokelumne and Cosumnes Rivers and countless small meandering waterways. This land was a vast tule marsh comprised of islands, sloughs and rivers with occasional broad, low hills and natural river levees. Most of this country was a low plain, averaging just 25 feet above sea level (Bennyhoff 1977, 1, 5).

In this watery world Utian-speaking peoples developed a culture centered on the rivers and wetlands (Foster 1996, 89). These ancestral Plains Miwok created a very successful life amidst the vast plant and animal resources of the Delta.

Basketry flourished here and was the most impressive Plains Miwok art. Only a small number of documented Plains Miwok baskets survive, but they offer a glimpse of a fine art.

Archeological Plains Miwok Baskets

Bamert Cave (Ama-3), an archeological site in Amador County located near the boundary of Plains Miwok and Northern Sierra Miwok country, held both coiled and twined basketry. Because of its border location, it was difficult to determine which culture made these baskets. However, Lawrence Dawson made a careful analysis of these baskets and was able to determine that both Plains Miwok and Sierra Miwok baskets seemed present. This is not surprising since the Bamert Cave site dates from the period after European arrival, and this was an era when Plains Miwok people took refuge with the Northern Sierra Miwok.

Among the baskets recovered, a coiled winnowing tray is almost certainly Plains Miwok. This basket has a leftward work direction with the work face on the concave side. The warp foundation was of the three-rod type, with the top rod larger than the bottom two rods. Weft fag ends were concealed in the foundation and the moving weft ends bound under successive stitches. The rim was plain wrapped. There were no designs. In most respects this basket was comparable to a Northern Sierra Miwok basket, but with some significant exceptions: the stitches were split on the back face of the basket and were not the interlocking stitches typical of the Sierra Miwok. Furthermore, a Plains Miwok basket in the Hearst Museum of Anthropology collection has similar split stitches and closely resembles the Bamert

Cave archeological tray in terms of spacing of weft stitches and texture (Dawson in Heizer and Hester 1973, 83-84).

Another archeological find from Bamert Cave was a large fragment of a diagonally twined conical burden basket with a coiled patch. The concepts found in this Bamert Cave burden basket are those of the Sacramento Valley, not the Sierras. This basket has chevron designs that cross the middle of the fragment. The designs were done in a dark material, possibly the root of horsetail or Indian scouring rush plant (*Equisetum*). This material is highly unusual in a burden basket and the basket did not compare to any documented basket in the extensive Hearst Museum of Anthropology collection at UC Berkeley.

In the Hearst collection, one undocumented basket of general Miwok type had the same unusual root material (Dawson 1973, 85-86). The only Central California people to regularly use equisetum for black weft material were the Ohlone. This use of equisetum is interesting since both linguistic and mtDNA studies suggest that the Plains Miwok and Ohlone share a common ancestry and were anciently once one people (Callaghan 2002, 2005; Eshleman 2002).

While it is possible that this fragment could be from an Ohlone burden basket brought to the area by refugees fleeing the Spanish missions, the designs on the Bamert Cave burden basket point to a Central Valley origin. Diagonally twined burden baskets with chevron designs were typical of the Sacramento Valley Patwin and the Valley Maidu. It is most likely that this basket fragment is a Plains Miwok burden basket.

Plains Miwok Coiled Basketry Technical Features

Basketry awls are common archeologically in Plains Miwok territory indicating that coiled baskets were very important (Bennyhoff 1977, 12, 49). Based on rare surviving Plains Miwok baskets and on archaeological findings, we have valuable insight into Plains Miwok coiled basketry.

Technical Features of Plains Miwok Coiled Basketry

Tight spiral starting knots were used. Work direction was to the left. Foundations were of three-rods, typically of willow. Single rod foundations may have been used too, but this is based only on a lone attributed basket. Grass bundle foundations were not used (Aginsky 1943, 417-418; Elsasser

1978, 633; Dawson p.c.; Bates 1982, 9; Deisher collection at University of Pennsylvania Museum of Archaeology and Anthropology).

Wefts were of sedge root. Weft stitches were generally split on the basket's back face, but some interlocking stitches were used as well. **Weft fag ends** were normally concealed in the foundation. On some baskets (which may be trade pieces) weft fag ends were trimmed. **Moving ends** were bound under. **Coil endings** were either tapered or blunt (Dawson p.c.; Bates 1982, 8).

Designs were typically black bracken fern root on a background of buff colored sedge root. Only black weft patterns were said to be used (Aginsky 1943, 418). Feathers, abalone pendants and eventually glass European trade beads were also used to ornament fancy baskets. There were usually no designs on the bottoms of baskets.

Rim finishes included herringbone shaped over-stitched rims and plain wrapped rims. The herringbone-type over-stitched rims were common on feather baskets, but less frequent on cooking pots. On Plains Miwok baskets the herringbone-shaped rim finish usually ran all the way around the rim, although it was sometimes only used at the coil ending (Mokelko Plains Miwok baskets, Deisher collection notes, University of Pennsylvania Museum of Archaeology and Anthropology; Bates 1982, 8-9; also see Mowat, et. al. 1992, 56-57, fig. 56).

Plains Miwok Coiled Basket Types

The Plains Miwok made fine **feather baskets**. These baskets typically had a distinctive herringbone rim finish all the way around their rim. They were globular in shape with a constricted mouth. Some had quail plumes attached and/or strings of glass beads strung on fiber with abalone pendants. Mallard, meadowlark and other kinds of feathers were used for decoration. European glass trade beads were also attached to the feather baskets. There were no designs on the bottom of these baskets (Dawson p.c.; Bennyhoff 1977, 13; Deisher collection, University of Pennsylvania Museum of Archaeology and Anthropology).

Cooking Pots typically had herringbone rim finishes all around the rim. Designs were black bracken fern root on a sedge root background. The coiling ending was tapered. On one basket the bottom was repaired with leather.

The Plains Miwok had large **feast baskets**, at least up to 26 inches in diameter and 18 inches in height. One example has the classic Plains Miwok herringbone overstitched rim.

The University of Pennsylvania's feast baskets, in contrast, have plain wrapped rims. Having more than one type of rim finish occasionally occurs in Central California.

Aginsky stated both coiled and twined cooking pots were made, but twined cooking pots seem unlikely. He made the same statement about all the Sierra Miwok groups and twined cooking baskets were absent there (Aginsky 1943, 417). It should be noted that Aginsky's Miwok information was gathered long after Plains Miwok culture had been subjected to great changes.

Dipping Baskets were made to dip acorn soup and other liquids from larger baskets (Callaghan 1984, 245).

Coiled Winnowers, Sifters and **Gambling Trays** were present (Aginsky 1943, 417; Callaghan 1984, 234).

Small Watertight Baskets, apparently of globular shape, were noted (Aginsky 1943, 418; Callaghan 1984, 234).

Special Mortuary Baskets were made for funerals (Bennyhoff 1977, 13).

Bottleneck Treasure Baskets and **Water Bottles** were probably absent. Aginsky stated that the Plains Miwok and Sierra Miwok made coiled bottleneck treasure baskets and twined water bottles. This seems very unlikely based on all other research, but if they were actually present they would likely have been late borrowings (Aginsky 1943, 417).

THE PLAINS MIWOK AND THE NORTHERN SIERRA MIWOK

Some surviving Plains Miwok people found refuge with the Northern Sierra Miwok around Ione in Amador County.

So many meals were prepared in this well-worn Plains Miwok cooking pot that it needed a leather repair on its bottom. This mush boiling basket was made by the wife of Mokelmo Chief Maximo, who lived near Stockton. Black bracken fern root designs were the artist's chosen design material. D: 17.5", H: 9.5" (University of Pennsylvania Museum of Archaeology and Anthropology, #NA 8013)

A large Plains Miwok cooking pot with black bracken fern designs on a sedge root background. Note the over-stitched rim done in the distinctive Plains Miwok herringbone style. (Southwest Museum of the American Indian, Autry National Center, #811-G-2274)

A detail of the Plains Miwok herringbone over-stitched rim. When present on coiled baskets, over-stitching can be seen atop the uppermost coil at the rim. (Southwest Museum of the American Indian, Autry National Center, #811-G-2274)

The Plains Miwok could have influenced the basketry of the Northern Sierra Miwok people of the Ione area with respect to use of herringbone rim finishes, sedge root wefts, moving ends bound under, three-rod foundations and certain types of starting knot.

However, the Northern Sierra Miwok of Ione trimmed their weft fag ends and, unlike the Plains Miwok, rarely concealed weft fag ends in the foundation so there was a continuation of two separate basketry traditions. Still, there was much in common between the two cultures' basketry. Some shared basketry techniques did develop, but this may have occurred only after European contact.

TWINED PLAINS MIWOK BASKETS

Both close-twined and openwork **burden baskets** were woven (Aginsky 1943, 417). Plain twined conical burden baskets are documented. In addition, archeological evidence strongly supports the presence of diagonally twined burden baskets. Having both plain twined and diagonally twined types of burden baskets would not be surprising. For example, both types occurred among the Pomo and Maidu (see archeological basketry section above).

Storage Baskets were used to store fish and other food (Aginsky 1943, 401). These were probably openwork baskets.

Winnowers were done in plain twined openwork weaving. Close-twined winnowers would not have been needed because the Plains Miwok made coiled winnowers.

Seedbeaters were oval or triangular in shape and were plain twined with parallel warps (Aginsky 1943, 417).

Berry Baskets were said to be plain twined (Aginsky 1943, 418).

Fish Scoops were oval, winnower-shaped baskets used to scoop fish from the water (Aginsky 1943, 400).

Fish Traps were long and conical, with an opening at the end to allow fish to enter (Aginsky 1943, 399).

Cradles of the lying type with hoods were made (Aginsky 1943, 419; Callaghan 1984, 234).

Tule Bags are reported, but it is not stated whether these were true bags or were baskets (Aginsky 1943, 418). The Plains Miwok lived in a rich marshland where vast numbers of tule reeds grew. Tule was an important basket material and it is likely that a variety of utilitarian tule baskets were made.

Hats were not made (Aginsky 1943, 417).

Comments

Plains Miwok coiled basketry has ties not only to Northern Sierra Miwok basketry, but also to the Patwin, Maidu and possibly San Francisco Bay area peoples.

The Plains Miwok occupied an important central location in California. The Delta of the Sacramento and San Joaquin Rivers has been suggested as the birthplace of Central Californian Indian culture. If so, the Plains Miwok would have had a very influential role. Their contributions may have been far more important than we presently know. We do know that Plains Miwok feathered and beaded baskets and cooking pots were among the finest in Central California.

Perhaps the most spectacular Maidu coiled baskets were huge feast baskets. Feast baskets were owned by leading families and were used to serve large numbers of guests at Big Time celebrations and other occasions. Certain Maidu villages specialized in making these feast baskets. This Valley Maidu feast basket features black bracken fern root designs on a sedge root background. D: 22", H: 16" (Private collection)

This huge feast basket has redbud designs on a background of maple wefts. This is a classic Sierra Nevada basket. Foothill and Mountain Maidu coiled baskets used wefts of maple or other peeled shoot material, while the Sacramento Valley Maidu used sedge root wefts. D: 27.5", H: 17" (Collection of the Pacific Grove Museum of Natural History, #4-1053)

MAIDU BASKETRY

The Maidu are the people of the northern Sierra Nevada Mountains and the east side of the Sacramento Valley. Maidu country ranges from the low marshlands of the Great Central Valley to the High Sierras. The Feather, Yuba, Bear and American Rivers all flow through Maidu land.

The Maidu people form three major groups based on language and culture. The Nisenan (Southern) Maidu occupy the southern portion of Maidu territory around Sacramento, Marysville, Nevada City, Auburn and Placerville. The Nisenan are people of the eastern Sacramento Valley and the Sierras. The Konkow (Northwestern) Maidu are also an eastern Sacramento Valley and Sierran people. The communities of Chico and Oroville are in Konkow country. The Mountain (Northeastern) Maidu live in the mountain meadows and high valleys in the Sierra Nevada Mountains. The towns of Quincy, Greenville and Susanville are in traditional Mountain Maidu territory. We will refer to the Mountain Maidu, Konkow and Nisenan collectively as the Maidu since their basketry is so closely related.

Maidu Coiled Basketry History

The three Maiduan groups are believed to have migrated south to California from the Columbia River region of Washington and Oregon. The Maidu people probably arrived in California via Nevada in several migrations. This migration theory is based on basketry research, but is supported by linguistic and archeological studies as well (Moratto 1984, 55; Foster 1996, 90; Dawson p.c.).

Prior to entering California, the Maidu seem to have spent time in the western Great Basin in Nevada. Maidu coiled basketry has connections with the ancient archeological basketry of western Nevada, including that of the early Lovelock culture. Some of the coiled baskets found northeast of Reno are said to date as far back as circa 4,200 years (Adovasio 1986, 199-200; E. Jolie 2004).

Some of the ancient archeological basketry found in Nevada dry caves has significant Maidu characteristics. These include the weaving of coiled cooking pots, coiled winnowers, the use of split weft stitches and three-rod coiling foundations, the presence of coiled feather baskets, the type of feather designs selected and other features.

Western Nevada archeological basketry has important ties to both the Sierra Miwok and the Maidu. However, the characteristics the Maidu and Sierra Miwok have in common with the ancient Nevada basketry are not all common to both cultures. This indicates separate introductions of coiling into California from western Nevada. The Maidu brought some coiling techniques into California while other techniques came in with the Sierra Miwok. (The history of Great Basin coiled basketry ancestral to Maidu and Sierra Miwok coiling is also discussed in the Sierra Miwok chapter.)

Maidu designs are not those of ancient western Nevada. Many Maidu designs were apparently developed earlier along the Columbia River when ancestral Maidu lived in that region. These designs are related to Columbia River twined baskets, not to the imbricated coiled baskets of that

A Nisenan Maidu woman using her seedbeater and burden basket to gather small seeds. Close-twined burden baskets were necessary to collect large quantities of tiny seeds. This early photo was taken near Placerville in El Dorado County. (Phoebe Apperson Hearst Museum of Anthropology and Regents of the University of California)

region. This is because the imbricated coiled basketry of the Klickitat and other Washington tribes did not arrive at the Columbia River until after ancestral Maidu had left that region. The Maidu brought only twining designs with them as they moved south (Dawson, n.d.).

After arriving in western Nevada and eastern California, the Maidu adopted coiled basketry from Lovelock culture people. Many Nevada archeological baskets are very much like Maidu baskets in their technological features. In terms of designs, however, the Maidu tended to use their old twining designs on their coiled baskets (Baumhoff and Heizer 1958; Dawson 1988, 2; and Dawson, n.d.).

Once in California, the Maidu elaborated their coiled basketry, added features and forms and ultimately created what would become perhaps the single most influential North Central California coiling tradition. The Maidu were not only one of the people to bring coiling into the Golden State, but their coiled baskets were admirable and inspiring in the eyes of other cultures. The Patwin, Nomlaki, Pomo, Wappo, Lake Miwok, Plains Miwok, Ohlone/Costanoan and Huchnom all either directly or indirectly adopted Maidu coiling ideas. While each of these tribes developed their own artistic coiling styles and unique features, but the underlying technical features of all these culture's coiled baskets are largely Sacramento Valley Maidu.

The Maidu were in a key location to influence others. The Maidu began expanding into the northern Sierra Nevada Mountains. They displaced Yana and perhaps Washoe. By around A.D. 1300 the Nisenan Maidu had expanded so far south through the Sierras that they were moving into northern Sierra Miwok country (Moratto 1984, 562; Foster 1996, 90).

Meanwhile, the Patwin moved into the western edge of Maidu country. The Patwin expansion reached the southern Sacramento Valley, eventually extending Patwin territory as far as San Francisco Bay along the lower Napa River estuary and Suisun Bay. The arrival of the Patwin in the Sacramento Valley resulted in the Maidu strongly influencing Patwin coiled basketry. The Patwin, Pomo and others transmitted Maidu type coiling even further. Via these other cultures, Sacramento Valley Maidu-type coiling spread as far as the coast.

The Sacramento Valley Maidu consisted of both Konkow and Nisenan Maidu living on the east side of the Sacramento Valley. Since surviving Valley Maidu basketry is largely Konkow and few Valley Nisenan baskets survive, the Valley

Maidu baskets referred to in this chapter are largely Konkow. Important Maiduan basketry characteristics often do not correspond with language divisions. This is because Maidu basketry was strongly affected by geography (the Sacramento Valley versus the Sierra Nevada mountains and foothills) and by neighboring cultures.

MAIDU COILED BASKETRY

All Maidu groups made both coiled and twined baskets. To understand Maidu basketry, we need to recognize not only the three linguistic branches of Maiduan peoples— the Nisenan (Southern) Maidu, Konkow (Northwestern) Maidu and Mountain (Northeastern) Maidu—but the major basketry differences between the Maidu living in the Sacramento Valley and those Maidu living in the Sierras. We begin by looking at coiling.

Maidu coiling has beautifully even wefts. Although the weft strands are typically broad compared to many other Californians, the wefts are so evenly and closely sewn that they give Maidu baskets a smooth, refined surface. Beneath this surface are strong foundation rods that provide Maidu coiled baskets with a feeling of strength. The weft covered foundation rods give a "corrugated texture" to the surface. Maidu baskets proudly proclaim that they are coiled work.

Maidu design layout was superbly tasteful. Fairly large diagonal or zigzag patterns were common; isolated scattered patterns uncommon. Bold designs using strong, fairly wide patterns were done in either red or black on a light buff background. Each basket had designs that make a strong, pleasing artist's statement, a result of both color contrast and very careful spacing. The whole side of the basket was the artist's "canvas." It is rare to see a well made Maidu basket that does not make you want to stop and admire its beauty.

TWO COILING TRADITIONS: SACRAMENTO VALLEY MAIDU COILING VERSUS MAIDU COILING IN THE SIERRA FOOTHILLS AND MOUNTAINS

The most prominent feature of Maidu coiled baskets is the distinction between the coiling of the Valley Maidu and that of the Sierra Maidu of the foothills and mountains. This was not a difference based on language, for Konkow and Nisenan of the Sacramento Valley made coiled baskets differently from the Konkow and Nisenan of the Sierras. The differences were largely based on a valley homeland versus a mountain and foothill homeland.

A Nisenan Maidu feast basket. Note the rim ticks (stripes) at the coil ending on the rim. When they chose to use rim ticks, Maidu weavers traditionally used them only at or near the coil ending. As with nearly all Maidu coiled baskets, the designs stop just below the top coil. This basket has redbud designs on a maple background. Purchased on the Bear River near Colfax, Placer County, in 1902. D: 21", H: 13" (C. Hart Merriam Collection, University of California at Davis, #270)

The coiled baskets of the Valley Maidu look quite different from those of Sierra Maidu. Such differences, particularly difference in choice of weft material, make it easy to distinguish the two basic types of Maiduan coiling. For wefts, the Valley Maidu used sedge root while the Sierra Maidu typically used peeled redbud or maple.

It is significant that the Konkow Valley Maidu traded chiefly with the Patwin (Dixon 1905, 202). Valley Maidu coiled basketry and Patwin coiled basketry are very similar, sometimes even indistinguishable. Sacramento Valley Maidu coiling and Patwin coiling both used sedge root for their wefts and typically bound some or all moving ends under the wefts on the interior of the basket. This practice results in a slightly bumpy appearance on the basket's back face (usually the interior side). This feature links Valley Maidu coiling to that of the Patwin rather than to that of the Sierra Nevada Maidu. In contrast, Foothill and Mountain Maidu coiling does not use sedge root for background wefts, but ordinarily uses redbud, maple or other peeled material. Sierra Maidu weft moving ends also are trimmed and lack the raised "bumps" of Valley Maidu weft moving ends.

At first glance, Sierra (Foothill and Mountain) Maidu coiling often looks most like finer Yuki work, which uses peeled redbud wefts and unpeeled redbud designs. Valley Maidu coiling with its use of sedge root wefts, in contrast, looks much more like Patwin, Pomo and Wappo coiling.

TECHNICAL FEATURES OF MAIDU COILED BASKETRY

Maidu coiling is invariably done in a **leftward work direction,** as seen from the weaver's perspective. **Starting knots** are typically shaped somewhat like a spiral with a small

One of the largest coiled Central California baskets ever made, this Konkow Maidu feast basket is thirty inches in diameter. It has redbud designs on a split shoot background (probably maple) with a three-rod foundation of willow. D: 30", H: 19.5" (California State Parks, Bidwell Mansion State Historic Site, #139-19-1)

bundle of shredded material inside. Foundation rods were added beginning by about the third coil. Most starting knots were round, but an oval starting knot was sometimes used by the Valley Maidu around Chico (Bates and Bibby 1983, 52). This oval starting knot may also have been used among other Maidu and perhaps some Patwin (Bibby p.c., 2005).

Nearly all Maidu coiling **foundations** were three-rod. These three sturdy rods give the "corrugated" appearance so apparent on Maidu coiled baskets. Single rod foundations were rare, although a single-rod bowl made by the Hill Maidu was noted by the early researcher C. Hart Merriam (Merriam 1967, 412). Single-rod foundation basketry may have been a fairly late adoption by the Maidu since three-rod foundations were standard in every type of Maidu coiled basket. Single-rod foundations could have been adopted as a result of contact with the Paiute and Washoe, both of which regularly made single-rod foundation baskets as well as three-rod ones (Bates and Bernstein 1982, 193).

Maidu stitch work is characterized by **split stitches** on the back face (usually the inside) of the basket. All Maidu

groups split the weft stitches on the back face (non-work face) of their baskets carefully and regularly. These split stitches can easily be seen by looking inside any coiled Maidu bowl or cooking pot.

Splitting of stitches is accomplished by piercing the weft material with the awl and drawing the weft material through. The Maidu carefully split the wefts on the back face of their baskets with remarkable regularity and evenness, unlike some tribes who intermittently and unevenly split their weft stitches. The Mountain (Northeastern) Maidu were said to be especially careful in their splitting of stitches (Bates and Bernstein 1982, 193), although finely split stitches were found among the other Maiduan peoples, too.

It is important to note that Maidu stitches were split on the back face of the basket, not on the smoother work face. The Maidu work face was on the exterior of bowl-shaped baskets and on the upper side of plate-like trays.

Maidu **weft fag ends** were concealed in the foundation bundle on both Sierra Maidu and Valley Maidu baskets. One southern Nisenan Maidu group trimmed the fag ends on the basket's work face, a feature perhaps borrowed from their Sierra Miwok neighbors (Bates and Bernstein 1982, 193). Sierra Maidu **weft moving ends** were generally trimmed. Valley Maidu moving ends were bound down under one to several weft stitches. These Valley Maidu moving ends are usually conspicuous as regular bumps on the back face of Valley Maidu baskets.

A few Foothill Hill Maidu groups mixed these weft trimming and concealing techniques, even on the same basket. They occupied a transition zone in terms of basketry between the Valley and the Sierras (Bates and Bernstein 1982, 193).

The Maidu **rim finish** used plain weft wrapping on the final coil at the rim on the vast majority of their coiled baskets. The coiling ending tapers fairly quickly, but does not end abruptly.

A back-stitched over-stitch atop the coil ending is found on a few Sacramento Valley baskets from the Valley Maidu, Patwin and possibly the Nomlaki. This over-stitching can extend from the coil ending back along the coil for up to an inch or so. The over-stitching is narrow and does not cover the entire surface of the coil top.

Decorative Features of Maidu Coiled Basketry

Maidu coiling has major distinctive decorative features. The entire last coil at the rim is almost always left undecorated, in contrast to the Pomo, Wappo and the Yuki who often had designs on the rim. Maidu baskets where the design extends to include the top coil are likely either innovations or baskets purchased before they were finished, something which usually happened over the protests of dedicated weavers that "the basket was not done yet."

The Maidu did, however, occasionally use one distinctive kind of rim decoration. The Maidu occasionally added "rim ticks" at the coil ending. Rim ticks are alternating stripes placed in the final inch or so at the coil ending. Later, less traditional baskets occasionally were made with rim ticks extending all the way around the top coil, but this practice was uncommon.

The Maidu rarely place designs on the bottoms of their traditional coiled baskets (flat trays are an exception due to their form). This contrasts with the Patwin, Pomo and Yuki who commonly put designs on their basket bottoms.

Maidu wefts are blockier looking than the very narrow wefts of the Pomo and Wappo, a feature the Maidu shared with the Yuki. But despite wider wefts, Maidu designs and workmanship were so well thought out and carefully done

that these baskets rank among the most beautiful in all California.

Maidu Coiled Basketry Materials

Maidu baskets were made with yellowish-brown colored background wefts and traditionally decorated with designs of only a single color, either red or black. On Sierra Maidu baskets, the design color is either the red of redbud bark (*Cercis occidentalis*) or less commonly the black of bracken fern root (*Pteridium aquilinum*). Bracken fern roots were often found growing in old logs where the roots grew nice and long and made good weft material (Beals 1933, 342; Potts 1977, 36-39).

Like Sierra Maidu groups, the Valley Maidu also used redbud bark for red designs and bracken fern root for black designs. In addition, the Valley Maidu sometimes used *Smilax californica* for black designs. *Smilax* has tiny bumps on its surface, resulting in its common names of greenbriar, wart root or briar root. The River Patwin and Nomlaki also used this material, but only infrequently (Bates and Bernstein 1982, 196).

The Valley Maidu rarely used dyed bulrush root (*Scirpus*) for black designs. In contrast, other north Central Californians such as the Patwin, Pomo, Wappo, Lake Miwok and Huchnom regularly used dyed bulrush root for their black designs (Beals 1933, 342; Bates and Bernstein 1982, 196; Mathewson 1998, 189, 197).

For the background weft material, peeled redbud or maple (*Acer macrophyllum*) were most commonly preferred by the Sierra and Foothill Maidu. Maple was particularly popular as a weft material among Maidu living in Nevada and Butte Counties (Bates and Bernstein 1982, 194). Used for background wefts, maple wefts were practically white when new but changed to a pleasing yellow or cream buff color with age. Fresh maple shoots were prized by the Maidu for these coiled wefts (Beals 1933, 343). The Sierra and Foothill Maidu burned maple thickets to produce new-growth basketry material. Unlike the Sierra and Foothill Maidu, the Sacramento Valley Maidu used sedge root for their weft background material.

Willow was used as a weft material in extreme eastern Maidu territory around Susanville and in El Dorado County, probably due to Washoe and Paiute influence. The Honey Lake Maidu, for example, made a coiled tray with both weft and warp of willow for seed processing (Riddell 1978, 18; Bates and Bernstein 1982, 194).

Maidu foundation rods were most commonly of willow (*Salix*), ceanothus (*Ceanothus*) or dogwood (*Cornus*) (Mathewson 1998, 152).

The Valley Maidu made feathered baskets using red woodpecker feathers and/or green mallard feathers. Some of these baskets were decorated with abalone shell pendants. The bases of Maidu feather baskets were usually left un-feathered (Kroeber 1929, 262; Bates and Bernstein 1982, 200).

A special basket with red woodpecker feathers was also woven. This was a small feather basket about the size of an egg, open at each end, that was worn at dances and other gatherings. It was entirely covered with red woodpecker feathers (Kroeber 1929, 262).

MAIDU DESIGNS

Maidu coiling designs include diagonals, crisscross patterns, up and down zigzags, vertical patterns, isolated units, step designs and others. Despite differences in weft materials between valley and mountain groups, many coiled basketry designs were shared among the Maidu people. There were a great variety of traditional designs to choose from throughout Maidu country. Knowledge of these designs was widespread and only comparatively minor differences in coiling designs existed from one major Maidu group to another (Dawson p.c.).

Significantly, however, the Maidu had separate design traditions for twining and coiling. In fact, Nisenan twining and coiling have almost no designs in common (Dawson p.c.). This results from coiling and twining having two different histories. Nisenan Maidu work illustrates this quite well. Nisenan twined baskets, such as their burden baskets,

A Maidu globular storage bowl. Its redbud designs are on a buff colored background, probably maple. D: 9.5" (Private collection)

For family meals, cooking pots rather than feast baskets were used. Cooking pots were smaller than feast baskets, but equally beautiful and made with the same care. This much used Valley Maidu cooking pot's interior has been worn through the wefts to the foundation rods by cooking stones being stirred to heat countless meals. This basket has redbud designs and a background of sedge root on a three-rod willow foundation. It has an oval starting knot. D: 14", H: 8" (Private collection)

were decorated with horizontal bands. Nisenan coiling, in contrast, were decorated with diagonal, vertical and other designs. Unlike coiling, Maidu twined designs in most areas were largely limited to horizontal bands (Dawson p.c.). Extensive variations in twining designs were only common among the Mountain Maidu, whose twined patterns were strongly influenced by the neighboring Atsugewi and Achumawi.

Yet, as among all Californian people, individual women had their own artistic tastes and some baskets could be identified by a weaver's personal design choices (Beals 1933, 342). There was no ownership of designs, rather daughters tended to learn beloved designs from their mothers or other female relatives and carry them on (Riddell 1978, 18).

There were also some differences between the designs from one village or valley to the next. Sometimes designs could also even be pinpointed to specific villages. Production of certain types of baskets might be a specialty of a village. One village was well known, for instance, for making feast baskets.

But even with these kinds of variations, Maidu coiled basketry was a cohesive artistic tradition. For a people occupying so large a territory, there was remarkable standardization in coiling designs (Dixon 1902, 13).

As mentioned, all early Maidu weaving had red or black designs, but not both. Baskets using red designs outnumber those with black designs in Maidu coiled basketry. After about 1910, three-color (red, black and buff) designs began appearing among the Northeastern Maidu as sale pieces for non-Indians (Bates and Bernstein 1982, 191). Three-color patterns were a late innovation among the Maidu.

MAJOR TYPES OF MAIDU COILED BASKETS

Feast Baskets

Feast baskets were huge, deep cooking pots used to serve large numbers of people when important ceremonies and social gatherings were held (Bibby 1996, 61-62). Feast baskets could reach 30 inches in diameter. These baskets were beautifully decorated with designs in redbud or bracken fern root. They had linear, flaring sides (Merriam 1967, 312).

Acorn mush was cooked in ordinary size cooking pots and then poured into the large feast baskets in what was certainly a dramatic scene. Feast baskets were so large and heavy that several men would be needed to lift a full feast basket. For lifting, a flexible sapling would be cut and wrapped around the exterior of the feast basket, allowing a good grip on the basket when it was heavy with acorn mush.

To add to the elegance of the presentation, affluent Valley Maidu women made decoratively matched sets of finely coiled culinary baskets such as servers and sifters with the same designs, rather like the place settings common at fine dinner parties (Wilson and Towne 1978, 394; Bates and Bernstein 1982, 190).

Cooking Pots

Like feast baskets, Maidu cooking pots usually have flaring sides that are straight with little or no curve to them. They are generally higher in proportion to their width than Patwin cooking pots.

Maidu cooking pots were good-sized baskets (often 12 to 18 inches in diameter), but were smaller than the gigantic feast baskets. Unlike the feast baskets, cooking pots were used for everyday cooking. Maidu cooking pots were often decorated with designs of great beauty, most often in redbud and occasionally in bracken fern root. They rarely used bulrush root designs. Designs did not extend to the bottom of the basket.

Small Mush Bowls or Dippers

A smaller round bowl was made to dip out liquids from the cooking pots. These dipping and serving baskets were used for acorn mush, soup, water and for any similar purpose where a cereal bowl-sized basket was useful. Oval bowls were sometimes made, but were uncommon.

Small Globular Baskets

These were Maidu signature pieces and are probably the most common Maidu baskets seen today. They have a globular shape that curves inward toward the mouth. These baskets held valuables, small seeds and other objects (Merriam 1967, 312).

Sifting/Winnowing/Parching Trays

Coiled, round trays were made by all Maidu groups. These rather flat, coiled trays were used for winnowing, sifting and parching. They were also used as platters for serving fish and meat. Various sizes were made. All Maidu made these circular trays, except possibly some of the Mountain Nisenan people (Voegelin 1942, 3, 78).

Storage Baskets

Merriam (1967, 312) mentions storage baskets. These large, broad baskets were used for storing food and may also have occasionally served as cooking pots.

Shamans' Baskets

This was apparently a small globular basket, easily held in the hand, used by Indian doctors during their curing rituals. The Patwin may have made a similar basket.

MAIDU TWINED BASKETRY

Despite being very much a coiling people, the Maidu produced a wide variety of twined baskets. **Types of twining** included plain twining, diagonal twining and wrapped twining. **Starting knots** were either the cross warp type or the fan-shaped type start with warps bent into a single warp section near the center of a fan-shaped knot. At the rim, warps were often turned down and bound into the wefts. Sometimes the warps were used to attach a reinforcing rod at the rim. **Warps** were of maple (*Acer*) or willow. **Wefts** were of conifer root, willow, redbud or wild grape, the latter especially for wrapping reinforcing rods. A **double overlay** of beargrass (*Xerophyllum tenax*) was a distinctive Maidu design technique (Elsasser 1978, 629-631).

Maidu twining primarily has a down-to-the-right **slant of weft twist.** Up-to-the-right slant of twist was also done in Maidu twining, but was rare (Dawson p.c.).

Twining and coiling were the main Maidu basketry techniques. Wickerwork was little used, except for some seedbeaters and a type of broad, shallow bowl (Dawson p.c.).

Twined basketry was probably brought with the Maidu as they migrated south over the centuries from the Columbia River region of Oregon and Washington. Supporting this view is the fact that there is a continuous distribution of designs from the Wasco and Wishram on the Columbia River south to the Maidu. Most convincingly, the Maidu share more designs with the Wasco and Wishram than

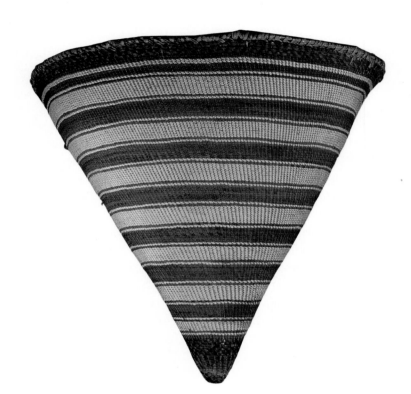

The most common Maidu burden baskets were plain twined. The yellow bands on this fine Mountain (Northeastern) Maidu burden basket are done with a double overlay of beargrass on a brown conifer root background. Maidu burden baskets were conical, unlike the bell-shaped burden baskets of the Pomo. (Private collection)

they do with such Northwestern Californians as the Yurok, Hupa and their neighbors. Many Maidu designs are absent in Northwestern California (Dawson p.c.). Maidu twining, thus, almost certainly had interior Columbia River, not coastal, origins. However, the Maidu innovated greatly, and Maidu basketry in California became very different from the Wasco-Wishram basketry.

With the major exception of the differences between Valley Maidu coiling and Sierra Maidu coiling, Maidu coiled basketry was actually fairly uniform. Maidu twining, on the other hand, was more diverse (Dawson p.c.). Twined burden baskets illustrate this point particularly well and will be discussed in detail later.

Only the Mountain (Northeastern) Maidu, among the Maiduan peoples, adopted the beargrass overlay twining of the Achumawi and Atsugewi with all its features, including virtually the full set of materials: hazel warps, pine root wefts, beargrass overlay, maiden hair fern stems and redbud. It is a significant case of one group of Maidu adopting an entire twining complex and establishing it along with a Maidu coiling tradition (Kroeber 1925, 415).

There was, however, a unique Mountain (Northeastern) Maidu twining feature not shared with either the Achumawi or Atsugewi or with any other Maidu group. Called double overlay, this technique normally involved using two layers of beargrass, one placed perfectly atop the other, and used as design overlay atop the pine root background wefts (Dixon 1905, 147-148; Mathewson 1998, 202; Dawson p.c.).

Bracken fern root (rhizome) strands were occasionally combined with the beargrass overlay to create black designs. During the weaving, the black bracken fern root was brought in front of the white beargrass layers to form the designs (Mathewson 1998, 202).

MAJOR TYPES OF MAIDU CLOSE-TWINED BASKETS
Maidu Twined Burden Baskets

Plain twined conical burden baskets for gathering seeds were made by all Maiduan groups (Voegelin 1942, 78). There was fascinating variation in burden baskets, and nothing illustrates the rich regional diversity of Maidu twining better than burden baskets.

Close-twined **Mountain (Northeastern) Maidu burden baskets** were unique in that they were overlayed with two layers of beargrass (*Xerophyllum tenax*) over the conifer root weft background material. This double overlay contrasts with the single strand beargrass overlay on conifer root wefts so characteristic of both Northwestern and Northeastern California tribes.

The double overlay of beargrass was apparently confined to the Mountain (Northeastern) Maidu (Dixon 1905, 147). In this unique type of overlay, two strands of beargrass were stacked on each other so skillfully that you have to look carefully to see that two are present. Beneath the double overlay the weft was of conifer (usually pine) root. The conifer root weft is often a rich, dark brown color. Warp sticks were of hazel.

Mountain Maidu burden basket designs were either solely of beargrass or with beargrass used as a background for designs done in either redbud or black bracken fern root. When only beargrass was used for designs, the conifer root weft served as background material. But when beargrass served as the background for either red or black designs, then little of the pine root weft was allowed to show. Red and black designs were not used together on the same basket, but only in combination with beargrass. Redbud was not used to wrap rims.

Burden basket rims were not braided as in Northwestern California. Instead, Mountain Maidu warp sticks were bent down, often in pairs, under a reinforcing rod at the rim. Heavy-duty wefts were wrapped over the reinforcing rod and beneath the bent warp sticks, firmly attaching them to the basket. This was essentially coiling the rim to the twined structure of the basket. Just below the rim, a few rows of diagonal twining or plain twining over two warps were used. Below these rows was the entire central portion of the basket, the vast majority of the basket, which was done in plain twining.

The bottom tips of these baskets were done with diagonal twining often mixed with some plain twining over two warps. The use of diagonal twining at the base and again just below the rim suggests that the Mountain (Northeastern) Maidu may have once made burden baskets entirely of diagonal twining, as the Valley Maidu continued to do. This use of diagonal twining at two key points in their burden basket construction suggests that at some time in the past

a switch occurred from diagonally twined to plain twined burden baskets.

Some Mountain Maidu burden baskets used horizontal bands of beargrass as designs on a background of conifer root weft. Horizontal bands were the standard design layout found in other Maidu groups as well and probably are the oldest type of Maidu design. But when red or black designs are used on a background of solid beargrass overlay on Mountain Maidu burden baskets, they look more like those of the Atsugewi and Achumawi.

There was intermarriage and trade in baskets between the Northeastern Maidu and the Atsugewi (Davis 1966, 35; Bibby p.c., 2005). This resulted in the Mountain Maidu adopting some basket features from the Atsugewi. Mountain Maidu burden baskets show some shared concepts of design, form and material with many Atsugewi and Achumawi burden baskets. Mountain Maidu concepts that seem to be derived from the Atsugewi and Achumawi include: (1) conifer root wefts, (2) beargrass overlay, (3) plain twining, (4) zigzag designs, (5) covering the entire side of some baskets with

This Mountain (Northeastern) Maidu burden basket has black bracken fern root designs on a background consisting of a double overlay of yellow beargrass. The reinforcing rod at the rim is wrapped with peeled willow. Neighboring Atsugewi and Achumawi designs probably inspired the Mountain Maidu use of diagonal designs on this burden basket. H: 16.5", W: 18" (California Academy of Sciences, #464-3)

This Nisenan Maidu burden basket was purchased in 1902 from a Maidu weaver on the north side of Bear River, about four miles from Colfax in Nevada County, California. Most Maidu groups made such plain twined burden baskets, often with horizontal band designs. H: 20″, W: 20″ (C. Hart Merriam collection, University of California at Davis, #316)

own. For example, Mountain Maidu burden baskets lack the conspicuous horizontal design band just below the rim that is a characteristic feature of so many Achumawi and Atsugewi burden baskets. Mountain Maidu and other Maidu either did not use, or removed, the interior lattice rods that are sometimes found on the inside of Achumawi, Atsugewi and Wintu burden baskets. These small interior reinforcing rods were placed well down inside the burden basket and are not to be confused with the large rod at the rims.

Lastly, it should be mentioned that there are probably ancient connections between Mountain Maidu burden baskets and Klamath-Modoc basketry. For example, these tribes share the down-to-the-right slant of weft twist, conical

The Sierra Nevada and Sacramento Valley homeland of the Maidu people is as varied as their great art. This diagonally twined Valley Maidu burden basket has redbud designs and a sedge root background. The basket also has plain twining over two warps just below the reinforcing rod at the rim. Diagonally twined burden baskets extended from the Sacramento Valley Maidu through the Patwin country to the Pomo. H: 18″, D: 19″ (California State Parks, Bidwell Mansion State Historic Site, #139-19-40)

beargrass overlay, and (6) using somewhat similar starts to those of the Achumawi and Atsugewi.

But Maidu burden baskets remained distinct in most technical features and so they can be easily distinguished from those of the Atsugewi and Achumawi. Maidu concepts that remain uninfluenced by the Atsugewi and Achumawi include: (1) the Maidu beargrass double overlay, (2) the extensive Maidu use of horizontal band patterns, (3) the Maidu use on burden baskets of a down-to-the-right slant of weft twist as opposed to the up-to-the-right slant of twist of the Atsugewi, Achumawi and others, (4) the differences in Maidu rim selvages from those of the Atsugewi and Achumawi, (5) the Maidu avoidance of redbud as rim wrapping material on burden baskets in contrast to the Atsugewi and Achumawi who used it, and (6) the Mountain Maidu use of diagonal twining at the top and bottom of their burden baskets.

Interestingly, even when they borrowed burden basket designs from the Atsugewi and Achumawi, the Mountain Maidu changed the overall patterns and made them their shape and some design concepts. But such a connection is from the distant past and was long ago altered by the Maidu people's own artistic concepts and by later Atsugewi and Achumawi influence.

The **Foothill Nisenan Maidu** made two types of burden baskets. One was plain twined, often with a leather-covered point to stick in the ground. There was sometimes a distinctive narrow design band at the top and/or bottom of this style of burden basket. The second type of Foothill Nisenan burden basket was diagonally twined with a leather-covered base.

In the Sacramento Valley, the **Konkow Valley Maidu** made yet another type of burden basket. The Konkow Valley Maidu burden basket was diagonally twined with designs done in spiral lattice binding, a feature also found on Pomo and Patwin diagonally twined burden baskets. However, Valley Maidu and Patwin burden baskets were conical, not bell-shaped like Pomo burden baskets. The Valley Maidu burden basket also had large, coarse over-stitching around the base for strength and durability. Although diagonal designs were sometimes used, the Valley Maidu burden baskets usually had horizontal band designs. The Patwin also used horizontal bands on their burden baskets. The Patwin and some Valley Maidu burden baskets used chevron-shaped designs in their bands, as did some Nisenan Maidu burden baskets (Dawson p.c.). These chevron designs had the point of the chevron horizontally arranged and placed close together so as to form a cohesive band. All these characteristics serve to underscore a close connection between Valley Maidu diagonally twined burden baskets and those of the Patwin. Pomo diagonally twined burden baskets with their bell-shape and diagonal designs are a bit more distantly related.

Either the Pomo or the Valley Maidu first developed the North Central California type of diagonally twined burden basket. It then spread to the Patwin after their arrival in the Sacramento Valley. What is so distinctively Maidu in twined burden baskets is the use of three to seven or eight horizontal bands for the design. These striking bands are found with varying degrees of frequency in all Maidu groups and occur on both plain twined and diagonally twined burden baskets. Another striking Maidu feature is the near perfect cone shape of their plain twined burden baskets.

It should be mentioned that Riddell (1978, 18) reported a diagonally twined burden basket from the Mountain Maidu at Honey Lake "with overlay design." If this statement is accurate, this would be a fifth type of Maidu burden basket, one that is very different in concept from the Valley Maidu diagonally twined burden basket.

No other diagonally twined Maidu burden baskets used overlay designs. The Susanville Mountain Maidu had extensive interaction with the Northern Paiute and the Paiute made diagonally twined burden baskets, but Paiute patterns were not done using overlay. It is possible that in the Susanville area, the Maidu did make diagonally twined burden baskets, too. However, the mention of overlay in conjunction with diagonal twining would be a major departure from the standard Mountain Maidu practice. If it occurred at all, it would probably be a late adaptation.

Small Burden Baskets

A smaller burden basket was made by some Mountain Maidu, probably for collecting seeds to be poured into the big, full-size burden basket and carried home (Riddell 1978, 18). This small conical basket was made of willow with bracken fern root and redbud designs.

Mortar Hoppers

Twined mortar hoppers are nearly universal in Northern California and extend well into Oregon. But among the Maiduan peoples, apparently only the Northeastern Maidu and foothill Konkow Maidu made mortar hoppers (Dixon 1905, 179; Beals 1933, 352; Voegelin 1942, 74).

The absence of mortar hoppers from the Valley Maidu and Nisenan Maidu and their apparent rarity among other Maidu groups is interesting. Mortar hoppers were almost indispensable bottomless baskets used to keep acorn particles from flying out of the mortar during pounding. They were also useful for keeping debris from being blown into the acorn flour during processing. The mortar hopper was so widespread and essential to acorn processing in Central California that we would expect it among all the Maidu.

Even the limited presence of mortar hoppers among Mountain Maidu seems to be the result of influence from tribes to the north (Kroeber 1973, 60). The Mountain Maidu twined mortar hoppers are almost certainly derived from the Atsugewi or Achumawi (Kroeber 1935, 415; Riddell 1978, 18; Dawson p.c.; Bibby p.c., 2005). It has been suggested that mortar hoppers may have arrived among the Plumas County Maidu through intermarriage with Atsugewi and Achumawi women. This supports the view that mortar hoppers collected from Maidu people might: (1) be an introduced tradition, (2) be trade pieces, or (3) be the result of intermarriage with non-Maidu women. Many Plumas County Maidu families have Atsugewi and Achumawi ancestors in their genealogies

Some Nisenan Maidu twined seedbeaters, such as this one, also served as trays for drying acorns. Purchased from a Nisenan woman at her camp at Yankee Jim, Placer County, in 1902. L: 17", W: 16.5" (C. Hart Merriam collection, University of California at Davis, #317)

Ranges and adjacent valleys. In the Coast Ranges and valleys, compared to the Sierras, there are comparatively few flat rock outcrops where bedrock mortars could be established. In contrast, the Sierra Nevada Mountains offer vast numbers of flat rock outcrops where bedrock mortars could be conveniently established. With an abundance of broad, flat rock outcrops in their land, mortar hoppers were less essential to the Maidu and Miwok people. Mortar hoppers spread well inland only in northeastern California among the Achumawi, Atsugewi and Yana. This may have been because their territory is in the volcanic lava country of the Cascade Range where granite bedrock is a less common than in the Sierras.

Mortar Hopper Start Baskets

Mortar hopper start baskets were used to begin the mortar hopper and then cut out after the mortar hopper was finished. Having a hole in the bottom necessitated that mortar hoppers have some kind of temporary starting knot and supporting structure where the hole was to be located.

and these two cultures regularly made mortar hoppers (Bibby p.c., 2005).

Anthropologist Roland Dixon collected a mortar hopper from the Plumas County Maidu about 1900 (Dixon 1905, 179, fig. 44a). This twined hopper is lower and broader than many Atsugewi and Achumawi mortar hoppers. This Maidu mortar hopper also has narrow horizontal bands. The narrow horizontal band designs are similar in concept to horizontal patterns found on Maidu burden baskets. Atsugewi and Achumawi hoppers, in contrast, tend to have diagonal patterns or broader horizontal designs. This suggests Maidu origin rather than a trade item.

Mortar hoppers were used less by the Maidu than among any other Central Californians, except the Sierra Miwok. The limited use of mortar hoppers partly must have been the result of geography. Mortar hoppers were a Coast Range invention, originating among the Pomo and Yuki. Mortar hoppers primarily spread north and south along the Coast

The most common Maidu seedbeater was twined. This Mountain (Northeastern) Maidu twined seedbeater is made of maple wefts with willow warps. L: 25", W: 19" (Turtle Bay Exploration Park, Redding, California #1963.1.32)

The solution was to make a temporary start basket comprised of the starting knot and warps to support the beginning of the mortar hopper.

Stewart Culin collected a twined mortar hopper start basket (Brooklyn Museum 08.491.8794) from a Maidu family near Quincy in 1908. It consisted of a slightly flaring, handle-like woven bundle of willow warp sticks. This bundle-like basket of close-twined conifer root wefts was woven in plain twining. The weft slant is up-to-the-right for the conifer root weft section. But a lower section has three courses of cloth rags for wefts with a down-to-the-right weft slant. The Maidu did use both these slants of weft twist (Elsasser 1978, 633; Bibby p.c., 2005).

Twined Cooking Pots

Only the Mountain Maidu made twined cooking pots. These were similar to those of the Atsugewi and Achumawi (Dawson p.c.). The Mountain Maidu also made coiled cooking pots. All other Maidu groups made only coiled cooking pots.

Close-Twined Sifters

The Nisenan Maidu made close-twined triangular sifters with a very short handle. This basket was also used to dry acorns (C. Hart Merriam notes, University of California at Davis; Voegelin 1942, 193). It is rather seedbeater-like in appearance.

Trays and Scoops

Various types of trays and scoop-shaped baskets were woven using both plain twining and diagonal twining (Voegelin 1942, 77). Both close-twined and openwork forms were probably made.

On these scoop-shaped forms, the starting knot was well inset from the basket's rim rather than being placed at the edge. It was located toward the narrower end of the scoop. This inset starting knot was unusual, as the vast majority of scoop-shaped baskets in California had their starting knot near the edge at one end.

Cups

The Mountain Maidu made twined cups of the Achumawi and Atsugewi type for acorn soup and mush (Riddell 1978, 18). These cups were probably used for other drinks as well.

Basketry Hats

Mountain Maidu women are said to have worn a twined tule hat similar to those of the Klamath, Modoc and Eastern Atsugewi (Riddell 1984, 375). The Mountain Maidu traded coiled baskets for twined ones with the Atsugewi and that may have been the source of these hats (Davis 1966, 35).

Seedbeaters were vitally important for gathering small seeds. The Maidu made both wickerwork and twined seedbeaters. Wickerwork seedbeaters were used by Maidu groups in the Sacramento Valley and adjacent Sierra Foothills. These seedbeaters are related to Pomo and Patwin wickerwork seedbeaters. This Konkow Maidu wickerwork seedbeater is made of ceanothus and was collected in 1911 at Mooretown, east of Oroville in Butte County. L: 17", W: 13" (Oakland Museum of California, #H16.1556)

One writer claimed that the Mountain Maidu and Foothill Konkow Maidu made coiled basketry hats (Voegelin 1942, 70, 86). A twined hat would seem more likely, especially among the Mountain Maidu. Coiled hats were not characteristic of any North Central California tribe. Coiled hats were a South Central and Southern California trait. They also appear archeologically in the western Great Basin in Nevada (Burgett 2004).

MAIDU OPENWORK TWINED BASKETS AND WICKERWORK BASKETS

Twined and Wickerwork Seedbeaters

Maidu seedbeaters were a variable group, although they all generally had relatively short handles (Dixon 1905, 188, fig. 47). There were at least two types of twined seedbeaters, one plain twined and the other diagonally twined. There was also a wickerwork seedbeater. Maidu plain twined seedbeaters were oval, shallow baskets with a short handle. The Maidu diagonal twined seedbeaters were made using openwork diagonal twining on zigzag warps of willow (California Academy of Sciences 1980, 25, plate 46). Interestingly, the Nisenan reportedly made both openwork and close-twined seed beaters (Voegelin 1942, 193).

Twined seedbeaters were widespread, but wickerwork seedbeaters were collected only from the Valley and Foothill Maidu. Voegelin's Maidu consultants reportedly denied having wickerwork seed beaters (Voegelin 1942, 164).

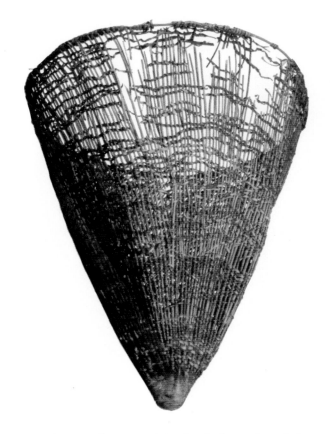

This Konkow Maidu openwork burden basket is the only known early example of an openwork burden basket from the Konkow people. The basket is made of ceanothus. Collected in 1911 at Pleasant Valley, Butte County. H: 21", D: 20" (Oakland Museum of California, #H16.1693)

However, Dixon actually saw wickerwork seedbeaters being used by Konkow Maidu during his 1905 visit. In fact, he said that among the Konkow Maidu, wickerwork seedbeaters were the most common type (Dixon 1905, 148 and 188, plate 47) and at least one example survives (Oakland Museum basket, #H16.1556). Dixon worked with an earlier generation of Maidu consultants than did Voegelin and it is likely that disagreement results from wickerwork seedbeaters being discontinued before plain twined ones stopped being made.

The Maidu wickerwork seedbeater was oval with a short handle. A reinforcing rim surrounded the edge of the oval portion. The warp sticks were gathered together in the short handle. This handle broadened at its upper end. These short-handled, wickerwork seedbeaters are reported from some, but not all, Valley and Foothill Nisenan and Konkow Maidu groups (Barrett 1996, 80; Elsasser 1978, 629). For other Maidu groups, the plain twined seedbeater was the standard seedbeater type (Voegelin 1942, 77).

The Extent of Wickerwork Among the Maidu

Both Lawrence Dawson and Alfred Kroeber reported wickerwork baskets among the Maidu. Dawson noted that besides wickerwork seedbeaters, the Valley Maidu made broad, low wickerwork baskets shaped rather like an old fashioned shallow washbasin (Kroeber 1925, 244, 415; Dawson p.c.).

Openwork Twined Burden Baskets

The Maidu made rough, openwork diagonally twined and plain twined burden baskets. These baskets had warps bent down and bound under the rim wrapping to attach the rim's reinforcing rod. The starting knot was ruggedly made for durability.

This openwork basket was, like the closed twined Maidu burden basket, conical in shape with V-shaped sides. Among the Valley Nisenan Maidu, rough openwork carrying baskets were made of willow by men (Kroeber 1929, 262). These were coarse and uneven compared to the fine, close-twined burden baskets made by the women. Rough openwork carrying baskets were used to carry acorns or firewood.

Gathering Baskets

Gathering baskets were carried in the hand and when full, the contents were poured into a larger burden basket. Openwork gathering baskets had less pointed bottoms than burden baskets. Gathering baskets reached their broadest diameter about two-thirds of the way up the side of the basket. The sides then incurved slightly from there to the rim. These twined baskets had warps cut off at the rim; the slant of weft twist was down-to-the-right (Dawson p.c.). Modest horizontal bands might be used as designs, but these openwork baskets were probably often left undecorated.

Openwork Sifters

All Maidu groups made twined openwork sifting baskets (Voegelin 1942, 77). These baskets were of at least two types. Some were oval and shallow with one end nearly flat (Dixon 1905, 179, fig. 43). Others were rough workbaskets with a short, crude handle. (See also "Trays and Scoops" in the close-twined section.)

Openwork Storage Baskets

Women and youngsters gathered acorns and stored them in large openwork storage baskets in the houses (Dixon 1905, 184).

Wickerwork Shallow, Basin-Shaped Baskets

As mentioned previously, the Valley Maidu made shallow, wickerwork basin-shaped baskets (Oakland Museum collection #16-1619; Dawson p.c.). These baskets and seedbeaters were the only type of wickerwork baskets made by the Maidu.

Scoops

Some Maidu groups, including the Valley Maidu, made scoop baskets for various purposes such as scooping up fish from streams or drying acorns (Voegelin 1942, 55). These scoops undoubtedly had other purposes as well and there may have been more than one type of scoop. Surviving examples have a short handle and are larger than seedbeaters. Merriam described scoops as looking like modern dustpans in form (Merriam 1967, 412). Dawson noted that on at least some Maidu scoops the starting knot is inset from the basket's edge, and not at the very edge of the basket as commonly practiced by other groups.

Cradles

All Maidu groups made lying-type cradles, some with sunshades. The Mountain Maidu and some Foothill Konkow Maidu used a Y-frame type cradle with a rod arching over the top of the two arms of the "Y," which made for a convenient handle (Dixon 1905, 200; Kroeber 1925, plate 40). Other similar Y-shaped cradles simply had the reinforcing rod arch over the top. Some cradles had a point at the lowest end of the "Y" to stick the cradle in the ground for stability and to help the child remain upright. Typical materials included the oak reinforcing rod, willow warps, and wefts of willow, redbud and/or pine root (Gladys Mankins quoted in Riddell 1960, 59; Bibby 2004, 103-104).

Typically, two cradles were made for each child. A newborn baby's receiving cradle was used for about 28 days. Then a second larger cradle replaced it, which was used for about a year (Voegelin 1942, 79, 119).

Basketry Bird Traps

Foothill Konkow Maidu and Northeastern Maidu made basketry traps to catch quail and various other birds (Voegelin 1942, 52).

Fish and Meat Trays

Openwork twined serving trays, ranging in shape from an oval to nearly a triangular shape, were used for serving fish and meat (Fang and Binder 1990, 198). The starting knot was within the narrow end of the tray inside of the reinforcing rod (Dawson p.c.).

Cone Shaped Fish Traps

The Mountain Maidu and Foothill Konkow Maidu made conical fish traps, usually in plain twining (Dixon 1905, 147; Voegelin 1942, 55). Fish traps were made of willow (Potts 1977, 35).

Funeral Baskets

Some Maidu groups occasionally put the corpse in a basket before cremation or burial (these baskets may have been close-twined). Deceased infants and children up to two or three years old might be placed in their cradle (Voegelin 1942, 135, 228).

Trade Pieces

The Nisenan and other Maidu also occasionally traded for carrying baskets, seedbeaters and winnowing trays from the Paiute and probably the Washoe (Davis 1966, 42). These are very different looking baskets from Maidu baskets and are unlikely to be confused with Maidu work.

Comments

The Maidu had an exceptionally important role in the development of North Central California coiled basketry. As a result of the long presence of coiling in their culture, the Maidu had come to use coiled basketry for many purposes. They created a fully developed, beautiful basketry tradition that had great appeal to other cultures. These factors plus a strategic geographical location resulted in an unsurpassed Maidu influence in introducing coiled basketry into North Central California.

Maidu basketry was much admired by other cultures. Sacramento Valley Maidu coiled basketry techniques and some forms directly influenced the Patwin and indirectly influenced the Pomo, Nomlaki, Huchnom, Lake Miwok, Wappo, Coast Miwok, Plains Miwok and Ohlone/Costanoan. The coiled basketry of all these groups has some Valley Maidu roots. The coiling of all these cultures is similar enough that we can speak of it as belonging to a Valley Maidu-Patwin-Pomo tradition.

It was the Maidu of the Sacramento Valley who influenced so many others. Most Sierra and Foothill Maidu basketry had an artistic character quite distinctive from their neighbors. Nevertheless, Sierra Maidu influence can be seen in Miwok feast pots, certain Washoe designs and probably in many ways among the Valley Maidu themselves.

Maidu people were also, of course, influenced by other cultures. For example, Mountain (Northeastern) Maidu twined basketry seems to have borrowed extensively from the Atsugewi and Achumawi. Yet, overall, the Maidu produced some of the most distinctive coiled and twined basketry in California. They played a key role in the development of North Central California coiled basketry.

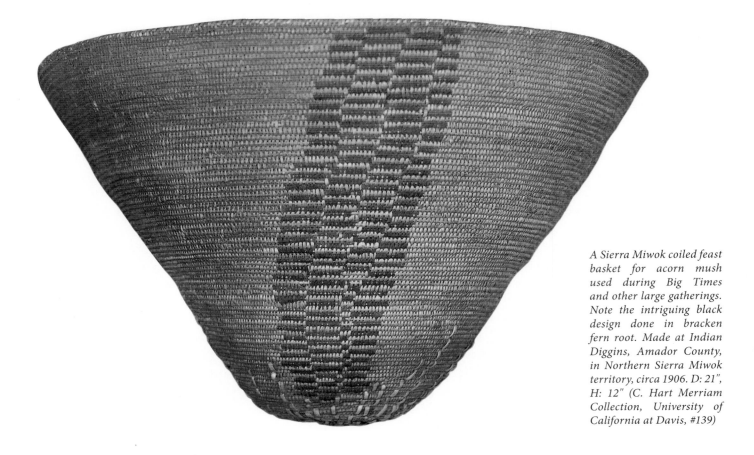

A Sierra Miwok coiled feast basket for acorn mush used during Big Times and other large gatherings. Note the intriguing black design done in bracken fern root. Made at Indian Diggins, Amador County, in Northern Sierra Miwok territory, circa 1906. D: 21", H: 12" (C. Hart Merriam Collection, University of California at Davis, #139)

The Sierra Miwok made both single-rod and three-rod foundation coiled baskets. This Sierra Miwok basket has a single-rod coiled foundation. Note how the edges of the black bracken fern root designs intermix with the buff colored background like the teeth of a comb. On three-rod foundation baskets the edges of designs do not have this serrated look, but instead have straight edges. Purchased in 1902 at Murphys, Calaveras County, in Central Miwok territory. D: 14.5", H: 7" (C. Hart Merriam Collection, University of California at Davis, #157)

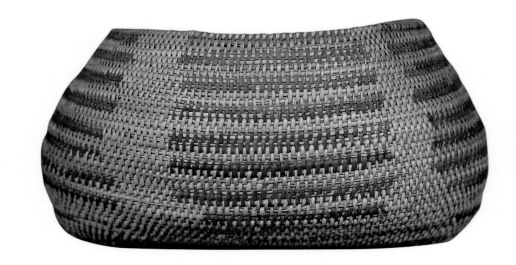

SIERRA MIWOK BASKETRY

Sierra Miwok country extends from Amador County southward beyond Yosemite to Mariposa. This land includes rolling foothills with oak and pine and the heavily forested Sierra Nevada Mountains. Numerous rivers such as the Mokulumne, Calaveras, Stanislaus, Tuolumne, Merced and Chowchilla rush down from the High Sierras to the Great Central Valley.

The Sierra Miwok people spoke three related languages (Northern, Central and Southern Miwok), plus various dialects. The Sierra Miwok were, and remain today, comprised of politically independent communities. However, based on similar basketry and culture, we can speak of the Sierra Miwok as an ethnic group.

There are, of course, other Miwok people besides the Sierra Miwok. To the northwest of the Sierra Miwok were the Plains Miwok of the Great Central Valley and the Delta. Adjoining the Plains Miwok were the Bay Miwok of Mount Diablo and the Diablo Valley. Farther west, the Coast Miwok lived from the Golden Gate north to Bodega Bay. Farthest north were the Lake Miwok, whose homeland was near Clear Lake. The Coast Miwok and Lake Miwok were the most distant in language and location from the Sierra Miwok. The basketry of all the other Miwok speaking peoples – Coast, Lake, Bay and Plains – was different from the basketry made by the Sierra Miwok.

A Great Miwok Land

The Miwok have a long and amazing history. At one time ancestral Miwok and Ohlone (Costanoan) were probably one people. Their languages are clearly related and are grouped by linguists under the name Utian. Basketry research suggests that ancestral Miwok-Ohlone long ago entered California from western Nevada, probably after having been a part of the ancient Lovelock culture northeast of Reno (Moratto 1984, 552; Callaghan 2002, 2; Dawson, n.d., "The Spread of Coiled Basketry in California").

Preliminary mitochondrial DNA evidence also links early western Great Basin people to the Miwok. Ancestral Miwok people were in Nevada prior to arrival of the Numic speaking Paiute and Shoshone. The mtDNA[1] evidence indicates an ancient western Nevada population with mtDNA very similar to modern Miwok, Ohlone and Yokuts people. This, along with basketry studies, supports the view that ancestral Miwok lived in the western Great Basin prior to coming into California (Eshleman 2002; Callaghan 2002).

There is disagreement as to how long ancestral Miwok have been in Central California. One view held is that there is archeological evidence that between 4,000 and 2,500 years ago ancestral Miwok/Ohlone people were living in the Sacramento Valley Delta and the foothills to the east and west. Some Sierra Miwok families spread along the southern Sierra foothills and the mountains. Other Miwok people migrated far westward, reaching the Pacific Ocean in Marin and southern Sonoma Counties. By around 2,500 years ago, archeological and linguistic evidence also suggests that ancestral Ohlone/Costanoan separated from the Miwok and began moving into the San Francisco Bay and Monterey Bay areas (Breschini 1983; Moratto 1984, 553-554; Foster 1996, 89-90; Breschini and Haversat 2005, 192-193).

A second view is based on preliminary mtDNA research. This suggests a later migration date of only about 2,000 years ago for ancestral Miwok-Ohlone coming into the Central Valley (Eshleman 2002, 75). The mtDNA evidence also suggests a relation between the Miwok and early western Nevadans dating back before the arrival of the Paiute (Eshleman 2002).

This would mean that ancestral Miwok arrived later in California. It has been suggested that the differences in the dates proposed for arrival in Central California may result from differing interpretations of archeological dates (Breschini p.c., 2005).

While the dates of the Miwok expansion are debatable, that fact that it occurred is not. Ancestral Miwok-Ohlone crossed the Sierras at some point in time before arriving in the Central Valley and surrounding foothills. Additionally, it is almost certain that the Miwok did not all migrate at once. Miwok basketry suggests different Miwok groups arrived at different time periods.

For centuries Miwok territory stretched from the Sierras to the Pacific Coast. This continuous, but probably

---

[1] The term mtDNA stands for mitochondrial DNA. DNA is the molecule that encodes genetic information. Mitochondria are tiny energy producers within cells that have their own DNA molecules. Mitochondrial have their own DNA molecules and are much shorter than nuclear DNA (see: Eshleman 2002; Breschini and Haversat 2004).

These coiled Sierra Miwok bowls illustrate a variety of Sierra Miwok designs. (Lawrence Dawson)

periodically changing, Miwok territory lasted until the arrival of the Patwin in the southern Sacramento Valley and the expansion of the Wappo in to the Napa Valley. Movements by the Patwin and Wappo separated the Coast Miwok and Lake Miwok from the main body of Miwok, perhaps around fifteen hundred years ago (Whistler 1977, 157, 161-163; Hattori 1982, 208; Moratto 1984, 552, 562-563; Foster 1996, 90).

As a result, the Miwok became separated into two linguistic and geographic divisions. The western Miwok became the Coast and Lake Miwok. The eastern Miwok became the Bay, Plains and Sierra Miwok. The Sierra Miwok basketry is the heart of this chapter.

The Origins of Coiled Basketry: California, the Great Basin and the Southwest

The history of basketry is more difficult to trace than, say, pottery. Basketry is perishable and rarely found in California archeological sites. But in the dry caves of western Nevada and elsewhere in the Great Basin, numerous ancient examples of twined basketry, coiled basketry and wickerwork survived. This gives us insight into what we might find in California if more complete archeological preservation had been possible.

In western Nevada, twined baskets appeared long before coiling. Twined basketry was found at Skinner's Site A at Nevada's dry Winnemucca Lake that dates back approximately 10,000 to 11,000 years (Rozaire 1969, E. Jolie 2005, p.c.). Coiled basketry found at the Kramer Cave site on the northwest shore of Lake Winnemucca in western Nevada sites dates back at least 4,200 years (Adovasio 1986, 199-200; E. Jolie 2004, 162; E. Jolie p.c., 2005).

Even older coiled basketry appears in the eastern Great Basin at Hogup Cave, Utah, about 8,500 years ago (Aikens 1970; Adovasio 1970; E. Jolie 2004, 179-180). Coiling apparently spread from eastern Nevada and Utah to western Nevada (Adovasio 1986, 203; E. Jolie 2004, 179-180). It is uncertain, but possible that coiled basketry developed even earlier in New Mexico, west Texas and northern Mexico and then spread up the Rio Grande Valley and on into Utah and Nevada.

Twined basketry pre-dated coiling throughout the Great Basin, as it did in California. Over time, however, in the Great Basin coiled baskets begin surpassing twined basketry in frequency in archeological sites (E. Jolie p.c., 2005). Similarly, in Central and Southern California coiled baskets replaced twined baskets for certain purposes.

Linguistics provides an interesting insight into Miwok basketry history. The Miwok verb "to twine" is a very ancient proto-Miwok word dating from the time when all Miwok languages were one. This is not surprising since twining is quite old, long pre-dating coiling. In contrast, the Sierra Miwok verb "to coil" is a more recent word (Catherine Callaghan p.c., 2005). This supports the view that the Miwok people twined well before they began to weave coiled basketry.

Archeological evidence also supports the view that twined basketry came into California long before coiled basketry. Archeological research in Central California indicates a virtual absence of bone awls of the type necessary to make coiled baskets prior to at least 3,000 years ago (Elsasser 1978, 634). Before that time, primarily twined basketry and perhaps wickerwork basketry were made within the state. Thus, if the absence of basketry awls is a reliable indicator and if the dating is accurate, coiled basketry was not made in California until after the Early Horizon Period, which ended around 3,000 years ago (Baumhoff and Heizer 1958, 55; Elsasser 1978, 634; Moratto 1984, 181-183; Breschini p.c., 2005). The key point is that coiled basketry arrived in California thousands of years after twined basketry.

Ancient Coiled Basketry in Western Nevada and Its Relationship to North Central California

California coiled basketry is not all the same. Nor does it all have the same origin and history. Miwok, Maidu and Washoe coiling are all directly related to the ancient coiled basketry in western Nevada.

Three cultures border the general area where the ancient Lovelock culture once flourished. The Sierra Miwok and Maidu are close to western Nevada and the Washoe actually live in that state. The coiled baskets of these three peoples have clear ties to the ancient archeological basketry found in the western Nevada caves. The ancient basket weaving culture located there has been called the Lovelock culture, named after Lovelock Cave, which is one of the most important archeological sites in the area.

Significantly, the basketry of the Paiute and other present day Numic speaking people of Nevada is unrelated to that made by the Lovelock culture (Adovasio 1986, 204-205; Fowler and Dawson 1986, 728-729). The basketry of the Sierra Miwok, Washoe and Maidu, however, is related and does have important features in common with the coiled baskets of the ancient Lovelock culture (Dawson p.c.).

What is striking about the Lovelock culture coiled basketry is that it is very much like North Central California basketry. In fact, it was so Central Californian that it was at first thought that these baskets could be trade pieces from California (Baumhoff and Heizer 1958, 54-55). But later studies strongly suggest that these baskets were made in western Nevada and were not trade pieces. What seems likely is that this type of coiling developed in the Great Basin, probably in western Nevada, and was brought into California by ancestral Miwok, Maidu and possibly Washoe (Tuohy 1974, 28-39; Dawson, n.d.; Dawson p.c.; see also Burgett 2004).

Western Nevada Archeological Coiled Baskets: A Grandmother of Coiling in California?

Lawrence Dawson's studies led him to conclude that ancient Lovelock culture's coiled baskets had many features in common with Sierra Miwok baskets. Shared features include some basket forms (such as round winnower trays and truncated cone-shaped cooking pots, for example), leftward work direction, several kinds of starting knots, three-rod foundations (and the occasional use of single-rod foundations), herringbone-type over-stitched rims, split stitches, interlocking weft stitches, the use of duck feathers and designs using weft substitution. Most of these characteristics are also found among Maidu and Washoe coiled basketry. Dawson also concluded that Maidu and Washoe basketry was related to ancient Lovelock basketry (Dawson, n.d. and Dawson p.c.).

Feather baskets, cooking pots and winnowing and parching trays were major types of coiled archeological baskets found. The Sierra Miwok and the Maidu made such baskets. Feather baskets from Nevada archeological sites also have designs spread about the basket surface in a manner similar to the Sierra Miwok style. These feather baskets may date back as far as 2,500 years (Adovasio 1986, 199; Dawson 1988).

The technique of concealing weft fag ends in the foundation occurs in the ancient Lovelock archeological baskets and in Sierra Miwok, Sierra Maidu and Washoe work. Split stitches are common on the Lovelock area baskets and these are found in Maidu, Plains Miwok and occasionally Sierra Miwok work. The practice of splitting weft stitches was an important link to the Lovelock culture that was less common among the Sierra Miwok, but was usual among the Maidu and Plains Miwok.

As mentioned previously, early historic examples of Sierra Miwok and Washoe coiling are nearly identical and clearly share a common ancestry (Fowler and Dawson 1986, 729; Dawson p.c.). But unlike the Sierra Miwok, the Washoe have different mtDNA from the ancient western Nevada sample (Eshleman 2002). Basketry studies, however, suggest that the Washoe coiling is related to the Lovelock culture. For example, Washoe openwork twined baskets were made with whole shoot wefts. This twining is neither Sierra Miwok nor Paiute. It is, however, an important basketry feature that only the Washoe share with the Lovelock culture (Fowler and Dawson 1986, 729).

The Maidu were either a part of the Lovelock people or came in contact with them (Dawson 1988, 2; Dawson, n.d.; see also Bates 1982, 33-34; Burgett 2004 and the Maidu chapter in this volume). Maidu coiled baskets have important differences from Sierra Miwok and Washoe coiling, but they also have many features in common with Lovelock basketry.

Ancestral Miwok and Maidu women brought different versions of Lovelock inspired coiling into Central California. Interestingly, there are differences in the coiled basketry among Miwok cultures. The Sierra Miwok and Washoe made coiled baskets almost identical in their technical features. In contrast, Coast Miwok, Lake Miwok and Plains Miwok coiling are all more closely related to the basketry of the Maidu. How could this happen?

The differences in Sierra Miwok coiling from that of other Miwok cultures could be the result of any of several events. The Coast, Lake and Plains Miwok may have simply adopted the general Maidu-style coiling of various neighbors, such as the Maidu, Pomo, Patwin and others. The Sierra Miwok may have been less influenced by neighboring California cultures and simply continued to make their older type of Lovelock-style coiling. Alternatively, the Sierra Miwok could have adopted coiling from the Washoe after moving into the Sierras. This possibility cannot be ruled out, but an ancient Sierra Miwok link directly to their western Nevada ancestors seems more likely. Another possibility is that the Sierra Miwok simply remained in Nevada longer than other Miwok groups, retained their old style coiling and brought it with them when they moved over the Sierras. What actually happened is uncertain.

Sierra Miwok Coiled Basketry

TECHNICAL FEATURES

Sierra Miwok technical features are especially interesting as they may be the features of some of the earliest coiled basketry in California. Starting knots were most typically round, spiral "clock spring" starts where a strand of material was tightly wound around itself like a clock spring. The start was then wrapped with a weft and stitched over with stitches that radiated to the outer edge of the starting knot. There was often a hole remaining in the center of the starting knot. This hole was frequently plugged and/or stitched over to close it. Oval starts, when needed, were made by bending a foundation rod back against itself and wrapping it with weft materials (Elsasser 1978, 630; Bates and Lee 1990, 52).

The coiled basketry of the Miwok people of the Sierra Nevada Mountains is one of the oldest coiling traditions in California. Coiled basketry came into California from western Nevada with Sierra Miwok and Maidu people. This coiled cooking pot is a fine example of a Sierra Miwok basket. An elder at Rich Gold Rancheria near West Point, Calaveras County, in Northern Sierra Miwok country owned this basket. When Merriam purchased this basket from the Sierra Miwok weaver in 1903, it was full of delicious acorn mush. The basket has a three-rod foundation with designs done in bracken fern root. D: 12", H: 5.5" (C. Hart Merriam Collection, University of California at Davis, #158)

Work Direction: Sierra Miwok work direction was leftward (Elsasser 1978, 633; Bates and Lee 1990, 52).

Foundations were most commonly either three-rod or single-rod. These foundation types predominated through Sierra Miwok country among the Northern, Central and Southern Miwok. Two-rod foundations were rare and were sometimes merely used on the final coil. Grass bundle foundations were among the foundations used by the Central and Southern Miwok. Bates and Lee reported a few utilitarian Miwok baskets with a foundation of a rod and two grass stems. Dawson suggested that grass bundle foundation baskets, such as cooking pots collected among the Southern Sierra Miwok, may have been trade pieces from the Yokuts or Western Mono. At the very least, grass bundle foundations were likely adopted from these neighboring peoples. However, some Sierra Miwok traditionally made one type of basket, a coiled winnowing/sifting tray, which had a grass bundle foundation (Dawson p.c.; Barrett 1933, 239; Elsasser 1978, 630-633; Bates and Lee 1990, 52; Polanich 1996, 187).[2]

---

[2] Lawrence Dawson made notations for me that several of the coiled baskets illustrated by Barrett and Gifford (1933) were probably not Sierra Miwok, but trade pieces from the Western Mono or possibly the Yokuts. These baskets were: plate L, fig. 5; plate XLIV, figs. 3 and 4; plate XLIII, fig. 9 and plate XLI. These baskets appear to be Western Mono baskets with grass bundle foundations.

Coiling Stitches were overwhelmingly the **interlocking type stitch** (Elsasser 1978, 633). Interlocking stitching gives a basket a distinctive weft arrangement. If viewed carefully with your eye aligned along the basket's side, you can see tiny spaces between stitches extending away from the eye in a V-pattern. By following the same viewing procedure with non-interlocking stitches, the space between the wefts will line up nearly perpendicularly to the rim.

Occasional Sierra Miwok baskets using split-stitches and/or non-interlocking stitches have been purchased from Miwok people (Barrett and Gifford 1933, 239; Bates 1982, 7; Bates and Lee 1990, 51-52). Non-interlocking Miwok baskets generally have grass bundle foundations rather than rod foundations. It has been suggested that most of these baskets were either trade pieces or fairly recent introductions inspired by the Yokuts and/or Western Mono. Sierra Miwok winnowing trays, however, were the exception. Winnowing trays made using grass bundle foundations were definitely an old time Sierra Miwok practice (Dawson p.c.).

Weft fag ends were concealed in the foundation on the back face or simply trimmed on the work face. **Weft moving ends** were trimmed flush on the back face or were bent and bound under the weft stitches and hidden in the foundation. The **work face** on Sierra Miwok baskets was on the convex (generally smoother, exterior) side of the basket.

Rims on coiled baskets had either of two kinds of selvages. Rims might be plain wrapped (self rims) with a tapered coil ending. Other rims were over-stitched atop the final coil using a diagonal over-stitching or a herringbone over-stitching (Barrett and Gifford 1933, 239; Elsasser 1978, 630; Bates and Lee 1990, 54-55, figs. 88-91).

Surfaces were sometimes lumpy and a bit rough resulting from an uneven foundation (Moser 1987, 48). The Sierra Miwok did not produce exceptionally fancy coiling until the tourist trade developed after about 1910 (Dawson p.c.). Yet even some early baskets were beautifully made. Early Sierra Miwok baskets and early Washoe coiled baskets look much alike, but the Miwok surface was generally a bit less even than those of the Washoe.

Designs

The Sierra Miwok traditionally used only single color designs on each basket. The designs were done in either black or red. Rarely, a second color might be sparingly used. Some coiled cooking pots and even feast baskets were occasionally made without designs (C. Hart Merriam collection, UC Davis; Bates and Lee 1990, 56). After about

Diagonally over-stitched rims such as this one are found on some Sierra Miwok baskets. (Southwest Museum of the American Indian, Autry National Center, #811-G-2274)

1910, combining red and black in basket designs became increasingly common. This was primarily a response to non-Indian buying tastes.

Traditional Sierra Miwok designs included narrow horizontal lines or bands, narrow lines that crisscross forming open diamonds, small rectangles or squares, closely placed triangles alternately pointing upward and downward, various types of zigzags, diamonds and others. Another arrangement consisted of vertically stacked narrow horizontal lines, often with a vertical line running through the center of the horizontal lines. Sierra Miwok designs also might use scattered, floating blocky elements. Northern Sierra Miwok baskets show a preponderance of horizontal designs and, secondarily, vertical designs (Kroeber 1905, 149). This contrasts with their neighboring Nisenan Maidu designs where diagonals and zigzags were so frequently found. (Kroeber 1922, 77; Barrett and Gifford 1933, 243-245; Merriam 1967, 330-331; Dawson p.c.).

Some Miwok baskets had no designs at all for a good reason. C. Hart Merriam pointed out that while some Sierra Miwok baskets had very little or no designs, they had another virtue. These undecorated baskets were "extraordinarily hard, strong and compact and well made" of gray (bull) pine roots (*Pinus sabiniana*) (Merriam 1967, 335). Some design materials, such as bracken fern root, were weaker than pine root background wefts. Having no designs added strength to a basket and allowed it to be woven faster. Single rod cooking pots without designs were also made (Bates and Lee 1990, 56).

Coiled Basketry Materials

Sierra Miwok coiled basketry **foundations** commonly were willow shoots (*Salix*). Other foundation materials included ceanothus (*Ceanothus cuneatus* and *Ceanothus intergerrimus*), sumac or sourberry (*Rhus trilobata*) and hazel (*Corylus*). Deer grass (*Muhlenbergia rigens*) was often favored for winnowers/sifters and possibly some other baskets (Barrett and Gifford 1933, 229, 236-237; Elsasser 1978, 630; Bates and Lee 1990, 43; Mathewson 1998, 148).

For coiled basketry **wefts**, Barrett observed that the Sierra Miwok used redbud (*Cercis occidentalis*), sedge (*Carex barbarae*), maple (*Acer macrophyllum*), sumac (*Rhus trilobata*), and occasionally other materials. Split twigs of gray (bull) pine (*Pinus sabiniana*) were used, at least on single rod baskets (Barrett and Gifford 1933, 237-239; Levy 1978, 496; Mathewson 1998, 164). The Southern Sierra Miwok also used willow for wefts on coiled baskets, although it was mostly obtained from the Mono Lake Paiute in trade (Barrett and Gifford 1933, 237; Bates and Lee 1990, 43; Dawson p.c.).

Weft design materials were bracken fern root (*Pteridium aquilinum*) for black designs and redbud for red designs. Black designs were a bit more common than red designs. As noted earlier, these colors were not often used together on baskets until Euro-American tourism influenced cultural changes after 1910.

The **weft appearance** of Sierra Miwok coiled baskets is fairly distinctive. Sierra Miwok coiled baskets often have flat, rather broad wefts. Miwok wefts typically look broader and flatter than on many other coiled Central California baskets.

Mends

Extensive mending was common on Sierra Miwok baskets. In fact, worn out baskets from the Western Mono were obtained by the Sierra Miwok who repaired them and continued to use them (Polanich 1994, 169).

Designs are an easily transmitted cultural feature of basketry. Weaving techniques are much more resistant to change and are far more helpful in identifying baskets than relying on designs alone. This Sierra Miwok basket has contrasting horizontal and vertical patterns, a classic Western Mono design arrangement. But all its technical features, the choice of materials and the horizontal designs are Sierra Miwok. This feast basket was purchased at Tuolumne Meadows in 1910. It is very similar to a documented coiled basket from Murphys in Central Miwok country. The basket shown here has designs done in bracken fern root, a peeled shoot background material, interlocking stitches and a three-rod foundation. D: 18", H: 12". (Private collection)

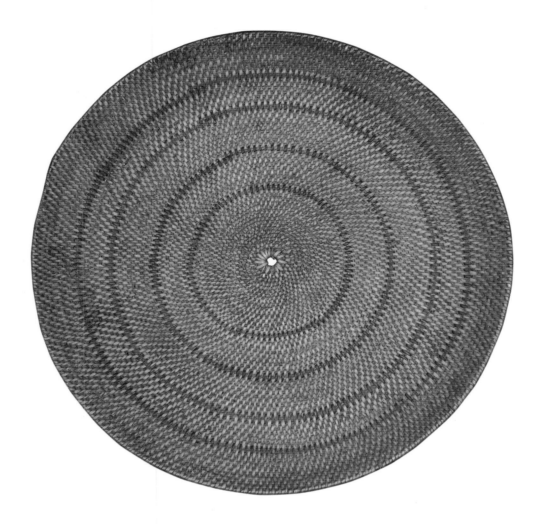

A Central Sierra Miwok tray from Tuolumne County. Coiled winnowing trays were an important Miwok contribution as they and the Maidu were the first people to introduce winnowing coiled trays into Central California. Purchased in 1902. D: 14.5", H: 1" (C. Hart Merriam Collection, University of California at Davis, #177)

Major Types of Sierra Miwok Coiled Basketry

Cooking Pots

Early Sierra Miwok and early Washoe cooking pots both had truncated cone shapes, flaring sides and sometimes over-stitched rims. Washoe cooking pots generally had a more even surface than did those of the Sierra Miwok (Dawson p.c.). Designs were simple, but attractive.

Feast Baskets

Sierra Miwok feast baskets were huge, some being over two feet deep. They were tall with flaring sides, close to Maidu feast baskets in shape. These giant baskets, when filled, were so large and heavy that several men were needed to lift them. To lift such a heavy basket, straps made of saplings were wrapped around the basket to provide a grip for the men doing the lifting. Once the feast baskets were properly positioned, the prepared food was then dipped out by women using smaller baskets and served. These big feast baskets were owned by the village leader and were not communally owned (Barrett and Gifford 1933, 241).

Dipping Baskets, Food Servers, Drinking Cups and Other Small Bowls

Small, shallow dipping, serving and storage bowls were made with sides that could be globular, straight or flaring. These baskets were often decorated with simple horizontal band designs. Some had three-rod foundations, but others were made using single-rod foundations. Among this type of basket were the low, broad bowls about nine inches in diameter and several inches high that held water during the weaving process to keep materials moist (Barrett and Gifford 1933, 315, plate 45, figs. 1-4 and 321, plate 48; Merriam 1967, 350; Bates and Lee 1990, 58-59).

Winnowing and Parching Baskets

Round, coiled Miwok winnowers were very common and important baskets. Their form was a flat, coiled tray. Miwok used sumac warps (*Rhus trilobata*) for foundation rods on at least some coiled winnowers (Mathewson 1998, 154). Most trays for sifting acorn meal had three-rod foundations. However, the Southern Sierra Miwok around Mariposa and probably others groups often used grass bundle foundations in their winnowers (Dawson p.c.).

Oval Small Storage Baskets

Lovely, finely sewn oval baskets for holding valuables were made with a rim finished with backstitching all around the top. Other less fancy, oval baskets were made, too; some using single-rod foundations. Some oval baskets, perhaps innovations, had lids (Silva and Cain 1976, 51).

Treasure Basket

A globular basket was made to hold valued possessions (Dawson p.c.).

Feather Baskets

Lovely, coiled feather baskets were made. A variety of feathers were used on these feather baskets including quail, woodpecker, mallard, meadowlark and blackbird (Barrett and Gifford 1933, 238; Bates 1982, 25-28, 34-35; Bates and Lee 1990, 57).

Sierra Miwok designs using duck feathers resemble those of the Washoe and ancient Lovelock people in western Nevada (Fowler and Dawson 1986, 729). One distinctive Miwok feather basket studied had only quail topknots scattered about its sides.

Sierra Miwok feather baskets were similar to some Valley Maidu baskets with the bottoms not feathered, frequent use of a low bowl-shape and the common use of mallard and woodpecker feathers. Pomo feather baskets were less similar in feather placement, shape and design layout.

Basket Types Not Traditionally Made by the Sierra Miwok

The Sierra Miwok did not make mortar hoppers, either in coiling or twining (Kroeber 1925, 448; Barrett and Gifford 1933, 208-209, 229-243). There is a vague, unconfirmed report of the Sierra Miwok using worn out baskets as mortar hoppers on rare occasions (Dawson pc.). If true, then old coiled cooking pots with their bottoms removed would have been the likely choice.

There are four types of baskets reported by a single source (Aginsky 1943) that were almost certainly absent among the Miwok, except possibly as trade pieces. Aginsky conflicts with all other sources and our own research. This could be because his information was gathered at a relatively late date. Intermarriage and the adoption of new basketry forms to please non-Indian buyers were causing changes in Miwok basketry. Aginsky reported water bottles, bottleneck baskets, hats and twined cooking pots as being made by some or all Sierra Miwok groups (Aginsky 1943, 417). In fact, the Sierra Miwok did not traditionally make the Yokuts-style hat, the "bottleneck" shouldered treasure basket or the mortar hopper (Kroeber 1925, 446, 448; Barrett and Gifford 1933, 209). Miwok cooking pots were definitely coiled, not twined, and numerous documented examples survive. Water bottles were widespread in the Great Basin, but absent in Miwok country, except perhaps as trade pieces. If present, these four types of baskets were either trade pieces from the Paiute, Western Mono and/or Yokuts or were recent innovations.

Regional Variations in Coiled Basketry Technical Features

Basketry of the Northern Sierra Miwok and Plains Miwok was said to be related to North Central California. Central and Southern Sierra Miwok basketry was, at least in later years, stylistically influenced by the Yokuts, Western Mono and Paiute (Barrett 1933, 229; Levy 1978, 406; Bates and Lee 1990 and 1993).

Northern Sierra Miwok

Northern Sierra Miwok starting knots were usually the clock spring or tight spiral type. The Northern Sierra Miwok around Ione used a tight spiral start and sedge root weft. These were features shared with the Plains Miwok.

Northern Sierra Miwok weft fag ends were typically stitched over, concealed in the foundation or trimmed. Moving ends were either trimmed or bound under (Dawson p.c.). Weft materials included maple, pine root (*Pinus sabiniana*) and sedge root. Bracken fern root was used for black designs.[3]

The Northern Sierra Miwok made both three-rod and single-rod coiled baskets. Foundation warps were of willow, ceanothus, honeysuckle, hazel or dogwood. Grass bundle foundations were used by some Northern Miwok, but only for coiled winnowers/sifters. Around the Jackson area about half the coiled baskets were three-rod and half were single-rod. Northern Miwok rims were mostly plain wrapped rims, but herringbone or over-stitched rims occurred (Barrett and Gifford 1933, 236-239; Bates 1982, 8-15; Bates in Moser 1987, 56).

Central Sierra Miwok

The Central Sierra Miwok coiled baskets used the clock spring start on round baskets. Oval starting knots had a start of long, bent warps. Plain or overstitched rims were used on single-rod and three-rod baskets. Foundations were of ceanothus, willow or sumac (in later times non-native straw was sometimes substituted). Grass bundle foundations were used on winnowers/sifters and a few other baskets. Moving ends were bound under or trimmed. Weft fag ends were trimmed or concealed. Weft background materials included maple, pine (*Pinus sabiniana*) and sedge root. Bracken fern root was widely used for black designs. Redbud was also used for designs (Barrett and Gifford 1933, 236-239; Bates 1982, 16-19).

Southern Sierra Miwok

The clock spring start was found on round baskets. Fag ends were trimmed, bound under or concealed in the foundation (Dawson p.c.). Trimmed moving ends occurred on some baskets as well, although this may have been a newly introduced practice.

In the Mariposa area, three-rod and single-rod foundations were generally of mock orange (*Philadelphus lewisii*), ceanothus or willow. The Southern Sierra Miwok around Mariposa used grass bundle foundations for winnowers/sifters. Wefts were of maple, redbud (peeled and brownish-yellow colored), willow or pine (*Pinus sabiniana*) and less commonly of sedge. Bracken fern and redbud were used for design materials. Plain wrapped rims and several types of over-stitched rims were present.

In the Chowchilla River area, Yokuts influence was evident and both Miwok-style and Yokuts-style baskets intermingled. Grass bundle foundations were common here, although some Yokuts-style baskets may have been trade pieces. Wefts were of sedge root, pine, ceanothus or maple. Black bracken fern designs were common. Around Yosemite,

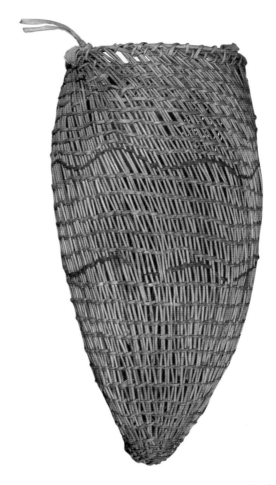

Twined hanging baskets were a very ancient type of basket made by some California Native Americans. Remnants of the Native string used to hang the basket can be seen at the rim. This Central Sierra Miwok basket was used for gathering and storing small foods. Purchased at Murphys, Calaveras County, in 1902. L: 18", D: 7.5" (C. Hart Merriam Collection, University of California at Davis, #182)

bracken fern root was used for black; redbud designs were rare on early baskets.

After about 1910, Mono Lake Paiute influence became so strong in the Yosemite area that mixed Miwok-Paiute baskets and technical features emerged. About that date, willow wefts began being frequently traded by the Mono Lake Paiute to Yosemite Miwok. Complex new patterns emerged. Some of the patterns were inspired by beadwork

---

[3] Basketry of the Railroad Flat area used maple as the most common weft material and redbud was occasionally chosen for some designs. Due to intermarriage, Railroad Flat style basketry may actually be Central Miwok rather than Northern Miwok, as once thought (see: Bates 1993, 14). These materials are, in fact, more likely Central Miwok than Northern Miwok.

designs and other outside influences (Dawson and Shanks 1974).

Southern Miwok basketry shows Paiute, Yokuts and Western Mono influence as well as Miwok innovation. What was originally Southern Miwok and what were borrowings can be complicated to determine, especially around the Chowchilla River and Yosemite areas (Barrett and Gifford 1933, 236-239; Bates 1982, 19-25; also see: Bates and Lee 1990).

Sierra Miwok Twined Basketry

Sierra Miwok Twining and Its Relation to Other People

Twining pre-dates coiling in California. Sierra Miwok twined baskets were almost solely utilitarian openwork or semi-openwork baskets. In terms of close-twined basketry, only a large storage basket and a twined triangular winnower adopted from the Paiute or Washoe were present (Barrett and Gifford 1933, 230-231).

The general type of twining historically used by the Sierra Miwok was also done by the Yokuts, Western Mono, Washoe, Paiute and, to a limited extent, by the Achumawi, Atsugewi and some Maidu (some close-twined burden baskets). All these people have one very significant thing in common: the Paiute were their neighbors (Dawson p.c.).

It could be that Paiute twined basketry ideas spread to their neighbors after they arrived in the region. The Paiute had a very strong, well-developed twining tradition. Paiute twined baskets were admired by their neighbors both for function and beauty. Given the geographical distribution of this twining in eastern California and western Nevada, its spread must have been influenced by the Paiute settlement of the adjacent Great Basin. Some tribes continued the pattern of adopting a few Paiute basket types even after the arrival of non-Indians. Miwok openwork twining was only partly related to the Paiute-type twining tradition. Paiute twining ideas clearly spread to others.

Virtually all Miwok household twined utility baskets are done in openwork. While the Miwok did not have the close-twining of the Paiute and Washoe, their openwork was similar (Dawson p.c.).

There was an earlier twining tradition dating prior to Paiute arrival in the Great Basin that eastern California and western Nevada tribes adopted in varying degrees. Prior to the arrival of the Numic-speaking Paiute and Shoshone, some early Great Basin twining was made using tule, cattail and juncus. For example, archeological twined basketry with twined cordage warps of tule (*Scirpus*) from southeastern Oregon predates the Paiute expansion into Nevada and Oregon. Archeologists have discovered tule, cattail and Indian hemp (*Apocynum*) twined baskets in the western Great Basin. Additionally, twined baskets of juncus and sagebrush also have been found in archeological sites in the northwestern Great Basin (Adovasio 1986, 203).

Technical Characteristics of Sierra Miwok Twined Basketry

Twined starting knots were fan-shaped or the crossed warp type. The slant of weft twist was primarily up-to-the-right. Rim selvages involved either: (1) trimming off the warp ends, (2) turning the warps sticks horizontally at the rim and coiling or lashing them together to form a rim, or (3) attaching a reinforcing rod (Elsasser 1978, 630-633; Bates and Lee 1990, 45-46, figs. 6.0-6.1).

An up-to-the-right slant of twist was usual for Sierra Miwok openwork twining. Two plain twining techniques were used. Most common were two warps in each weft wrap, but a single warp was also done. Diagonal twining was also used (Barrett and Gifford 1933, 213). Diagonal twining was widely used not only by the Sierra Miwok, but also by the Paiute and Washoe (Fowler and Dawson 1986, 705).

Sierra Miwok Twining Materials

Twining **warps** were made from a variety of plant materials including willow (*Salix*), hazel (*Corylus*), western chokecherry (*Prunus Virginian, var. demissa*), Sierra bitter cherry (*Prunus emarginata*), redbud (*cercis occidentalis*), sumac or sourberry (*Rhus trilobata*), maple (*Acer macrophyllum*) and pine root. The Sierra Miwok occasionally used ceanothus (*Ceanothus cuneatus*) for both warps and wefts on rough twined utility baskets. Willow was the most common twining **weft** material. But other twined weft materials were also used. These included maple bark, redbud, sumac, hazel, and pine root. Wild grape (*Vitis*) was sometimes used to wrap rims. Willow wefts were sometimes treated to give a desired color. Brownish or red-brown "sun burned" willow was baked in the sun while damp to give it a rich, warm color. Shoots of peeled and unpeeled redbud were both utilized (Barrett and Gifford 1933, 231; Elsasser 1978, 630-632; Bates and Lee 1990; Mathewson 1998, 150-160).

A coating of soap root (*Chlorogalum*) was applied to burden baskets (Barrett and Gifford 1933, 232; Bates and Lee 1990, 46). On these baskets the warps were very close together, but the weft rows were widely spaced. By applying the glue-like soaproot to the basket, the openings between warps were sealed to produce a very tight basket. This type of basket can be termed a semi-openwork basket because while the warps are tightly spaced, the weft rows are not. This practice of coating baskets with soaproot was a southern Sierra technique used by the Miwok, Yokuts and Western Mono.

Major Types of Sierra Miwok Twined Basketry

Nearly all Sierra Miwok twining was openwork or semi-openwork. Sierra Miwok twined baskets, except cradles, typically had reinforcing hoops of willow attached to their rims (Barrett and Gifford 1933, 230). Designs were either lacking or limited to stripes or narrow bands, but some were artistically done in a very attractive manner.

Burden Baskets

The Sierra Miwok essentially converted an openwork conical burden basket into a semi-openwork basket to make it tight. This was done by spreading gelatinous, glue-like soaproot (*Chlorogalum*) on both the inside and outside of the basket to coat it. The soap root was baked in hot ashes, dipped in water and then rubbed on the burden basket. Burden baskets covered with soaproot were tight enough to carry small seeds. Uncoated burden baskets were suitable only for carrying larger objects such as acorns.

Typically, four to six warp rods were twined together to form the burden basket's start. They were then bent upwards to form the beginning of the basket's side. Weft rows were

A Sierra Miwok burden basket with redbud designs. This Sierra Miwok burden basket shows the conical shape found in both Sierra Miwok and Maidu burden baskets. Purchased in Southern Sierra Miwok territory two miles north of Mariposa in 1902. D: 15", H: 17.5" (C. Hart Merriam Collection, University of California at Davis, #234)

carefully spaced about a half-inch apart leaving the warp sticks clearly visible.

Miwok burden baskets typically had designs done in narrow bands in either black or red colors. Sometimes clusters of the red-stemmed creek dogwood (*Cornus stolonifera*) were used as warps and this provided a vertical red design. Some burden baskets were undecorated. Background wefts could be willow, hazel or maple.

The burden basket's bottom was reinforced with either: (1) extra bundled warp rods, (2) three strand twining, or (3) a rawhide covering added at the tip for protection from wear.

The selvage of some burden baskets consisted of a mix of some warps trimmed off while other warps were bent over to the weaver's left and bound down. On other burden baskets warp rods were grouped in sets of four and a reinforcing rod (often of *Ceanothus cuneatus*) was coiled on top of this selvage. A row of coiled wrapping was used to attach the reinforcing rod to the basket (Barrett and Gifford 1933, 232-233, 332-333, plate LIV; Dawson p.c.; Bates and Lee 1990, 46-47).

Various Small Scoop-shaped Gathering, Sifting and Storage Baskets

The Sierra Miwok created two general types of gathering, sifting and storage baskets. One type was a deep form and the other kind was a low form. The deep form was deeper at one end. On the shallower form, starting warps were allowed to protrude from one to three inches at the start end of the basket

Sierra Miwok openwork baskets made in this distinctive shape could be used as storage baskets, as sifters or as gathering baskets. This particular basket had an attached string allowing it to serve as a hanging basket for storing food safely out of reach of animals. L: 11", H: 6" (C. Hart Merriam collection, University of California at Davis, #247)

to provide a lip type handle. These baskets could be round, oval, triangular or flat at one end. Warps were gathered in a bundle at one end of the basket. These baskets often had weft rows with alternating slants of weft twist from one row to the next. This resulted from the maker weaving across the basket and then turning the basket over to do the next row, resulting in the change of weft slant (Bryn Potter p.c., 2005).

Some of these baskets had interesting starting knots of over twenty parallel warps arranged perpendicularly to the rim using several rods bound securely at a right angle to the horizontal warps. Narrow band designs often decorated these baskets. A reinforcing rod was added for strength. Some baskets were coated with soap root to allow them to effectively hold small seeds. Uncoated baskets were good for gathering manzanita berries. (Barrett and Gifford 1933, 328-329, plate LII, 333; Bates and Lee 1990, 49, fig. 71, a,b,c; Levy 1978, 407, bottom fig. 6; Dawson p.c.).

Acorn Soup Ash Skimmer Baskets

The acorn soup skimmer was a clever and useful little scoop-shaped basket. It was about six inches in diameter. The shallow end had a short, broad handle. The opposite end was the deepest part of the basket, a little over two inches in depth and rounded. A reinforcing rod ran around the rim, but inside the little handle. This diagonally twined basket was used to skim ash, cinders or any other unwanted matter that appeared when cooking acorn soup. It was especially useful when the soup was beginning to boil and debris appeared on the surface. The ash skimmer was done in openwork so that as the liquid ran through it, any debris was caught and removed (C. Hart Merriam notes, UC Davis, basket #231).

Large Storage Baskets

Large flat-bottomed storage baskets were made to store food such as seeds, dried fish, dried meats, grasshoppers and greens (Levy 1978, 404). Both openwork and close-twined storage baskets were woven. Twined globular storage baskets were made by the Central Miwok and Southern Sierra Miwok, and perhaps by others (Barrett and Gifford 1933, 231, 234).

Winnowers

Openwork twined winnowers were most commonly used to separate seed husks and other unwanted materials by tossing the seeds into the air. The wind would blow away the husks and the seeds would fall back into the basket. Lacking handles, warp rods were bound together at the end to help form a grip. Winnowers included nearly round, oval and flat bottomed shapes.

A Sierra Miwok ash skimmer. When cooking acorn soup, this diagonally twined basket was used to carefully skim off any ash or cinders that appeared on the surface during boiling. The short, flat handle fits conveniently in the hand. The openwork weave allowed the acorn soup to flow through as the ash skimmer removed debris. This basket was purchased in Central Sierra Miwok territory at Bald Rock Rancheria, Tuolumne County, from the woman using it. L: 6.5", W: 6.5", Depth: 2.5" (C. Hart Merriam Collection, University of California at Davis, #231)

The triangular, close-twined winnower later adopted by some Sierra Miwok was a borrowing from the Paiute or Washoe. While the Miwok always made twined openwork winnowers, traditionally no close-twined winnowers were made. The traditional Miwok closely woven winnower was coiled, not twined (Barrett and Gifford 1933, 230; Bates and Lee 1990, 48).

Seedbeaters

There were several types of Sierra Miwok seedbeaters. Seedbeaters were used for knocking seeds from plants into a burden basket, a smaller gathering basket or occasionally used as scoops. One style of Sierra Miwok seedbeater was scoop-shaped with a straight handle that broadened at the very end. This seedbeater sometimes, but not always, had weft rows with alternating slants of weft twists (Dawson p.c.; Bates and Lee 1990, 48, fig. 68).

A second style of seedbeater was nearly flat. This seedbeater had a medium length handle and its opposite end was blunt rather than rounded (Barrett and Gifford 1933, 328-329, plate LII, fig.3).

A third Miwok seedbeater type was scoop-shaped, with a handle that either: (1) sharply curved upward and back toward the center of the basket, (2) ran straight up at a right angle to the scoop portion, or (3) curved upward at a sharp angle (Barrett and Gifford 1933, 331, plate LII, fig. 7; Dawson p.c.). A variation of this style had a short handle and a deep scoop. This type of seedbeater might be decorated with red creek dogwood warps gracefully arranged in broad stripes running from the handle base to the basket's tip.

Seedbeaters could also have designs done in bracken fern root, unpeeled willow or perhaps redbud. Miwok seedbeaters continued to be made after they had largely fallen out of use because they could be made quickly for sale (Bates and Lee 1990, 48; Bibby 1996, 25-26).

Unlike many tribes' undecorated seedbeaters, some Sierra Miwok seedbeaters had designs. There might be a white decorative band with the rest of the seedbeater done in the red color of unpeeled redbud or in the opposite color arrangement with red bands against a light background. Red warps of creek dogwood were used to produce red stripes. Black bracken fern root was also used to produce specks or narrow zigzag designs across the seedbeater (Dawson p.c.; Bates and Lee 1990, 47-48; Hedges 1997, 34, top left).

Hanging Baskets

Sierra Miwok made hanging baskets. These might be long and narrow, globular or egg shaped. They held awls, food, small tools and valuables. Some hanging baskets had designs (Barrett and Gifford 1933, 234; 331, figs. 1-3; Dawson p.c.).

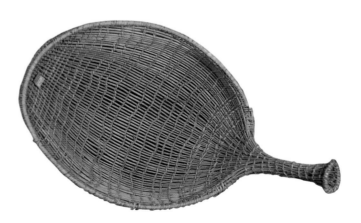

This Sierra Miwok twined seedbeater was made near Mariposa in Southern Sierra Miwok country. L: 18", W: 11" (C. Hart Merriam Collection, University of California at Davis, #251)

Ball Game Rackets

Women carried a pair of these rackets when playing "Indian football" games to catch a buckskin ball stuffed with deerskin. One racket held the ball and the other racket covered the ball and held it in place when the women ran with it (Barrett and Gifford 1933, 334-335, plate LV, figs. 1-2; Merriam 1967, 338).

Fish Traps and Fish Scoops

Most Sierra Miwok groups made fish traps. Fish traps were often used in conjunction with weirs. A winnower-shaped basket was used as a fish scoop (Aginsky 1943, 399-400; Levy 1978, 404).

Cradles

Sierra Miwok cradles traditionally had woven backs for babies to lie on. Sunshades to protect the baby were frequently used (Kroeber 1925, plate 39; Barrett and Gifford 1933, 231, 235-236, 372-373, plate 74; Bibby 2004, 107-108). Barrett and Gifford stated that some cradle sunshades were copies of Western Mono and Washoe sunshades (Kroeber 1925, 446, plate 39; Aginsky 1943, 419).

Beginning about 1900, some Sierra Miwok replaced their traditional twined-back cradles with a new type of cradle. These innovative cradles had backs made of wooden slats obtained from manufactured boxes, including dynamite boxes. Two oak sticks connected the horizontal wooden slats that formed the cradle back. The oak sticks extended up over the top of the cradle like a pair of large walking canes. This provided protection for the child's face, a mounting for a hood and a convenient handle (Barrett and Gifford 234-235, 372-373, plate 74, fig. 3; Bibby 2004, 107-108).

Sierra Miwok String Baskets

String baskets are neither coiled nor twined, although they have a look similar to coiled baskets. Instead, a kind of lattice bound weave of Native or commercial string was used to hold the string basket's coil foundation together. Numerous pairs of interlaced strings extended from the start up to the rim. Each pair of strings was spaced apart from adjacent paired strings so that the coil foundation was clearly visible. One string is passive while the other string actively encircles both the foundation coil and the passive string to hold the basket together. At the rim, the strings themselves are used to form a coil-like selvage.

String basketry is likely an old San Joaquin Valley Yokuts basketry technique that predates coiling (Dawson p.c.). String baskets are believed to have developed in ancient times among the San Joaquin Valley Yokuts and to have spread to

Sierra Miwok string baskets were typically bowl-shaped and well decorated. String baskets superficially resemble coiling, but are a distinct and ancient basketry technique. The coil is of iris leaf while the strings that serve as wefts are of cordage, perhaps of milkweed fiber. Remnants of black and red designs, probably of yarn, are barely visible. D: 6", H: 3" (Courtesy of the Maxwell Museum of Anthropology, University of New Mexico, #8223286)

the Sierra foothills prior to European arrival (Dawson p.c.; Bates and Lee 1990, 57-59).

In the Sierra foothills, the Sierra Miwok, Chukchansi Yokuts and Western Mono lavishly elaborated string baskets and made them art works. All or most Valley Yokuts string baskets were undecorated trays that had the brown color of tule. Sierra Miwok and Chukchansi Yokuts string baskets were quite different. Sierra Miwok string baskets often had a sheen that resulted from using iris leaf string rather than the tule the Yokuts favored (Pritchard 1970, 42; Dawson p.c.). In addition, Sierra Miwok and Chukchansi Yokuts string baskets were often highly decorated bowls rather than plain trays of the Valley Yokuts type. Quail topknots and, later, colorful commercial wool yarn were used to create designs. Designs done in yarn had a raised, three-dimensional quality. These designs were done in blocky zigzags, vertically arranged triangles and other patterns. Among Miwok groups, string baskets may have been done primarily by the Southern Miwok (Dawson p.c.).

In post-contact times a new type of basket developed from the ancient string baskets. By around 1900 a "needle and string" type of coiled basket developed among Sierra foothill weavers. This purposely resulted in an innovative type of basket that looked much like a string basket. Commercial cotton string and wool yarn were used to create designs inspired by string baskets and then embroidered on a completed coiled basket. Although these needle and string baskets are an innovation, they are pleasing baskets truly derived from ancient string baskets. They usually use string basket-type designs and have much of the look of string baskets, although technologically different (see: Tulloch and Polanich, 1999). Needle and string baskets could be called the grandchildren of string baskets.

Comments

Ancestral Sierra Miwok were one of the people who brought coiling into California. Sierra Miwok coiled basketry has a long history with roots in the ancient Lovelock culture of western Nevada.

Sierra Miwok coiled baskets have been said to be not as finely made as the finest Washoe, Maidu, Yokuts and Western Mono baskets (Barrett and Gifford 1933, 273). Yet there are many ways of looking at art and the Sierra Miwok made remarkable achievements. One way to appreciate an art is to recognize people who proudly carry on an ancient and admirable coiling style.

Sierra Miwok coiled basketry is closely related to the earliest known Washoe baskets. Sierra Miwok and Washoe cooking pots, for example, can be difficult to tell apart. Both cultures use interlocking weft stitches and had various other technical features in common. Additionally, a minority of Sierra Miwok coiling ideas were borrowed from Maidu, Yokuts, Western Mono, Plains Miwok or the Mono Lake Paiute basketry. These influences appear strongest in northern and southern Miwok territory.

Sierra Miwok string basketry was adopted from the San Joaquin Valley Yokuts prior to European arrival. Sierra Miwok string baskets, however, flourished and are among the most highly decorated and elaborate string baskets ever made.

Sierra Miwok twining has many distinctive features and a captivating charm of its own. This twining is a creative, varied art in its own right. It is subtly beautiful and includes memorable, graceful forms such as deep scoop-shaped storage baskets and decorative seedbeaters.

The Sierra Miwok have long made a wide variety of baskets with a sense of honoring one of the oldest coiling traditions in California.

Sierra Miwok coiled baskets were sometimes sparsely decorated, yet were still quite pleasing. This bowl has a diagonally over-stitched rim. D: 10", H: 4.75" (Southwest Museum of the American Indian, Autry National Center, #811-G-2274)

Early San Francisco Bay Area Baskets

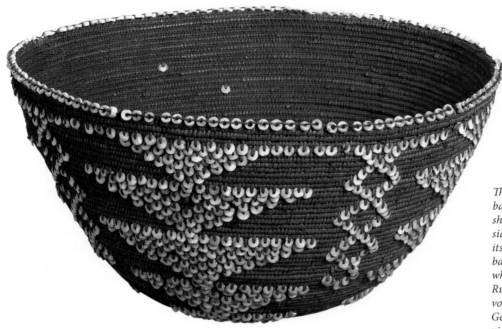

The San Francisco Bay origin of this basket is indicated by the olivella shell disc beads lavishly decorating its side, the clamshell disc beads sewn on its rim and its sedge root wefts. This basket was collected by Admiral Moller who as a young man accompanied a Russian sponsored around the world voyage under the command of the German, Otto von Kotzebue, which visited San Francisco Bay in 1816. This early basket is either Coast Miwok or Ohlone (Costanoan). D: 12", H: 6" (Courtesy of the Staatsliches Museum fur Volkerkunde, Munich; photo by Astrid Eckert; collection of the Ajaloomuseum, the Estonian History Museum, Tallinn, Estonia, K-1359)

Collected in 1865 or earlier, this San Francisco Bay Area basket seems most like Wappo baskets, but it could also be from one of the other Bay Area cultures. This sedge root weft basket has clamshell disc beads attached in the Wappo fashion along with European trade beads and abalone pendants. D: 10.5", H: 4" (Courtesy of the Staatsliches Museum fur Volkerkunde, Munich; photo by Astrid Eckert; collection of the Ajaloomuseum, the Estonian History Museum, Tallinn, Estonia, K-2136)

BIBLIOGRAPHY

Abel-Vidor, Suzanne, Dot Brovarney and Susan Billy
1996   *Remember Your Relations: The Elsie Allen Baskets, Family & Friends*, Grace Hudson Museum, Oakland Museum and Heyday Books, Berkeley

Adovasio, J.M.
1970   The Origin, Development and Distribution of Western Archaic Textiles and Basketry, *Tebiwa*, 13 (2)

Adovasio, J.M.
1986   Prehistoric Basketry, *Handbook of North American Indians*, vol. 11, Great Basin, Smithsonian Institution, Washington

Aginsky, B.W.
1943   Culture Element Distributions: XXIV, Central Sierra, *Anthropological Records*, 8(4), University of California Press, Berkeley and Los Angeles

Aikens, C. Melvin
1970   *Hogup Cave*, University of Utah Anthropological Papers No. 93, University of Utah Press, Salt Lake City

Aikens, C. Melvin
1993   *Archaeology of Oregon*, US Department of Interior (BLM), Portland, Oregon

Ashley, Ray
2004   From the Helm, *Mains'l Haul: A Journal of Maritime History*, 40(1), pp. 2-3, San Diego Maritime Museum, San Diego

Barnett, H.G.
1937   Culture Element Distributions: VII, Oregon Coast, *Anthropological Records*, 1(3), University of California, Berkeley

Barrett, Samuel A.
1910   The Material Culture of the Klamath Lake and Modoc Indians of Northeastern California and Southern Oregon, *University of California Publications in American Archaeology and Ethnology*, 5(4), Berkeley

Barrett, Samuel A.
1952   Material Aspects of Pomo Culture, Parts I and II, *Bulletin of the Public Museum of the City of Milwaukee, Vol. 20, Milwaukee*, Wisconsin

Barrett, Samuel A.
1996   *Pomo Indian Basketry*, Phoebe Apperson Hearst Museum of Anthropology, Berkeley

Barrett, Samuel A. and E. W. Gifford
1933   *Miwok Material Culture*, Bulletin of Milwaukee Public Museum, Milwaukee, Wisconsin (Reprinted by Yosemite Natural History Association)

Barrows, David Prescott
1967   *The Ethno-Botany of the Coahuilla Indians of Southern California*, Malki Museum Press, Banning, California

Bates, Craig D.
1982   Coiled Basketry of the Sierra Miwok, *San Diego Museum Papers No. 15*, San Diego

Bates, Craig D.
1983   The California Collection of I.G. Voznesenki, *American Indian Art Magazine*, 8(3), Scottsdale, Arizona

Bates, Craig D.
1987   Hechenu Pulaka: The Changing Role of Baskets in a Northern Miwok Family, in *Native American Basketry of Central California*, pp. 51-60, by Christopher Moser, Riverside Municipal Museum

Bates, Craig D.
1993   Scholars and Collectors Among the Sierra Miwok, 1990-1920: What Did They Really Find?, *Museum Anthropology*, 17(2), American Anthropological Association

Bates, Craig D. and Bruce Bernstein
1982   Regional Variation in Maidu Coiled Basketry Materials and Technology, *Journal of California and Great Basin Anthropology*, 4(2), Malki Museum, Banning, California

Bates, Craig D. and Brian Bibby
1983   Collecting Among the Chico Maidu: The Stewart Culin Museum Collection at the Brooklyn Museum, *American Indian Art Magazine*, 8(4), Scottsdale, Arizona

Bates, Craig D. and Martha J. Lee
1990   *Tradition and Innovation: A Basket History of the Indians of Yosemite-Mono Lake Area*, Yosemite Association, Yosemite National Park

Bates, Craig D. and Martha J. Lee
1993   Chukchansi Yokuts and Southern Miwok Weavers of Yosemite National Park, *American Indian Art Magazine*, 18 (3), Scottsdale, AZ

Baumhoff, Martin A.
June 20, 1957   Catlow Twine from Central California, *University of California Archeological Survey*, No. 38, Papers on California Archaeology: 50-62, pp.1-5, Department of Anthropology, University of California, Berkeley

Baumhoff, Martin A. and Robert F. Heizer
1958   Outland Coiled Basketry from the Caves of West Central Nevada, *University of California Archaeological Survey Reports*, 42, Berkeley

Beals, Ralph L.
1933   Ethnology of the Nisenan, *University of California Publications in American Archaeology and Ethnology*, 31(6), Berkeley

Bean, Lowell John
1978   Cahuilla, *Handbook of North American Indians*, vol. 8, California, Smithsonian Institution, Washington

Bean, Lowell John and Katherine Siva Saubel
1963   Cahuilla Ethnobotanical Notes: The Aboriginal Uses of the Mesquite and Screwbean, *Archaeological Survey Annual Report 1962-1963*, Department of Anthropology and Sociology, University of California, Los Angeles

Bean, Lowell John and Katherine Siva Saubel
1972   *Temalpakh: Cahuilla Indian Knowledge and Usage of Plants*, Malki Museum Press, Morongo Indian Reservation, Banning, California

Bean, Lowell John and Florence Shipek
1978   Cupeño, Luiseño and Serrano chapters in *Handbook of North American Indians*, vol. 8, California, Smithsonian Institution, Washington

Bean, Lowell John and Charles R. Smith
1978   Gabrielino, *Handbook of North American Indians*, vol. 8, California, Smithsonian Institution, Washington

Bean, Lowell John and Charles R. Smith
1978   Serrano, *Handbook of North American Indians*, vol. 8, California, Smithsonian Institution, Washington

Beckham, Stephen Dow
1971   *Requiem for a People: The Rogue (River) Indians and the Frontiersmen*, University of Oklahoma Press

Becker, Madison S.
1978   Esselen, *The Journal of California Anthropology Papers in Linguistics*, Malki Museum, Banning, California

Beeler, M.S.
1961   Northern Costanoan, International Journal of American Linguistics, vol. 27 no. 3, Chicago University Press

Benedict, Ruth Fulton
1924   A Brief Sketch of Serrano Culture, *American Anthropologist*, 26(3), 366-392

Bennyhoff, James A.
1977   *Ethnogeography of the Plains Miwok*, Center for Archeological Research at Davis, University of California, Davis

Benson, Foley
1993   From *Straw Into Gold*, Jesse Peter Memorial Museum, Santa Rosa Junior College, Santa Rosa, CA

Bernstein, Bruce
1985   Panamint-Shoshone Basketry, 1890-1960, *American Indian Basketry Magazine*, 5(3)

Bernstein, Bruce
1979   Panamint Shoshone Coiled Basketry, *American Indian Art Magazine*, 4(4)

Bernstein, Bruce
1990   Weaver's Talk, the Language of Baskets and the Meaning of Aesthetic Judgment: The Patwin of Central California, *The Art of Native American Basketry*, Greenwood Press, Westport, Connecticut

Bernstein, Bruce
2003   *The Language of Native American Baskets from the Weavers' View*, National Museum of the American Indian, Smithsonian Institution, Washington and New York

Bettinger, Robert L. and Martin A. Baumhoff
1982   The Numic Spread: Great Basin Cultures in Competition, *American Antiquity*, 47(3), pp. 485-503

Bibby, Brian
1996   *The Fine Art of California Indian Basketry*, Crocker Art Museum, Sacramento, California

Bibby, Brian
2004   *Precious Cargo: California Indian Cradle Baskets and Childbirth Traditions*, Marin Museum of the American Indian, Novato, California

Blackburn, Thomas C.
1963   Ethnohistoric Descriptions of Gabrielino Material Culture, *Archaeological Survey Annual Report 1962-1963*, Department of Anthropology and Sociology, University of California, Los Angeles

Blackburn, Thomas C. and Lowell John Bean
1978   Kitanemuk, *Handbook of North American Indians*, vol. 8, California, Smithsonian Institution, Washington

Blackburn, Thomas C. and Travis Hudson
1990   *Time's Flotsam*, Ballena Press Anthropological Papers No. 35, Ballena Press and Santa Barbara Museum of Natural History, Santa Barbara, California

Bocek, Barbara R.
1984   Ethnobotany of Costanoan Indians, California, Based on Collections by John P. Harrington, *Economic Botany*, 38(2), New York Botanical Garden, Bronx

Breschini, Gary S.
1983   *Models of Population Movements in Central California*, doctoral Dissertation reprint, Coyote Press, Salinas, California

Breschini, Gary S. and Trudy Haversat
2003   Ethnography of the Esselen, in *Ethnographic Overview for the Los Padres National Forest, US Department of Agriculture, Angeles National Forest*, Arcadia, CA

Breschini, Gary S. and Trudy Haversat
2004   *The Esselen Indians of the Big Sur Country*, Coyote Press, Salinas, California

Bretting, P.K. and Gary P. Nabhan
1986   Ethnobotany of Devil's Claw (*Proboscidea parvifolia ssp. parvifolia: Martyniaceae*) in the Greater Southwest, *Journal of California and Great Basin Anthropology*, 8(2)

Bright, William
1978   Karok, *Handbook of North American Indians*, vol. 8, California, Smithsonian Institution, Washington

Broadbent, Sylvia M.
1972   The Rumsen of Monterey: An Ethnography from Historical Sources, *Miscellaneous Papers on Archaeology, Contributions of the University of California Research Facility*, Berkeley

Burgett, Ruth B.
2004   *Coiled Basketry Designs from Charlie Brown Cave*, Western Nevada, Master's Thesis, University of Nevada, Reno

Cain, William C. and Justin Farmer
1981   Materials and Styles, in *Rods, Bundles and Stitches*, Raul A. Lopez and Christopher Moser, editors, Riverside Museum Press, Riverside, California

California Academy of Sciences
1980   *An Exhibition of Western North American Indian Baskets from the Collection of Clay Bedford*, San Francisco

Callaghan, Catherine A.
1965   Lake Miwok Dictionary, *University of California Publications in Linguistics*, vol. 39, Berkeley

Callaghan, Catherine A.
1978   Lake Miwok, *Handbook of North American Indians*, vol. 8, California, Smithsonian, Washington

Callaghan, Catherine A.
1984   Plains Miwok Dictionary, *University of California Publications in Linguistics*, vol. 105, Berkeley and Los Angeles

Callaghan, Catherine A.
2001   *Linguistic Archeology in California*, paper presented before the Anthropology Colloquium, University of California at Davis

Callaghan, Catherine A.
2002   *Yok-Utian Homeland and DNA Evidence*, Language Relatedness Group

Callaghan, Catherine A.
2005   *Yok-Utian Update*, handout from the paper read before the Linguistic Society of America, Jan. 6, 2005, Oakland, California

Cohodas, Marvin
1997   *Basket Weavers for the California Curio Trade: Elizabeth and Louise Hickox*, University of Arizona Press and The Southwest Museum

Collier, Mary E.T. and Sylvia Thalman, editors
1991   *Interviews with Tom Smith and Maria Copa: Isabel Kelly's Ethnographic Notes on the Coast Miwok Indians of Marin and Southern Sonoma Counties, California*, Miwok Archeological Preserve of Marin (MAPOM) Occasional Papers No. 6, San Rafael, California

Collings, Jerold L.
1979   Profile of a Chemehuevi Basket Weaver, *American Indian Art Magazine*, 4(4), Scottsdale, Arizona

Conn, Richard G. and Mary Schlick
1998   Basketry, *Handbook of North American Indians*, vol. 12, Plateau, Smithsonian Institution, Washington

Copeland, Margaret Ayr
1956   *An Analysis of Modoc Basketry*, Master's Thesis, University of Washington

Coville, Frederick Vernon
1892   The Panamint Indians of California, *American Anthropologist*, vol. 5, October 1892

Coville, Frederick Vernon
1904   Wokas, A Primitive Food of the Klamath Indians, *Annual Report of the Smithsonian Institution*, Washington

Craig, Steve
1966   Ethnographic Notes on the construction of Ventureno Chumash Baskets: From the Ethnographic and Linguistic Field Notes of John P. Harrington, *Annual Report, Archaeological Survey*, University of California, Los Angeles

Craig, Steve
1967   The Basketry of the Ventureno Chumash, *Annual Report, Archaeological Survey*, University of California, Los Angeles

Cressman, Luther S.
1942   *Archeological Researches in the Northern Great Basin*, Carnegie Institution of Washington, pub. 538

Dalrymple, Jerry
2000   *Indian Basketmakers of California and the Great Basin*, Museum of New Mexico Press, Santa Fe

Davis, James T.
1966   Trade Routes and Economic Exchange among the Indians of California, in *Aboriginal California*, University of California Archaeological Research Facility, Berkeley

Dawson, Lawrence E.
1968-2003   Personal Communications, Lawrence "Larry" E. Dawson was the senior museum anthropologist of the University of California's Hearst (formerly Lowie) Museum of Anthropology, Berkeley

Dawson, Lawrence E.
1973 ms.   Hypothesis Toward a Historical Interpretation of California and Great Basin Basketry, ms. on file with Ralph Shanks

Dawson, Lawrence E.
1973   *Description of Certain Basketry from Bamert Cave, Amador County, California* in *The Archeology of Bamert Cave, Amador County, California*, Robert F. Heizer and Thomas R. Hester, Archeological Research Facility, Department of Anthropology, University of California, Berkeley

Dawson, Lawrence E.
1988   Indian Basket Traditions of the Fresno Region, in *Strands of Time* by Linda E. Dick, Lorrie Planas, Judy Polanich, Craig D. Bates and Martha J. Lee, Fresno Metropolitan Museum, Fresno

Dawson, Lawrence E.
Various Dates   Lawrence E. Dawson notes on file at the Bancroft Library, University of California, Berkeley

Dawson, Lawrence E.
n.d.   *Fields of Clover: Larry Dawson's Years with the Lowie Museum Collection: The Spread of Coiled Basketry in California*, Lowie Museum, University of California, Berkeley

Dawson, Lawrence E. and James Deetz
1964   *Chumash Indian Art*, The Art Gallery, University of California, Santa Barbara

Dawson, Lawrence E. and James Deetz
1965   A Corpus of Chumash Basketry, *Archaeological Survey Annual Report*, Vol. 7, Department of Anthropology, University of California, Los Angeles

Lawrence E. Dawson and Ralph Shanks
1970-1975   Typed manuscripts on the Basketry of the Coast Miwok, Costanoan, Esselen, Salinan, Chumash and Gabrielino. Copies on file with Ralph Shanks and in the Lawrence E. Dawson notes at Bancroft Library, University of California, Berkeley

Dawson, Lawrence E. and Ralph Shanks
c. 1974   *Plains Beadwork Designs used in Eastern California as Basketry Designs*, Exhibit at Lowie (now Hearst) Museum of Anthropology, University of California, Berkeley

Dawson, Lawrence E., Vera Mae Fredrickson and Nelson H.H. Graburn
1974   *Traditions in Transition: Culture Contact and Material Change*, Lowie Museum of Anthropology, University of California, Berkeley

d'Azevedo, Warren L.
1986   Introduction, *Handbook of North American Indians*, vol. 11, Great Basin, Smithsonian Institution, Washington

d'Azevedo, Warren L.
1986   Prehistoric Basketry, *Handbook of North American Indians*, vol. 11, Great Basin, Smithsonian Institution, Washington

d'Azevedo, Warren L.
1986   Washoe, *Handbook of North American Indians*, vol. 11, Great Basin, Smithsonian Institution, Washington

Dean, Sharon E. and Peggy S. Ratcheson, Judith W. Finger, Ellen F. Daus and Craig D. Bates
2004   *Weaving a Legacy: Indian Baskets & the People of Owens Valley, California*, University of Utah Press, Salt Lake City

Deetz, James
1963   Basketry from the James-Abel Collection, *Museum Talk*, 38(2), Summer 1969, Santa Barbara Museum of Natural History, California

Dixon, Roland B.
1902   Basketry of the Indians of Northern California, *Bulletin of the American Museum of Anthropology*, vol. 18, part 1, New York

Dixon, Roland B.
1905   The Northern Maidu, *Bulletin of the American Museum of Natural History*, vol. 17(3), New York

Dixon, Roland B.
1907   The Shasta, *The Huntington California Expedition*, American Museum of Natural History, New York

Dixon, Roland B.
1907-1910   The Chimariko Indians and Language, *University of California Publications in American Archaeology and Ethnology*, Vol. 6, No. 5

Dozier, Deborah
1998   *The Heart is Fire: The World of the Cahuilla Indians of Southern California*, Heyday Books, Berkeley

Driver, Harold E.
1936   Wappo Ethnography, *University of California Publications in American Archaeology and Ethnology*, 36(3), Berkeley

Driver, Harold E.
1937   Culture Element Distributions: VI Southern Sierra Nevada, *Anthropological Records*, 1(2), University of California Press, Berkeley and Los Angeles

Driver, Harold E.
1939   Cultural Elements Distributions: X, Northwest California, *Anthropological Records*, 1(16), University of California, Berkeley

Drucker, Philip
1937a   Culture Element Distribution: V, Southern California, *Anthropological Records*, 1(1), University of California Press, Berkeley

Drucker, Philip
1937b   The Tolowa and Their Southwest Oregon Kin, *University of California Publications in American Archaeology and Ethnology*, 36(4), Berkeley

Drucker, Philip
1940   The Gentile System of the Siletz Tribes, *Journal of American Folklore*, vol. 3, pp. 227-237

Drucker, Philip
1941   Culture Element Distributions: XVII Yuman-Piman, *Anthropological Records*, 6(3), University of California Press, Berkeley

Du Bois, Cora
c. 1934   *Tututni (Rogue River) Field Notes*, ms., on file in the University Archives, Bancroft Library, University of California, Berkeley

Du Bois, Cora
1935   Wintu Ethnography, *University of California Publications in American Archaeology and Ethnology*, 36(1), Berkeley

Eisenhart, Linda L.
1990   *Hupa, Karok and Yurok Basketry, in The Art of North American Basketry*, Greenwood Press, Westport, Connecticut

Elsasser, Albert B.
1978a   Basketry, *Handbook of North American Indians*, vol. 8, California, Smithsonian Institution, Washington

Elsasser, Albert B.
1978 b   Mattole, Nongatl, Sinkyone, Lassik and Wailaki, *Handbook of North American Indians*, vol. 8, California, Smithsonian Institution, Washington

Elsasser, Albert B.
1978c   Wiyot, *Handbook of North American Indians*, vol. 8, California, Smithsonian Institution, Washington

Elsasser, Albert B. and Robert F. Heizer
1963   The Archaeology of Bowers Cave, Los Angeles County, California, *Reports of the University of California Archaeological Survey*, No. 59, Department of Anthropology, Berkeley

Eshleman, Jason Aaron
2002   *Mitochondrial DNA and Prehistoric Population Movements in Western North America*, Dissertation at the University of California, Davis

Essene, Frank
1942   Culture Element Distributions: XXI, Round Valley, *Anthropological Records*, University of California, Berkeley and Los Angeles

Fang, Madeleine W. and Marilyn R. Binder
1990   *A Photographic Guide to the Ethnographic North American Indian Basket Collection.* Peabody Museum of Archaeology and Ethnology, Cambridge, Massachusetts

Farmer, Justin F.
2004   *Southern California Luiseño Indian Baskets*, The Justin Farmer Foundation, Fullerton, California

Farmer, Justin F.
2005   Southern California Luiseño Indian Baskets, talk Feb. 26, 2005 at Marin Indian Art Show Symposium, San Rafael, California

Fields, Virginia M.
1993   *The Hover Collection of Karuk Baskets*, Clarke Memorial Museum, Eureka, California

Finger, Judith
2003   Fancy Coiled Caps of Central California, *American Indian Art Magazine*, 28 (3), Scottsdale, Arizona

Foster, George
1944   A Summary of Yuki Culture, *Anthropological Records*, 5(3), University of California Press, Berkeley and Los Angeles

Foster, Michael K.
1996   Language and the Culture History of North America, *Handbook of North American Indians*, vol. 17, Languages, Smithsonian Institution, Washington

Fowler, Catherine S.
1986   Subsistence, *Handbook of North American Indians*, vol. 11, Great Basin, Smithsonian Institution, Washington

Fowler, Catherine S. and Lawrence E. Dawson
1986   Ethnographic Basketry, *Handbook of North American Indians*, vol. 11, Great Basin, Smithsonian Institution, Washington

Fredrickson, David A.
1974   Cultural Diversity in Early Central California: A View from the North Coast Ranges, *Journal of California Anthropology*, 1(1)

Garth, Thomas R.
1953   Atsugewi Ethnography, *Anthropological Records*, 14(2), University of California Press, Berkeley and Los Angeles

Garth, Thomas R.
1978   Atsugewi, *Handbook of North American Indians*, vol. 8, California, Smithsonian Institution, Washington

Gayton, Anna H.
1948   Yokuts and Western Mono Ethnography, *Anthropological Records*, 10(1), University of California Press, Berkeley

Gifford, E.W.
1967   Ethnographic Notes on the Southwestern Pomo, *Anthropological Records*, Vol. 25, University of California Press, Berkeley

Gifford, E.W.
1932   The Northfork Mono, *University of California Publications in American Archaeology and Ethnology*, 31(2), Berkeley

Gifford, E.W. and A.L. Kroeber
1937   Culture Element Distributions: IV, Pomo, *University of California Publications in American Archaeology and Ethnology*, Vol. 37, No. 4, Berkeley

Gifford, E.W. and Stanislaw Klimek
1936   Culture Element Distributions: II Yana, *University of California Publications in American Archaeology and Ethnology*, 37(2), Berkeley

Goddard, Pliny Earle
1903   Life and Culture of the Hupa, *University of California Publications in American Archaeology and Ethnology*, 1(1), Berkeley

Goddard, Pliny Earle
1914   Notes on the Chilula Indians of Northwestern California, *University of California Publications in American Archaeology and Ethnology*, 10(6), Berkeley

Gogol, John
1980-1981   The Twined Basketry of Western Washington, *American Indian Basketry Magazine*, vols. 3 and 4, Portland, Oregon

Gogol, John
1983   Klamath, Modoc and Shasta Basketry, *American Indian Basketry Magazine*, 3(2), Portland, Oregon

Gogol, John
1984   Traditional Arts of the Indians of Western Oregon, *American Indian Basketry Magazine*, 4(2), Portland, Oregon

Gould, Richard A.
1978   Tolowa, *Handbook of North American Indians*, vol. 8, California, Smithsonian Institution, Washington

Gray, Dennis J.
1987   The Takelma and Their Athapascan Neighbors, *University of Oregon Anthropological Papers*, No. 37, Eugene

Grant, Campbell
1964   *Chumash Artifacts Collected in Santa Barbara County, California*, University of California Survey Facility, Survey No. 63, Berkeley

Grant, Campbell
1978   Eastern Coastal Chumash, *Handbook of North American Indians*, vol.8, Smithsonian Institution, Washington; also see in same volume: Chumash: Introduction, Island Chumash and Interior Chumash

Greenwood, Roberta
1978   Obispeno and Purisimeno Chumash, *Handbook of North American Indians*, vol.8, Smithsonian Institution, Washington

Grimes, John R., and Mary Lou Curran and Thomas Haukaas
2002   Uncommon Legacies, *American Indian Art Magazine*, 28(1), Scottsdale, Arizona

Griset, Suzanne
1988   *Historic Transformations of Tizon Brown Ware in Southern California*, Paper 13, Nevada State Museum, Carson City

Hansen, Harvey J. , Jeanne Thurlow Miller and David Wayne Peri
1962   *Wild Oats in Eden: Sonoma County in the 19th Century*, Santa Rosa, California

Harrington, John P.
Various years   Field Notes, courtesy of Lawrence E. Dawson and others

Harrington, John P.
1932   *Tobacco Among the Karuk Indians of California*, Smithsonian Institution, Bulletin 94, Washington

Harrington, John P.
1942   Culture Element Distribution: XIX, Central California Coast, *Anthropological Records*, 7(1), University of California, Berkeley and Los Angeles

Hattori, Eugene M.
1982   *The Archeology of Falcon Hill, Winnemucca Lake, Washoe County, Nevada*, Dissertation, Department of Anthropology, Washington State University, Pullman; also, Nevada State Museum Anthropology Papers, no. 18, Carson City

Hedges, Ken
1953   *Fibers & Forms: Native American Basketry of the West*, San Diego Museum of Man, San Diego

Heizer, Robert F.
1949-1953   The Archaeology of Central California. I: The Early Horizon, *Anthropological Records*, vol. 12, University of California, Berkeley (awls discussed, pp. 1-84)

Heizer, Robert F.
1952   California Indian Linguistics Records: The Mission Indian Vocabularies of Alphonse Pinart, *Anthropological Records*, 15(1), University of California, Berkeley and Los Angeles

Heizer, Robert F.
1953   The Archaeology of the Napa Region, *Anthropological Records*, 12(6), University of California Press, Berkeley

Heizer, Robert F.
1960   A San Nichols Island Twined Basketry Water Bottle, *Reports of the University of California Archaeological Survey*, No. 50, Department of Anthropology, University of California, Berkeley

Heizer, Robert F.
April-June 1968   One of the Oldest Known California Indian Baskets, *The Masterkey*, 42(2), Southwest Museum, Los Angeles Discussion of a Costanoan (Ohlone) Basket

Heizer, Robert F. and Albert B. Elsasser
1978   *The Natural World of the California Indians*, University of California Press, Berkeley

Heizer, Robert F. and Thomas R. Hester
1973   *The Archeology of Bamert Cave, Amador County, California*, Archeological Research Facility, University of California, Berkeley

Heizer, Robert F. and M.A. Whipple
1965   *The California Indians*, University of California, Berkeley

Herold, Joyce
1977   Chumash Baskets from the Malaspina Collection, *American Indian Art Magazine*, 3(1), Scottsdale, Arizona

Hester, Thomas Roy
1973   Chronological Ordering of Great Basin Prehistory, *Contributions of the University of California Archaeological Research Facility*, No. 17

Hester, Thomas Roy
1978   Esselen, *Handbook of North American Indians*, vol. 8, California, Smithsonian Institution, Washington

Hester, Thomas Roy
1978   Salinan, *Handbook of North American Indians*, vol. 8, California, Smithsonian Institution, Washington

Heye, George
1926   Chumash Objects from a Cave, *Indian Notes*, vol. 3, pp. 193-198, Museum of the American Indian, Heye Foundation, New York

Hinton, Cheryl
2004   Reuniting Families, Telling Stories: An Exhibition of San Diego County Baskets, *News From Native California*, 17(4), Berkeley

Hohenthal, William D., Jr.
2001   *Tipai Ethnographic Notes: A Baja California Indian Community at Mid-Century*, Baleen Press and The Institute for Regional Studies of the Californias, Novato, California

Holm, Bill
1990   Art, *Handbook of North American Indians*, vol. 7, Smithsonian Institution, Washington

Hoveman, Alice R. with contributions by Frank La Pena, Elaine Sundahl and Ronald M. Yoshiyama
2002   *Journey to Justice: The Wintu People and the Salmon*, Turtle Bay Exploration Park, Redding, California

Howard, Donald M.
1973   Test Archeology at the Smith Site, Mnt-463, *Monterey County Archaeological Society Quarterly*, 2(2), Carmel, California

Hudson, D. Travis
1984   Early Russian-Collected California Ethnographic Objects in European Museums, *American Indian Art Magazine*, 9(4), Scottsdale, AZ

Hudson, D. Travis and Thomas C. Blackburn
1982, 1983, 1985, 1986, 1987   *The Material Culture of the Chumash Interaction Sphere*, vols. I-V, Ballena Press/Santa Barbara Museum of Natural History, Santa Barbara, California

Hudson, D. Travis and Janice Timbrook
1974   Six Chumash Baskets: an important new acquisition, *Museum Talk*, 48(4), Santa Barbara Museum of Natural History, Santa Barbara, California

Iovin, June
1963   A Summary Description of Luiseño Material Culture, *Archaeological Survey Annual Report*, 1962-1963, Department of Anthropology and Sociology, University of California, Los Angeles

Israel, Claudia
1996   *Baskets and Weavers*, Clarke Memorial Museum, Eureka, California

Jacknis, Ira and Margot Blum Schevill, guest editors
1993   Museum Anthropology in California, 1889-1939, *Museum Anthropology*, 17(2), American Anthropological Association

Jackson, Thomas L.
1990   Prehistoric Ceramics of the Southwestern Sierra Nevada, California, *Anthropological Papers Number 22*, Nevada State Museum, Carson City

Jacobsen, Jr., William
1986   Washoe Language, *Handbook of North American Indians*, vol. 11, Great Basin, Smithsonian Institution, Washington

Johnson, Patty
1978   Patwin, *Handbook of North American Indians*, vol. 8, California, Smithsonian Institution, Washington

Johnson, Ron and Coleen Kelley Marks
1996   *Her Mind Made Up: Weaving Caps the Indian Way*, Reese Bullen Gallery, Humboldt State University, Arcata, California

Jolie, Edward A.
2004   *Coiled Basketry from Charlie Brown Cave, Western Nevada*, Master's thesis, University of Nevada, Reno

Kasner, Leone Letson
1980   *Siletz: Survival for an Artifact*, Confederated Tribes of the Siletz, Oregon

Kelly, Isabel T.
1930   Yuki Basketry, *University of California Publications in American Archaeology and Ethnology*, 24(9), Berkeley

Kelly, Isabel T.
1978   Coast Miwok, *Handbook of North American Indians*, vol. 8, California, Smithsonian Institution, Washington

Kelly, Isabel T. and Catherine Fowler
1986   Southern Paiute, *Handbook of North American Indians*, vol. 11, Great Basin, Smithsonian Institution, Washington

Kendall, Daythal
1990   Takelma, *Handbook of North American Indians*, vol. 7, Northwest Coast, Smithsonian Institution, Washington

Kent, William Eugene
1973   *The Siletz Indian Reservation*, Master's thesis, Portland State University

King, Chester and Thomas C. Blackburn
1978   Tataviam, *Handbook of North American Indians*, vol. 8, California, Smithsonian Institution, Washington

Kinkade, M. Dales and William W. Elmendorf, Bruce Rigsby and Haruo Aoki
1998   Languages, *Handbook of North American Indians*, vol. 12, Plateau, Smithsonian Institution, Washington

King, J.C.H.
1999   *First Peoples, First Contacts*, The British Museum, London

Kniffen, Fred B.
1928   Achomawi Geography, *University of California Publications in American Archaeology and Ethnology*, 23(5), Berkeley

Kojean, P.M.
1979   *Woven Vessels of the California Indians*, Miwok Archeological Preserve of Marin, MAPOM Paper No. 4, San Rafael, California. Translated by Wilma Follette

Kroeber, Alfred L.
1905   Basket Designs of the Indians of Northwestern California, *University of California Publications in American Archaeology and Ethnology*, 11(2), Berkeley

Kroeber, Alfred L.
1908   Ethnography of the Cahuilla Indians, *University of California Publications in American Archaeology and Ethnology*, 8(2), Berkeley

Kroeber, Alfred L.
1909   California Basketry and the Pomo, *American Anthropologist*, 11(2)

Kroeber, Alfred L.
1922   *Basket Designs of the Mission Indians*, (1967 reprint) Ballena Press, Ramona, California

Kroeber, Alfred L.
1925   *Handbook of the Indians of California*. Reprinted by California Book Company, Berkeley

Kroeber, Alfred L.
1929   *The Valley Nisenan*, *University of California Publications in American Archaeology and Ethnology*, 24(4), Berkeley

Kroeber, Alfred L.
1932   The Patwin and Their Neighbors, *University of California Publications in Archaeology and Ethnology*, 29(4), Berkeley

Kroeber, Alfred L.
1953   *Cultural and Natural Areas of Native North America*, University of California Press, Berkeley

Kroeber, Alfred L.
1973   *Basket Designs of the Mission Indians of California*, Ballena Press, Ramona, California, Reprint from 1922

La Pena, Frank
1978   Wintu, *Handbook of North American Indians*, California, vol. 8, California, Smithsonian Institution, Washington

Laird, Carobeth
1976   *The Chemehuevis*, Malki Museum Press, Banning, California

Latta, Frank F.
1999   *Handbook of Yokuts Indians*, Coyote Press, Salinas, California

Lee, Gaylen D.
1998   *Walking Where We Lived: Memoirs of a Mono Indian Family*, University of Oklahoma Press, Norman

Levy, Richard
1978   Eastern Miwok, *Handbook of North American Indians*, vol. 8, Smithsonian Institution, Washington

Liljeblad, Sven and Catherine S. Fowler
1986   Northern Paiute, *Handbook of North American Indians*, vol. 11, Great Basin, Smithsonian Institution, Washington

Liljeblad, Sven and Catherine S. Fowler
1986   Owens Valley Paiute, *Handbook of North American Indians*, Great Basin, vol. 11, Smithsonian Institution, Washington

Loeb, Edwin M.
1932   The Western Kuksu Cult, *University of California Publications in American Archaeology and Ethnology*, 33(1), Berkeley

Lopez, Raul and Christopher L. Moser
1981   *Rods, Bundles and Stitches*, Riverside Museum Press, Riverside, California

Luomala, Katherine
1978   Tipai-Ipai, *Handbook of North American Indians*, vol. 8, California, Smithsonian Institution, Washington

Mack, Joanne M.
1990   Siskiyou Ware: Hunter-Gatherer Pottery, It's Not Just for Cooking, *Anthropological Papers Number 22*, Nevada State Museum, Carson City

Mack, Joanne M.
1990   Changes in Cahuilla Coiled Basketry, in *The Art of Native American Basketry*, Frank W, Porter III, ed., Greenwood Press, Westport, Connecticut

Margolin, Malcolm
1981   *The Way We Lived*, Heyday Books, Berkeley

Mason, J. Alden
1912   The Ethnology of the Salinan Indians, *University of California Publications in American Archaeology and Ethnology*, 10(4), Berkeley

Mason, Otis Tufton
1902   *Aboriginal American Basketry: Studies in a Textile Art Without Machinery*, Smithsonian Institution, Washington

Mathewson, Margaret Susan
1998   *The Living Web: Contemporary Expressions of California Indian Basketry*, Dissertation at the University of California, Berkeley

McGuire, Thomas R.
1983   Walapai, *Handbook of North American Indians*, vol. 10, Smithsonian Institution, Washington

McGreevy, Susan Brown
2001   *Indian Basketry Artists of the Southwest*, School of American Research Press, Santa Fe, New Mexico

McKern, W.C.
1922   Functional Families of the Patwin, *University of California Publications in American Archaeology and Ethnology*, 13(7), Berkeley

McLendon, Sally
1993   Collecting Pomoan Baskets, 1889-1939, *Museum Anthropology*, 17(2), Journal for the Council for Museum Anthropology

McMinn, Howard E.
1970   *An Illustrated Manual of the Shrubs of California*, University of California Press, Berkeley

Meighan, Clement W.
1955   Excavation of Isabella Meadows Cave, Monterey County, California, *Reports of the University of California Archaeological Survey*, No. 29, Feb. 10, 1955, Department of Anthropology, University of California, Berkeley

Meighan, Clement W. and Martin A. Baumhoff
1953   Preliminary Excavation at the Thomas Site, Marin County; also in the same volume: Carbonized Basketry from the Thomas Site, *Reports of the University of California Archaeological Survey, No. 19*, Department of Anthropology, Berkeley

Merriam, C. Hart
1962   The Luiseño: Observations on Mission Indians, in *Studies of California Indians*, University of California Press, Berkeley

Merriam, C. Hart
1962   The Ko-too-mut Ke-hi-ah or Fiesta for the Dead in *Studies of California Indians*, pp. 77-86, University of California Press, Berkeley

Merriam, C. Hart
1966   Ethnographic Notes on California Indian Tribes, *Reports of the University of California Archaeological Survey*, UC Archaeological Research Facility, No. 68, Part I, Berkeley

Merriam, C. Hart
1967   Ethnological Notes on Northern and Southern California Indian Tribes, *Reports of the University of California Archaeological Survey*, No. 68, Feb. 1967, Part II, Berkeley

Merriam, C. Hart
1967   Ethnological Notes on Central California Indian Tribes, Reports of the *University of California Archaeological Survey*, No. 68, Part III, Berkeley

Merrill, Ruth Earl
1923   Plants Used in Basketry by the California Indians, *University of California Publications in Archaeology and Ethnology*, 20(13), Berkeley

Miles, Charles
1963   *Indian & Eskimo Artifacts of North America*, Bonanza Books, New York

Miller, Bruce
1988   *Chumash: A Picture of Their World*, San River Press, Los Osos, California

Miller, Jay and William R. Seaburg
1990   Athapaskans of Southwestern Oregon, *Handbook of North American Indians*, vol. 7, Smithsonian Institution, Washington

Miller, Virginia P.
1978   Yuki, Huchnom and Coast Yuki, *Handbook of North American Indians*, vol. 8, Smithsonian Institution, Washington

Miller, Virginia
1979   *Ukomno'm: The Yuki Indians*, Ballena Press, Socorro, New Mexico

Miller, Wick
1986   Numic Languages, *Handbook of North American Indians*, vol. 11, Great Basin, Smithsonian Institution, Washington

Moratto, Michael J.
1984   *California Archaeology*, Academic Press, Orlando, Florida

Morris, Earl H. and Robert F. Burgh
1941   *Anasazi Basketry*, Publication 533, Carnegie Institution, Washington

Moser, Christopher L.
1986   *Native American Basketry of Central California*, Riverside Museum Press, Riverside, California

Moser, Christopher L.
1989   *American Indian Basketry of Northern California*, Riverside Museum Press, Riverside, California

Moser, Christopher L.
1993   *Native American Basketry of Southern California*, Riverside Museum Press, Riverside, California

Mowat, Linda, Howard Morphy and Penny Dransart
1992   *Basketmakers: Meaning and Form in Native American Baskets*, Pitt Rivers Museum, University of Oxford, UK

Murray, Keith A.
1959   *The Modocs and Their War*, University of Oklahoma Press, Norman

Myers, James E.
1978   Cahto, *Handbook of North American Indians*, vol. 8, California, Smithsonian Institution, Washington

Naranjo, Reuben V. and Susan Lobo
2004   Reweaving the History of California Baskets: A Visit to the Museo de American, Madrid, Spain, *News From Native California*, 17 (2), Berkeley

Newman, Sandra Corrie
1974   *Indian Basket Weaving: How to Weave Pomo, Yurok, Pima and Navajo Baskets*, Northland Press, Flagstaff, Arizona

Nomland, Gladys
1935   Sinkyone Notes, *University of California Publications in American Archaeology and Ethnology*, 36(2), Berkeley

Nomland, Gladys
1938   Bear River Ethnography, *Anthropological Records*, 2(2), University of California, Berkeley

O'Neale, Lila M.
1995   *Yurok-Karok Basket Weavers*, Phoebe Hearst Museum of Anthropology, University of California, Berkeley. Reprint of 1929 study

Ortiz, Beverly R.
2000-2001   The Mountain Maidu Artistry of Ennis Peck, *News From Native California*, Winter 2000-2001, Berkeley

Peri, David W. and Scott M. Patterson
1967   The Basket is in the Roots: That's Where it Begins, *The Journal of California Anthropology*, 3(2), Malki Museum, Banning, California

Pilling, Arnold R.
1978   Yurok, *Handbook of the North American Indians*, vol. 8, California, Smithsonian Institution, Washington

Polanich, Judith Kessler
1994   *Mono Basketry: Migration and Change*, Dissertation at the University of California, Davis

Pollock, Hazel, editor
1971   Shasta Section, *Siskiyou Pioneer*, 4(4), Siskiyou County Historical Society, Yreka, California

Potts, Marie
1977   *The Northern Maidu*, Naturegraph, Happy Camp, California

Pritchard, William E.
1970   Archaeology of the Menjoulet Site, Merced County, California, *Archaeological Report No. 13*, California Department of Parks and Recreation (includes Lawrence Dawson's comments on string basketry, pp. 41-42)

Purdy, Carl
n.d., circa 1901-1902   *Pomo Indian Baskets and Their Makers*, Mendocino County Historical Society, Ukiah, California

Ray, Verne E.
1942   Culture Element Distributions: XXII Plateau, *Anthropological Records*, 8(2), University of California, Berkeley

Riddell, Francis A.
1978   Maidu and Konkow, *Handbook of North American Indians*, vol. 8, California, Smithsonian Institution, Washington

Riddell, Francis A. and William S. Evans
1978   Honey Lake Paiute Ethnography (Part 1); Ethnographic Notes on the Honey Lake Maidu (Part 2) and Maidu Genealogies, *Nevada State Museum Occasional Papers* No. 3, Carson City

Rozaire, Charles E.
1969   The Chronology of Woven Materials from the Caves at Falcon Hill, Nevada, Miscellaneous Papers of Nevada Archaeology, 1-8, Nevada State Museum Anthropological Papers #14, Carson City

Rozaire, Charles E.
1977   *Indian Basketry of Western North America: From the collection of the Bowers Museum, Santa Ana, California*, Brooke House, Los Angeles

Salazar, Eva
2002   Basketweaver Profile in *Roots and Shoots*, Newsletter 38, California Indian Basketweavers Association, Nevada City, California

Sapir, Edward
1907   Notes on the Takelma Indians of Southwestern Oregon, *American Anthropologist*, 9(2)

Sapir, Edward and Leslie Spier
1943   Notes on the Culture of the Yana, *Anthropological Records*, 3(3), Berkeley and Los Angeles

Sawyer, Jesse O.
1965   English-Wappo Dictionary, *University of California Publications in Linguistics*, Vol. 43, Berkeley

Sawyer, Jesse O.
1978 Wappo, *Handbook of North American Indians*, Vol. 8, California, Smithsonian Institution, Washington

Schevill, Margaret Blum
1993 Lim M. O'Neale and the Yurok-Karok Basket Weavers of Northwestern California, *Museum Anthropology*, 17(2), Journal for the Council for Museum Anthropology

Schevill, Margaret Blum
1995 Introduction, in *Yurok-Karok Basket Weavers* by Lia M. O'Neale, Phoebe Hearst Museum, University of California, Berkeley

Schlick, Mary Dodds
1994 *Columbia River Basketry: Gift of the Ancestors, Gift of the Earth*, University of Washington, Seattle

Schoenherr, Allan A. and C. Robert Feldmeth and Michael J. Emerson
1999 *Natural History of the Islands of California*, University of California Press, Berkeley

Schultz, Paul E.
1954 *Indians of Lassen Volcanic National Park*, Loomis Museum Association, Mineral, California

Shackley, M. Steven, editor
2004 *The Early Ethnography of the Kumeyaay*, Phoebe Apperson Hearst Museum of Anthropology, University of California, Berkeley

Shanks, Ralph
2004 An Esselen-Style Basket, in *The Esselen Indians of the Big Sur Country*, Coyote Press, 2004, pp. 136-139

Shanks, Ralph and Lisa Woo Shanks
1986 –1996 (five editions) *North American Indian Travel Guide*, Costaño Books, Novato and Petaluma, California

Silva, Arthur M. and William Cain
1976 *California Indian Basketry*, Cypress College Fine Arts Gallery, Cypress, CA

Silver, Shirley
1978a Chimariko, *Handbook of North American Indians*, vol. 8, California, Smithsonian Institution, Washington

Silver, Shirley
1978b Shastan Peoples, *Handbook of North American Indians*, vol. 8, California, Smithsonian Institution, Washington

Slater, Eva
2000 *Panamint Shoshone Basketry*, Sagebrush Press, Morongo Valley, California

Slaymaker, Charles M.
1972 *Cry for Olompali: An Initial Report on the Archaeological and Historical Features of Olompali*

Smith, Charles R.
1978 Tubatulabal, *Handbook of North American Indians*, vol. 8, California, Smithsonian Institution, Washington

Smith-Ferri, Sherrie
1993 Basket Weavers, Basket Collectors, and the Market: A Case Study of Josoppa Dick, *Museum Anthropology*, 17(2), American Anthropological Association

Smith-Ferri, Sherrie
1996 Human Faces of Pomo Indian Basketry, in *Pomo Indian Basketry* by Samuel A. Barrett, Phoebe Hearst Museum of Anthropology, Berkeley

Smith-Ferri, Sherrie
1998 *Weaving a Tradition: Pomo Indian Baskets from 1850 Through 1996*, Dissertation at the University of Washington, Seattle

Sparkman, Philip Steadman
1908 The Culture of the Luiseño Indians, *University of California Publications in American Archaeology and Ethnology*, 8(4), University of California, Berkeley

Spencer, Robert F.
1977 *The Native Americans*, Harper & Row, New York

Spier, Leslie
1923 Southern Diegueno Customs, *University of California Publications in American Archaeology and Ethnology*, Berkeley

Spier, Leslie
1930 Klamath Ethnography, *University of California Publications in American Archaeology and Ethnology*, Berkeley

Spier, Robert
1978 Foothill Yokuts, *Handbook of North American Indians*, vol. 8, California, Smithsonian Institution, Washington

Stern, Theodore
1966 *The Klamath Tribe*, University of Washington Press, Seattle

Stern, Theodore
1998 Klamath and Modoc, *Handbook of North American Indians*, vol. 12, Plateau, Smithsonian Institution, Washington

Steward, Julian H.
1933 Ethnography of the Owens Valley Paiute, *University of California Publications in American Archaeology and Ethnology*, 33(3), Berkeley

Stewart, Omer C.
1941 Culture Element Distributions: XIV Northern Paiute, *Anthropological Records*, 4(3), University of California, Berkeley and Los Angeles

Suquamish Museum
1985 *The Eyes of Chief Seattle*, The Suquamish Museum, Washington

Tac, Pablo
1958 *Indian Life at Mission San Luis Rey*, Edited by Inna and Gordon Hewes, Old Mission, San Luis Rey, California

Tanner, Clara Lee
1983 *Indian Baskets of the Southwest*, University of Arizona Press, Tucson

Thompson, Nile and Carolyn Marr and Janda Volkmer
1980 Twined Basketry of the Twana, Chehalis and Quinault, *American Indian Basketry Magazine*, 1(3), Portland, Oregon

Timbrook, Jan
1982 Use of Wild Cherry Pits as Food by the California Indians, *Journal of Ethnobiology*, 2(2)

Timbrook, Jan
1986 Chia and the Chumash: A Reconsideration of Sage Seeds in Southern California, *Journal of California and Great Basin Anthropology*, 8(1), 50-64

Tisdale, Shelby J.
2001 *Woven Worlds: Basketry from the Clark Field Collection*, American Indian Art Magazine, 26(3), Scottsdale, Arizona

Tulloch, Alice and Judith Polanich
1999 U'kuyus Basketry of Central California, *Bulletin of Primitive Technology*, Spring 1999, no. 17

Tuohy, Donald R.
1974 *A Cache of Fine Coiled, Feathered and Decorated Baskets from Western Nevada*, Archeological Papers, No. 16, Collected Paper 2, Nevada State Museum, Carson City

Turnbaugh, Sarah Peabody and William A. Turnbaugh
1997 *Indian Baskets*, Schiffler Publishing, West Chester, Pennsylvania

Utley, Robert M.
1988 Indian-United States Military Situation, 1848-1891, vol. 4, History of Indian-White Relations, *Handbook of North American Indians*, Smithsonian Institution, Washington

Van Camp, Gena R.
1979 *Kumeyaay Pottery*, Ballena Press, Socorro, New Mexico

Voegelin, Erminie W.
1938 Tubatulabal Ethnography, *Anthropological Records*, 2(1), University of California Press, Berkeley

Voegelin, Erminie W.
1942 Culture Element Distributions: XX, Northeastern California, *Anthropological Records*, University of California, Berkeley and Los Angeles

Wallace, William J.
1965 A Cache of Unfired Clay Objects from Death Valley, California, *American Antiquity*, 30(4)

Wallace, William J.
1978 Hupa, Chilula and Whilkut; Northern Valley Yokuts; Southern Valley Yokuts, chapters in *Handbook of North American Indians*, vol. 8, California, Smithsonian Institution, Washington

Wallace, William J.
1988 and 1990 *Another Look at Yokuts Pottery-Making*, Paper on the Hunter-Gather Pottery in the Far West for the 21st Great Basin Anthropological Conference, Park City, Utah and also pub. in: Anthropological Papers Number 22, Nevada State Museum, Carson City

Waterman, T.T.
1918 The Yana Indians, *University of California Publications in Archaeology and Ethnology*, 13(2), Berkeley

Whistler, Kenneth W.
1977 *Wintun Prehistory: An Interpretation Based on Linguistic Reconstruction of Plant and Animal Nomenclature*, Proceedings of the Berkeley Linguistics Society, Berkeley, California

Wilken, Michael
1987 The Paipai Potters of Baja California: A Living Tradition, *Masterkey*, Southwest Museum, Los Angeles

Wilson, Norman J. and Arlean H. Towne
1978 Nisenan, *Handbook of North American Indians*, vol. 8, California, Smithsonian Institution, Washington

Winther, Barbara
1985 Pomo Banded Baskets and their Dau Marks, *American Indian Art Magazine*, Autumn 1985, 19(4), Scottsdale, Arizona

Winther, Barbara
1996 More About Dau Marks: Visiting Four Pomo Basket Makers, *American Indian Art Magazine*, 21(4), Scottsdale, Arizona

Winther, Barbara
2000 Yuki and Yuki-Style Basketry. *American Indian Art Magazine*, 25(3), Summer 2000, Scottsdale, Arizona

Zigmond, Maurice
1978 Kawaiisu Basketry, *Journal of California Anthropology*, winter 1978, 5(2), Malki Museum, Banning, California

Zigmond, Maurice,
1977 Kawaiisu, *Handbook of North American Indians*, vol. 11, Great Basin, Smithsonian Institution, Washington

Zenk, Henry B.
1990 Siuslawans and Coosans, *Handbook of North American Indians*, vol. 7, Northwest Coast, Smithsonian Institution, Washington

INDEX

ACKNOWLEDGMENTS

In a way this book began when the Pomo Women's Club of Ukiah told me, at age twelve, that they were pleased someone so young would be interested in baskets. Over the years I learned that the best primary source materials are the baskets themselves. As respected Kashaya Pomo/Coast Miwok weaver Julia Parker told me, "The baskets talk to you." It is true. You may not hear words but by studying the baskets, sudden, remarkable insights occur. The saying that "the baskets will teach you" has truth in it. Many of my most valuable insights have occurred while quietly sitting alone at night with a group of baskets.

Over the decades many California Indian elders, weavers and cultural leaders (some of whom are all three) have helped with guidance, suggestions and information. I would never have continued my interest in baskets if it were not for the many Native American people whose kindness, wisdom and generosity continued to inspire and guide me. Some became friends and others helped, some demonstrated weaving techniques and a few simply took time to share their knowledge with us. These include Milton "Bun" Lucas (Kashaya Pomo/Coast Miwok), Lanny Pinola (Kashaya Pomo/Coast Miwok), Mabel McKay (Pomo), Geneva Mattz (Yurok), Isabel Cook (Northern Paiute), Laura Fish Somersall (Wappo/Pomo), Elsie Allen (Pomo), Sherrie Smith-Ferri (Southern Pomo), Margaret Baty (Western Mono), Bill Franklin (Sierra Miwok), Julia Parker (Kashaya Pomo/Coast Miwok), Lucy Parker (Mono Lake Paiute/Sierra Miwok/Pomo/Coast Miwok), Gene Buvelot (Coast Miwok), Eva Salazar (Kumeyaay), Axel Lindgren (Yurok), Justin Farmer (Ipai), Loren Bommelyn (Tolowa), and many other generous people.

It is important to remember that the Indian elders of generations past helped with so many of the publications listed in the bibliography. Many of the early publications are extremely valuable because the information came from elders born as early as the 1830s. We gratefully honor them and the scholars who cared enough to preserve their knowledge in writing. Certainly the work of Alfred L. Kroeber, C. Hart Merriam, Samuel Barrett, J.P. Harrington, and many others deserve to be recognized.

My wife Lisa Woo Shanks, editor of this volume, has been fellow researcher, principal photographer, computer guru and an exacting professional editor. It has been a massive and nearly overwhelming task. There would have been no book if it were not for Lisa's love, scholarship and dedication to excellence. We also thank our daughters Torrey and Laurel and my brother Donald Lacewell Shanks for their unfailing interest and support.

Over the decades the late Larry Dawson, museum anthropologist at the Phoebe Hearst (formerly Lowie) Museum of Anthropology at the University of California at Berkeley, spent years teaching me to be a basketry scholar. Larry and I began studying basketry together beginning in the late 1960s when I was a graduate student and continued through much of the 1970s. Then we worked again through the 1990s until his death in 2003. He was truly a great man, an inspired teacher, a brilliant scholar and a fine friend. No one has influenced the content and perspective of this book as much as Larry did.

Other important people repeatedly provided guidance and encouragement, shared their knowledge and helped in producing this book. Besides Larry Dawson, Bryn Potter of the Southwest Museum and BBP Museum Consulting, Sherrie Smith-Ferri of the Grace Hudson Museum, Lynn Murray of the Miwok Archeological Preserve of Marin (MAPOM), Beverly Kienitz of the Natural Resources Conservation Service and Lorna Johnson of Global Interprint read part or all of the manuscript and offered countless valuable suggestions, corrections and insights.

Gary Breschini of Coyote Press repeatedly offered valued archeological information, access to rare publications and suggestions. Lisa Deitz of the University of California at Davis was unfailingly kind and professional during our innumerable trips, phone calls and requests as we worked with the C. Hart Merriam collection.

The Miwok Archeological Board of Directors (MAPOM) was unfailingly supportive and enthusiastic. Several board members in particular deserve thanks. Sylvia Thalman believed in our project from the beginning and helped locate baskets and gave timely words of encouragement. Tim Campbell wrote eloquent introductory comments, Lynn Murray did invaluable proofreading, Betty Goerke and her husband Jon helped by sharing their outstanding photographs, Gene Buvelot provided valuable basketry information, Gae Canfield's husband Bob helped with professional photographic lessons, and other board members offered very much appreciated encouragement. Past MAPOM board members Lanny Pinola and Susie Moore also deserve recognition for their encouragement and support. We also want to thank the California Indian Basketweavers Association (CIBA), especially Julia Parker, Lucy Parker and Shannon Brawley, for their interest and help.

For production we thank Jacci Summers of Healdsburg, designer of the book, who worked with fine professionalism and much appreciated patience. Lorna Johnson of Global Interprint, Inc. of Santa Rosa, who managed our printing and binding, willingly shared her suggestions and her vast knowledge of publishing. We wish also to thank Mary Anderson of the University of Washington Press for her invaluable guidance and encouragement, especially as the book neared completion. Malcolm Margolin also graciously shared his extensive publishing knowledge and encouragement.

Others who helped with important insights and information include linguists Catherine A. Callaghan and Victor Golla who taught me much in a short time. Archeologists Gary Breschini, the late James Bennyhoff, and University of New Mexico graduate students Ed and Ruth Jolie all supplied highly valuable archeological information. Native American Studies scholar Brian Bibby very kindly provided helpful information and photographs.

We also deeply appreciate the generous help, professionalism and encouragement of the following individuals and institutions in the United States and Europe. Each provided wonderful research assistance, access to important baskets, photographic opportunities and/or all of the above. These are people and places that truly make research work. They include the American Museum of Natural History, esp. Peter M. Whiteley and Barry Landua; Antelope Valley Indian Museum, esp. Edra L. Moore; Logan Museum of Anthropology, Beloit College, Wisconsin, esp. Nicolette Meister; Benson Fine Art, San Patricio, NM, esp. Pete Benson; Coyote Press of Salinas, esp. Gary Breschini and Trude Haversat; The British Museum, esp. Alison Deeprose and Ivor Kerslake; the California Academy of Sciences, esp. Russell Hartman; California State Indian Museum, Sutter's Fort, Sacramento, esp. Michael S. Tucker; California State Parks, Bidwell Mansion State Historic Park, esp. Shirley Kendall and Judy Crain; California State Parks and Recreation, Monterey, esp. Kris Quist; State Museum Resource Center, California Department of Parks and Recreation, West Sacramento, esp. Betty Blue, Elizabeth B. Smart and John Rumming; Carmel Mission Museum, esp. Father John Griffin; Clarke (Memorial) Historical Museum, Eureka, esp. Pam Service and Rosemary Hunter; Cleveland Museum of Natural History, esp. Sharon E. Dean; Curry Historical Society, Gold Beach, Oregon, esp. P.J. Estlund; Eastern California Museum, esp. Beth S. Porter; Astrid Eckert, photographer, Munich; The Field Museum, esp. Isabel Tovar, Jerice Barrios and Jonathan Hass; Gienger Investments, esp. Bud Gienger and Roy Gienger; Grace Hudson Museum and Sun House, esp. Sherrie Smith-Ferri and Whitewolf; Philip Garaway Native American Art; Elizabeth B. Goerke, College of Marin; Peabody Harvard Museum of Archaeology and Ethnology, esp. Jeff Carr and Victoria Cranner; Phoebe Apperson Hearst Museum of Anthropology, esp. Douglas Sharon, Victoria Bradshaw, Anne Olney, Joan Knudsen, Larri Fredericks, Nicole Mullen, Frank Norick and the late Larry Dawson; Sandra Horn, Private Collector and Appraiser; Hupa Tribal Museum, esp. Lyle Marshall; Kania-Ferrin Gallery, Santa Fe, esp. John Kania; Klamath County Museum, esp. Judith Hassen and Sonny Matt; Russell Kloer of Clear Sky, Sonoma; Lassen Volcanic National Park, esp. Cari Kreshak; Len Wood's Indian Territory, Laguna Beach, California, esp. Len Wood and Matt Wood; Malki Museum, Morongo Indian Reservation; Marion Steinbach Indian Basket Museum and the North Lake Tahoe Historical Society, esp. Sara Larson; Maryhill Museum of Art, esp. Betty Long-Schleif and Mary Dodds Schlick; Maxwell Museum of Anthropology, University of New Mexico, esp. David A. Phillips, Jr., Kathryn Klein, Bruce Huckell and graduate students Ruth Burgett Jolie and Ed Jolie; Mendocino County Museum, County of Mendocino, esp. Rebecca A. Snetselaar; Michael Smith Gallery, Santa Fe, esp. Michael Smith; Milwaukee Public Museum, esp. Dawn Scher Thomae, Susan Otto and Athena Klotz; Mission San Antonio de Padua, esp. Father John E. Gini, OFM; Monterey County Historical Society, esp. Mona Gudgel and Gary Breschini; Museum of Indian Arts and Crafts, Museum of New Mexico, Santa Fe; Oakland Museum of California, esp. Diane Curry; Santa Barbara Museum of Natural History, esp. Jan Timbrook and the late Travis Hudson; Museum fur Weltkulturen, Frankfurt, esp. Mona B. Suhrbier; Musee de L'Homme, Paris, esp. Muguette Dumont; Janene Pete and Robert Pete; Museum of Anthropology and Ethnology, named after Peter the Great, St. Petersburg, Russia, esp. Natalia Taksami and Chuner Taksami; Gene Quintana; Pacific Grove Museum of Natural History, esp. Paul Finnegan; Santa Cruz Museum of Natural History, esp. Sally Legakis; Siskiyou County Museum, esp. Michael Hendryx; Smithsonian Institution, esp. Felicia Pickering; Southwest Museum of the American Indian, Autry National Center, esp. Bryn Potter and Kim Walters; Staatliches Museum fur Volkerkunde Munich, esp. Jean-Loup Rousselot; Turtle Bay Exploration Park, Redding, California, esp. Julia Pennington, Robyn Peterson; University of California, Davis, esp. Lisa Dietz and Robert Bettinger; Museum of Natural History/State Museum of Anthropology, University of Oregon, esp. Pamela E. Endzweig and Mel Aiken; University of Pennsylvania Museum of Archaeology and Anthropology, esp. Lucy Fowler Williams and William Wierzbowski; Vacaville Heritage Council, esp. Robert Allen; and Ray Volante. To many other kind individuals and institutions, your help is deeply appreciated. Thank you all very, very much.

Join the California Indian Basketweavers Association (CIBA)

In California, the displacement of Native people nearly destroyed our culture. Basket weaving was nearly lost because weavers were separated from the land; they were not allowed to practice their traditions. These cultural artists were not permitted to gather or manage the plants and animals integral to Native traditions and fine art. Basket weavers found their lands off-limits to gathering due in large part to private and public land laws.

In 1992, the California Indian Basketweavers Association (CIBA) was founded by eleven Native American women representing multiple tribes from throughout California. These women came together as individual leaders representing their tribes and also as carriers of their Native cultural knowledge. CIBA has empowered indigenous men and women to educate the public about the many issues surrounding basket weaving. This was the beginning of our organization setting in motion an effort to protect California Indian basket weaving traditions. CIBA continues to be the only statewide organization, which fosters this long-term artistic vision. CIBA is a "weaver of weavers" and serves a broader function than basketweaving alone might imply. The organization was founded to bring communities together to preserve, promote and perpetuate our traditions and also continues to vision for the future of basketweaving as a vital art form. Please help us in achieving our vision and become a member of CIBA.

CIBA VISION STATEMENT

The purpose of the California Indian Basketweavers Association is to preserve, promote & perpetuate California basket weaving traditions.

CIBA accomplishes this in the following ways:

- By promoting & providing opportunities for California Indian basket weavers to pursue the study of traditional basketry techniques & forms & showcase their work.

- By establishing rapport & working with public agencies & other groups in order to provide a healthy physical, social, cultural, spiritual, & economic environment for the practice of California Indian basketry.

- By increasing California Indian access to traditional cultural resources on public & tribal lands & traditional gathering sites, and encouraging the reintroduction of such resources & designation of gathering areas on such lands.

- By raising awareness & providing education for Native Americans, the public, public agencies, arts educational & environmental groups of the artistry, practices & concerns of Native American basket weavers.

- By promoting solidarity & broadening communication among Native American basket weavers and with other indigenous traditional artists.

- By monitoring public & private land use & encouraging those management practices that protect & conserve traditional Native resources.

- By monitoring & discouraging pesticide use in traditional & potential gathering areas for the safety of weavers, gatherers & others in tribal communities.

- By doing all of the above in a manner, which respects our Elders and Mother Earth.

For more information and a membership brochure contact:

CIBA
ciba@ciba.org
Visit our website: www.ciba.org

About the Author

Basketry scholar Ralph Shanks, M.A., is vice president of the Miwok Archeological Preserve of Marin (MAPOM). He began his basketry research as a graduate student working with Larry Dawson in the late 1960s. Dawson, a renowned basketry scholar, was museum anthropologist at the Phoebe Hearst (then Lowie) Museum of Anthropology at the University of California, Berkeley. Ralph continued to work with Larry well into the 1970s and again through the 1990s until 2003. Ralph Shanks has also been honored to work extensively with Native American cultural leaders, weavers and elders.

In addition, Ralph served as research associate in anthropology at Santa Barbara Museum of National History, and continued his basketry research at over fifty museums across the U.S. and Europe. During the 1980s and early 1990s, he and his wife Lisa spent seven years working with over 100 tribal offices researching their book, *The North American Indian Travel Guide*, a guide to Native American cultural activities, museums and events across the country.

Ralph Shanks is also a maritime historian. His recent book, *U.S. Life-Saving Service*, won the first Foundation for Coast Guard History Award in the category "Best Book on Coast Guard History." Ralph has served on graduate students' Master's Degree committees for the University of Oregon and presented lecture series there. His research and writings have centered on two topics, Native American Studies and maritime history. He has degrees from the University of California at Berkeley and San Francisco State University.

About the Editor

Lisa Woo Shanks is editor of the *Basketry of California and Oregon Series*. She has participated in basketry research across the United States in both museums and private collections. In addition, she is the photographer who produced most of the images of the baskets showcased here. With her husband Ralph, she produced the *North American Indian Travel Guide*, a comprehensive cultural guide to contemporary Native American events across the United States and Canada. Lisa works as Area Resource Conservationist for the Natural Resources Conservation Service. In that role, she has written articles published by the University of California at Davis and the University of Idaho. She has a B.S. degree from Humboldt State University. Lisa is a MAPOM director. The Shanks have two daughters, Torrey and Laurel.